Critical Social Theory:
Culture, Society and Critique

Critical Social Theory: Culture, Society and Critique

Tim Dant

SAGE Publications
London • Thousand Oaks • New Delhi

First published 2003

SAGE Publications Ltd
6 Bonhill Street
London EC2A 4PU

SAGE Publications Inc
2455 Teller Road
Thousand Oaks, California 91320

SAGE Publications India Pvt Ltd
B-42, Panchsheel Enclave
Post Box 4109
New Delhi 100 017

British Library Cataloguing in Publication data

A catalogue record for this book is available from the British Library

ISBN 0 7619 5478 x
ISBN 0 7619 5479 1

Library of Congress control number available

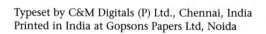

Typeset by C&M Digitals (P) Ltd., Chennai, India
Printed in India at Gopsons Papers Ltd, Noida

Contents

ONE

Criticism by Theory

Introduction: To criticise

We criticise what we don't agree with. When we disagree with other people's views or actions and tell them why, we criticise them. To be critical first involves establishing a perspective, a view of the world about how it is and how it should be, including how we, and others, should act. Secondly, it involves having reasons why that perspective is appropriate, and, thirdly, it involves being willing to articulate our views and reasons so that other people hear or read about them. The act of criticism situates us in a position in the world which has interests – ours and those of others that might be different from ours – and there is a link between our interests in that world and the perspective that we take when we are critical. The object of criticism may be the actions of another individual – as when criticising someone's driving – or it may be of an institution or other collective of people. Criticism involves a reflection, a standing back and responding to events and actions which have occurred. But these events or actions are always those which human volition has shaped in some way because it does not make sense to criticise non-human phenomena such as the weather or a mountain. We may criticise material objects, but when we do, we are criticising their design, manufacture or use – again it is the actions of human beings that have brought that thing to look or work in the way it does.

To criticise a social formation takes criticism to another level. It suggests that cumulative human actions have led to the particular social features that we dislike, but it often involves criticising the past actions of groups of people rather than identifiable individuals – although we may identify the architects of that social formation in our criticism. For example, if we criticise the law for favouring rich people over poor, two understandings are implicit: that past human action, probably by unspecified people, has shaped the law to discriminate in such ways; and that future human action can change the law in ways that will negate our criticism. We might, for example, feel that acts of fraud and misrepresentation should be punished as harshly as acts of theft or robbery in recognition that the harm done is equivalent and that the reason people committing the former types of crime receive lighter sentences is because they are likely to come from more privileged social strata. Without these two understandings there would be no more point in criticising the institution of the law than in criticising the weather. Of course, there is an argument that human actions have brought about changes in the weather – the debate on global warming – and we may wish to criticise those actions. However, when we do criticise the weather, we will attempt to distinguish between what is natural and what is caused by human action. The variability of the weather is produced by long-term climatic changes as well as the continuous flow of seasonal, daily, even hourly, fluctuations; what might reasonably be the subject of criticism are those human actions that alter what was a natural system of variability.

The criticism of social formations and their processes is the stuff of politics. Politicians and electors criticise the actions of those who govern the social formation and seek changes in the law, the economy and administrative practice. The study of politics, political science, political history and political philosophy will attempt to understand these processes. Such a study may distinguish between different systems of politics and may indicate the advantages and disadvantages of such systems and strategies of political action within the systems. But there is a distinction between the study of politics and the action of politics, although politicians may well find the study of politics useful in planning their actions. Now, criticism of whole social formations, the form of whole societies or even groups of societies implies that there are limits to the field of politics, both as a field of study and a field of action. To criticise the whole of a societal formation is to suggest that political action is not sufficient in itself to bring about changes in that formation. This is the rather strange situation that brings about critical theory in which there is an interest in, but also dissatisfaction with, the field of political action and an interest in, but dissatisfaction with, the study of social and political formations. Critical theory engages in a form of criticism of social formations that does not express itself as an agenda for political action. It arises precisely through the awareness of the failure of political action, even the most extreme and radical political action of revolution, to bring about the changes needed in political and social formations. But this is not a reason to abandon criticism; there is still much in the world to disagree with and dissent from. What is more, there is some point in expressing that disagreement, not merely by attacking specific perspectives or actions, but by trying to get to the roots of those perspectives or actions in the social formation.

This book concerns the development of critical theory in the twentieth century. There are a number of issues that need to be discussed to make clear what I mean by theory, and I will explore them in this chapter. The book will go on to draw out themes in the writing of critical theory that will link two not entirely discontinuous traditions. The first of these is originally Germanic (though much of the work I will refer to was written in the United States), usually referred to as the critical theory of the Frankfurt School, and includes in particular the writing of Adorno, Horkheimer, Marcuse and Benjamin. The second is an overlapping but slightly later Gallic tradition including the writing of Lefebvre, Barthes, Gorz, Touraine and Baudrillard. I have chosen to concentrate on the writing of these particular authors in order to sustain an argument that criticism by theory has become a feature of what we might call late modernity. There are many other writers from both the Germanic and the French traditions who could be included – and perhaps should be – but I will largely restrict my account to these writers, for a number of reasons.

Firstly, their works are well known, largely available in English, and there is a substantial secondary scholarly literature that refers to them. This means either that my readers will be familiar with the original works or that it will be easy for them to investigate them for themselves. One of my aims is to reinvigorate interest in criticism through theory and encourage the reading and rereading of what is a very substantial and powerful literature. Secondly, rather than trying to write a detailed investigation of the intellectual history of these two traditions – impossible in such a short book – I have chosen to emphasise the related contributions of their key figures. Thirdly, I wish to argue that there is a continuity between the Germanic and Gallic traditions, which are normally treated as somewhat separate. (This continuity has been commented on by others before me of course; see, for example, Dews 1989 and Jay 1996, both of whom cite others who have made similar connections among those within the traditions.) The term 'critical theory' is normally reserved for the approach of the Frankfurt School, but I wish to extend it to incorporate that of French writers who are neither part of a 'school' nor normally treated as a group. Fourthly, I will argue that this continuity can be seen in the work of the writers I have chosen to focus on, by the recurrence of a number of themes around which the chapters of this book are organised: myth, work, leisure, everyday life, sexuality, entertainment, art and knowledge. This list is far from exhaustive but I wish to argue they are the major spheres of social life in late modernity around which theory as criticism is formulated. Of course they overlap and they could have been articulated differently; they are not constituted as 'spheres' in the work of any of these writers and are purely an heuristic device for the purposes of the present argument. That said, a fifth reason for looking at these writers and these themes is to suggest that for the humanities and sociology in particular, these areas of social life are still ones that should be subject to theoretical criticism. Critical theory introduced many of the ideas that have produced debates about postmodernism and postmodernity (see especially the work of Fredric Jameson – 1990, 1991, 1998), but there has not been sufficient change to the modern world for it to be safe to declare the arrival of postmodern social formations. One of the reasons for revisiting critical theory is to suggest not that we have never been modern (as Latour 1993 and Delanty 2000 do in rather different ways), but that we are *still* modern. Critical theory continues to have much to say about the social world in which we live in the industrialised West

3

at the beginning of the twenty-first century, and yet it is often overlooked as displaced by more recent thinking.

It is worth saying a little more on who is excluded, and why, in my category of 'critical theorists'. All the authors I refer to take Marx's analysis of the mode of production as a starting point that needs to be developed to cope with the changes in capitalism that had become apparent by the middle of the twentieth century. What they have in common is an attempt to extend the 'critique of political economy' towards a broader critique of society and culture as a whole. In doing this, all the writers I will refer to accept the importance of political economy in shaping the form of late modern societies and in shaping the lives of individuals within those societies. But their emphasis shifts towards what we might call the 'culturalisation' of the economy: the way that modern culture follows the underlying rationale of the economy rather than, say, the tradition of religion or the inherited form of society as a monarchy or feudal class system. What emerges in both the Germanic and Gallic critical theory traditions is a concern to modify Marx's analysis, sometimes drawing on Freud, to mount a critique of culture and society beyond the critique of political economy. At times this critique is of society as *culture*, in distinction to Marx's critique of society as *political economy*, but consistent is a critique that addresses society as a totality and treats culture not as epiphenomenal, as Marx was prone to do, but as the form in which the modern mode of production resides.

There are many contenders for inclusion in this project who are excluded. The work of Jürgen Habermas, for example, in many ways continues the critical theory of the Frankfurt School, but his investigations into communicative action and social systems take him some way from the original tradition (1984, 1987) and to discuss his work would need too many caveats and distinctions to fit in such a short book. Similarly the writing of Michel Foucault has much that is 'critical' of society and culture and it emerges within the Gallic tradition that I refer to – his comments on sexuality (1978) and knowledge (1980) would be particularly relevant. However, Foucault's interests are rather more far-reaching, and by investigating the historical antecedents of modernity he undermines the 'critique of political economy' far more fundamentally than do the writers – such as Lefebvre, Gorz and Touraine – whom I will refer to. The themes of power, governance and discourse that are central to Foucault's work as a whole and have been inspirational for many later writers displace those of economy and ideology to provide a rather different foundation to the critique of society and culture. And then there is a strong feminist critique of society and culture that emerges from within second-wave feminism to address similar issues – sexuality, work, everyday life, art and so on – and also discusses and draws inspiration from many of the writers I will refer to. Much feminist writing is interesting and rewarding as a critique of society and culture but it is united by a theme, the situation and experience of women, that gives the critique a particular perspective and shape.[1] In this, feminist writing departs from the critical tradition that I am referring to, where the critique is a response to the social and cultural totality and resists prioritising the perspective of a particular class, gender, sexual, racial or ethnic group. The American tradition of critical theory that begins to address how political economy shapes society in cultural as well as social structural ways, could also have been included.[2] There are many others whose work has been excluded more on grounds of space and to retain the clarity of themes – amongst the Frankfurt School theorists, for example, I have ignored the writing of Erich Fromm, Siegfried Kracauer and Leo Lowenthal all of whom have much to say about society, culture and critique. In the Gallic tradition Louis Althusser, Guy Debord, Giles Deleuze, Jacques Derrida, Félix Guattari, Raoul Vaneigem and Paul Virilio also discuss many issues concerning society, culture and critique that would be interesting and relevant to explore. However, in such a short book that covers such a diverse range of themes, I have decided to give emphasis to the work of a few writers; I would encourage my readers to explore how the many other 'critical theories' they come across develop the themes that will be set out here.

The theme of culture as a social form that vies with the economy as a determinant of the form of society is not of course original to critical theory. Most famously, Max Weber's interest in religion can be seen as providing a contrast to Marx's emphasis on material interests and political economy. For Weber, culture, as traditionally expressed through religion, shapes the lives of people through the beliefs, ideas and practices that affect how they act and interact and provides the context for the arrangements of material life such as the economy. Weber wrote on law and music but his early essay *The Protestant Ethic and the Spirit of Capitalism* (1930), which showed how the culture of religion impacts on economy, was the beginning of his comparative study of religions that became a key component in his massive exploration of how different types of thought and action shape the trajectory of social forms (Weber 1978). Weber's contemporary in the founding of German theoretical sociology, Georg Simmel, also wrote on the sociology of religion but is more famous for his writing on aesthetic culture and its impact on social life and on society (see, for example, the collection edited by Frisby and Featherstone [1997]). His focus was more directly on the tension between culture and the life of the individual subject than was Weber's, and he explored how aesthetics was a dimension of interaction or 'sociability' and how the form of money affected human relationships. It is striking that the studies of culture by these two founders of sociology, whose influence waxes and wanes but has always been profound, has had little discernible impact on the critical theory tradition that I will address. This is for two reasons: Weber and Simmel engage in a form of sociology that would not claim to be 'critique', and neither takes the mode of production as of prime importance in understanding the relationship between culture and society.

While I do not intend to attempt to analyse the intellectual antecedents of critical theory, I will discuss some of the work of two seminal writers who began the project of criticising modern society: Marx and Freud. Marx transformed the Hegelian critique of social formations and fuelled a number of revolutions and revolutionary parties that failed to bring about the sorts of changes sought by critical theory. Critical theory can be seen as a retreat from revolutionary politics and from the field of political action, which attempts to build on Marx's critique but with a different strategy. Freud, in contrast, provides the murmurings of discontent with modern social formation that extends beyond the desire to escape from exploitation. Freud, as well as bringing into the field of critique issues of culture, sexuality and symbolism and the state of individuals, provides a tone for critical theory, a sense of dismay that withdraws from direct action into writing: criticism by theory.

Critique

Criticism may take the form of, as Raymond Williams puts it, 'fault finding' (1976: 75), in which specific issues or facts are disputed. He discovers the origin of the term in the Greek word *kritos*, 'a judge'. Criticism involves making a judgement, of bringing powers of judgement to bear on some form of utterance, and for Williams criticism is used in the context of judging literature – literary criticism – from the seventeenth century. The notion of fault finding entails a negative judgement: something is wrong which could be right, something could be better than it is. But Theodor Adorno (1998: 282) finds a different Greek origin in the word *krino*, 'to decide', from which a range of words are derived, including 'criticism', 'critique', 'critic' and 'crisis'. The critic is one who is in a position to make judgements, who decides whether something is good or bad, who points to the faults that, if rectified, would lead to something better.

Williams's interest is in the origins of literary criticism but Adorno's is in the origins of 'critique', which has a slightly different set of connotations. Clearly literary criticism is more than fault finding – Williams points to the task of commentary on literature, which describes and summarises it, linking one text to another, and the task of judgement of the writing of the piece as a whole. And this broader view of criticism begins to take us towards the approach that is normally referred to as 'critique'. It is critique that is the central method of critical theory and it is the sustaining of critique that makes it distinctive. Adorno was particularly concerned to be clear about what critique involves and discusses what it entails a number of times. In a late piece of writing (Adorno 1998), first published in 1969 but prepared originally for a radio programme broadcast in Berlin earlier that year, he sets out the political basis of critique.

For Adorno, critique is essential to democracy. What makes democracy democratic is a separation of powers of the legislature, executive and judiciary such that each can subject the others to critique. Critique provides the system of checks and balances that prevent democracy from drifting towards despotism. It builds in the possibility of resistance: to established views and opinions; to the taken-for-granted presumption of institutions to decide; to simple acceptance on the basis of convention or established authority. What is implicit here is that critique means not only fault finding but setting up a line of opposition, one that deals not just with the detail but rather with the whole system. Faults are not the result of mistakes, correctable once they are pointed out, but are the result of the workings of established systems. Critique begins to challenge whole systems rather than identify failings. A critique of society confronts the form of society as a whole, perhaps identifying particular features but treating them as consequent upon the underlying character of the social system. Adorno points to the link between critique and reason in enlightenment thought as exemplified by Kant's teaching of autonomous thinking ('judgement according to one's own insight' – Adorno 1998: 282), of engaging with dogmatism and confronting established rationalistic systems.

The notion of critique involves both criticism and reasoned reflection – it can be contrasted with spontaneous thought or revelatory thought, in which knowledge is acquired directly. Critique derives two elements from German idealist philosophy: from Kant, the notion of a *reflection on the foundations of knowledge;* and from Hegel, a *liberation from the constraints on our thought.* Critique involves reflection on the way we know things and the freeing of knowledge from illusions imposed from outside.

Marx: Alienation

Adorno reminds us that Marx's main work, *Capital,* is subtitled 'The Critique of Political Economy'. Marx's mode of critique was born out of a transformation of Hegel's philosophy and offers not only a thorough-going critique of society but also a model of what is involved in engaging in such a critique. If Kant's enlightenment challenge was to think autonomously, Hegel promoted a method that accepted a higher authority, the totality, the force of history, which is necessarily greater than any one mind. Although Marx rejected his idealism, he discovered within Hegel's dialectic the means of mounting a critique that could be sustained beyond mere criticism. Phenomenology, in the Hegelian tradition, begins from the recognition that knowledge, in the form of propositions and claims, is constituted in social relationships. As Hegel puts it: 'Self-consciousness exists in and for itself when, and by the fact that, it so exists for another; that is, it exists only in being acknowledged (1977: 111)'.

Knowledge may always be social, but self-certainty, truth, only comes through the negation of the other's claim to truth. The Hegelian dialectic involves the estrangement of consciousness from sense experience, in which the struggle to grasp the nature of estrangement leads to the possibility of self-conscious understanding. But Marx sees the limitations of Hegelian philosophy in the way that it begins to re-create religious thinking in terms of the absolute knowledge arrived at through self-conscious thought. ('The appropriation of man's objectified and estranged essential powers is therefore firstly only an *appropriation* which takes place in *consciousness*, in pure thought, i.e. in *abstraction*' – Marx 1975: 384.[3]) There is in the Hegelian dialectic a tool that can be utilised for critique, but in Hegel's hands it is used to plot the movements between consciousness and self-consciousness. Taking up Feuerbach's criticism of Hegel, Marx wants to use the dialectical method for critical effect in relation to the world of people; critique will not be achieved by philosophy alone. At the philosophical level, however, the critique of religion does provide the basis for social critique in that it puts man rather than God at the centre of the world 'so that he will think, act and fashion his reality like a man who has discarded his illusions' (Marx 1975: 244). Marx asserts a primacy of the natural world and of human being as an objective, sensuous, suffering and passionate being ('Passion is man's essential power' – Marx 1975: 390), but it is the social relation of people being objects for each other that begins to unwind Hegel's Idealism. Instead of having purely formal relations that are grasped in consciousness, human beings are confronted by the lived relations that are present to their senses, including hunger and suffering from the actions of another. Nonetheless, Marx reaffirms the importance of history as the understanding of human experience at the level of consciousness: '... everything natural must *come into being*, so man also has his process of origin in *history*' (1975: 390).

It is from a critique of Hegel's system of philosophy that Marx derives the means to critique political economy. He provides a summary of Hegel's text which criticises and links to texts of others, including Feuerbach and Bauer. This would be criticism in Williams's sense of the criticism of literary texts, but Marx goes further because he takes much from Hegel's writing: a dialectical method; a concern with the process of history and the centrality of the emergence of the modern state; a recognition of labour as the self-confirming essence of man; and, most importantly, the notion of human alienation. Marx argues that it is through following the logic of Hegel's argument about the process of abstraction that consciousness is confronted with nature, something that lies beyond human existence and is independent of it (1975: 397). Critique, then, such as Marx's of Hegelianism, has a form that builds on as well as criticises, incorporates as well as rejects. When applied to social formations this is an eminently sensible strategy because history cannot be cast aside as easily as a philosophy or a text. A critique, when applied to the tangible form of people's lives and their social and political relations, must recognise the interrelated components of those lives. To change one thing has consequences for other things, and changing the whole at once is fraught with risks.

Marx's critique of political economy attempts to show the consequences of the capitalist mode of production in people's lives. He shows that capitalism is not a simple form of domination and exploitation of one group by another – it is a social system in which all are embroiled and constrained, although some more than others. For Marx, the social relations of capitalism alienate human beings from the world around them: from their products, their work, their fellow workers and their 'species being' (1975: 324–7 – see Chapter 3, p. 62). The concept of alienation for Marx, writing in 1844, expressed the separation of individuals from what gives a human life meaning: actions in the world that makes that world his. Because labour under capitalism is external to the worker – is not part of his essential being – 'he does not confirm himself in his work, but denies himself, feels miserable and not happy, does not develop free mental and physical energy, but mortifies his flesh and ruins his mind' (Marx 1975: 326). It is a system of belief – political economy – that sustains the social system of capitalism just as religions have sustained the ideological power of shamanistic classes and belief in the specialness of royal blood-lines have sustained monarchies. Political economy as a system of ideas that locates economic value in commodities (objects, goods and services) independent of the human work that went into creating them is subject to critique by Marx as the 'fetishism of commodities'. By treating the commodity as something alienated from humans in the process of its production, political economy then reappropriates it as an idea, an abstraction, as something that has intrinsic value that 'transcends sensuousness' (Marx 1976: 163). The commodity takes on a mystical character in which its properties appear as 'natural' when they are in fact the result of the human labour that produced them. The relations between objects – their relative exchange values – appear to be just as independent of human labour as do the powers of fetishes. Goods do have a 'sensuous' value in the lives of people, which Marx calls their use value, but this is obscured in the process of commodity exchange. Marx argues that bourgeois economics began with the analysis of price and took money to be the expression of value: 'It is however precisely this finished form of the world of commodities – the money form – which conceals the social character of private labour and the social relations between individual labour, by making those relations appear as relations between material objects, instead of revealing them plainly' (1976: 168–9).

This, of course, is just the beginning of Marx's extensive critique of capitalism, which goes on to take in money, capital, surplus value, the division of labour, wages and capital accumulation (and that's just Volume 1). But what is important here is the parallel between the way Marx subjects Hegel's philosophy to critique and then critiques political economy. As Marx engages with the writings of the political economists, such as Ricardo and Smith, he finds points of agreement which he incorporates and gathers up as he moves on. It is the cumulative effect of Marx's debate with a series of economists, in which he accepts some ideas while rejecting or modifying others, that amounts to a critique of political economy as a whole.

There is in Marx's form of critique a dialectic: a recognition that disagreement involves two poles in tension and that progress requires the emergence of a third position, deriving in part from the previous two. Criticism as disagreement or fault finding suggests that the opponent is to be dismissed or dealt with by setting out the critical judgement. Critique is concerned not to reach a final judgement but to take the initial force of disagreement to discover something more complex and fundamental, something lying behind what produces disagreement. Ironically, Marx's critique was linked most famously to a revolutionary politics that, when it overthrew oppressive political and economic structures, established new ones that created their own forms of suffering. The critique associated with critical theory has generally avoided practical politics, including the radical politics of the revolution, to turn the tools of critique on society as a whole. Rather as Marx had critiqued Hegel and political economy, much of the effort of critical theory is applied to existing texts and ideas (including those of Marx and Hegel). However, the Frankfurt School learns from Marx that critique should not be directed simply at the *ideas* of society but should be a dynamic, thorough-going critique of society itself, of the very form of society. Marx's critique of society is complex and wide-ranging, but the key points I wish to take forward can be summarised like this:

- Industrialisation extends the values of private property to economic relationships of capital accumulation, the employment of labour and commodity production.
- Work under capitalism alienates individuals from their nature as human beings.
- Political economy attributes value to commodities rather than to the labour that produced them – the illusion of commodity fetishism.
- The exchange value of commodities is at some remove from their use value in lived experience.
- It is not through changing ideas alone, but through changing material relationships that modern society will be transformed.

Freud: Discontent

Another analyst who mounted a critique of the whole social formation of modernity was Sigmund Freud, famous as the originator of psychoanalysis. He is distinctive in the history of the thought of the twentieth century for attempting to understand individual human beings in relation to their social environment. His theories were based on clinical work with people whose physical suffering – ticks, pains, headaches, vomiting, coughs, inability to perform tasks – had no apparent physical cause. As his psychoanalytical therapy tried to cure them, he reflected on the 'neuroses' that caused a departure from the ordinary state of human being. Like Marx, Freud's account begins to fill the gap left by the failure of religion as an explanatory system for the way that the human world is. He attempts to understand the complexity of an animal with a mind (both species and individual) that lives in societies. He was not a sociologist, but towards the end of his working life he began to think through how the suffering of individuals resulted from the state of society rather than their particular interpersonal relationships. For Freud, the civilised societies of modernity produced a general state of unhappiness not explicable by economic exploitation – he identified the cause in culture, civilisation itself.

Freud's detailed and systematic account of the modern self recognised both the conscious and the unconscious workings of the mind in relation to a person's body. The self was not simply a mind; it was a thinking and dreaming machine linked to a body that could feel hunger, sexual desires, pleasure, aggression and pain. The self of the individual had a structure – of id, ego, super-ego – whose components were in tension with each other as well as with the world of other beings and the material environment beyond. The body of an individual self was itself an object for the desires and fears of other selves, and as Freud's account developed, it became clear that the happiness of the individual depended on her or his social context; culture and society bore back on the individual, affecting that person's life. Two particular aspects of Freud's theory of the individual incorporated this recognition: the 'reality principle' and the 'super-ego'. The reality principle says that seeking pleasure brings unwanted consequences from outside, particularly from other people and social institutions, which may not lead directly to pain but nevertheless need to be managed (see Chapter 5). Super-ego is the internalisation of external authority: the parents' restrictions on the child's behaviour; the law or moral code on the adult's. Culture or civilisation as a model of approved action and a system of censure and constraints is expressed in the individual in the form of the super-ego, which inhibits the ego from seeking pleasure regardless of others.

Religion can be seen as an expression of emotions and feelings – love, for example – that Freud's theory of the complex individual sought to understand. But he argued that while religions purport to explain the riddles of the world and protect the individual from life's frustrations, they are in fact based on an illusion (Freud 1928). In 1930 he published *Civilization and its Discontents* (1962), in which he argued that religion restricted the lives of people who were unable to see through it as no more than a palliative based on fiction: 'The whole thing is so patently infantile, so foreign to reality' (Freud 1962: 21). Of course religion was the source of many of the constraints of the reality principle because following a religion involves internalising external authority, accepting not simply that sins, once committed and discovered, have to be atoned for, but also that the believer takes on a responsibility not to commit sins. Religion restricts individual choice and the possibility of adapting to change – but Freud did recognise that it spared people from some individual neuroses.

In *Civilization and its Discontents* Freud took on not just religion but culture itself, including the system of rules, both formal and informal, by which a society organises itself. He argues that the restrictions of civilisation – or *'kultur'* in the original – produce unhappiness (*'unglück'*, meaning uneasiness or discomfort – translated as 'discontent') in people because they constrain and frustrate them. The unhappiness is rather unspecific; it is not deep or agonising and is the result of a general condition – rather like Marx's understanding of alienation – that the individual may not be aware of. For Freud, the point of human life is a rather irreligious, modern, sensuous, pursuit of happiness: 'The feeling of happiness derived from the satisfaction of a wild instinctual impulse untamed by the ego is incomparably more intense than that derived from sating an instinct that has been tamed' (1962: 26).

Freud sees sexual pleasure as the prototype of all happiness, even though love carries the risk of rejection (see Chapter 3). Modern civilisation tames the individual, reducing satisfaction and increasing frustration, by sublimating instincts and redirecting desire for excitement into other forms: art, science and culture. Religion, however, involves not so much a sublimation as a 'delusional remoulding of reality' (Freud 1962: 28). One of Freud's reasons for rejecting religion is that it disconnects the search for pleasure in love from genital love, with the result that there is no risk of rejection but an inhibition of real pleasure seeking. It also universalises love, requiring the religious to love everyone, to 'love thy neighbour'.

Freud understands happiness as episodic, flowing from the satisfaction of needs that have been dammed up (1962: 23). When the satisfaction of needs is prolonged but consequently diluted, he says it produces 'mild contentment'. Unhappiness is much less difficult to experience; it is the pain and frustration that derives from the limitations of our own body, the external world and our relations with other people. Our search for happiness is guided by the pleasure principle but modified by the reality principle, which seeks to avoid unhappiness, with the paradoxical effect that happiness may be experienced as the avoidance of unhappiness (see Chapter 3). Civilisation is good for avoiding unhappiness because it protects us from the ravages of nature and brings protection in a variety of forms. So, medicine and health care limit unhappiness derived from the body, and technology provides us ever more effectively with food and shelter and protects us from the external world. Civilisation also brings the regulation of human societies that limits the unhappiness we suffer through the actions of others. The cost of this protection is the frustration of our own desires and need for pleasure, and we may believe that a return to primitive social forms would bring more happiness. This idea is lived out by those who try to opt out of modernity to emulate the lifestyles of Druids, Native Americans or other pre-modern cultures of which they have read. Civilisation, however, brings culture as well as protection: science, aesthetic appreciation of beauty, the development of law, of cleanliness, hygiene and religion.

The religious injunction to love everyone, Freud points out, attempts to repress the way the ego discriminates between those who are worthy of love and those who are not. As he puts it, the human being's neighbour is not only a potential helper or sexual object, 'but also someone who tempts them to satisfy their aggressiveness on him, to exploit his capacity for work without compensation, to use him sexually without consent, to seize his possessions, to humiliate him, to cause him pain, to torture him and to kill him' (Freud 1962: 58). Civilisation is threatened by these instinctual impulses in the individual and seeks to contain them, and channel them by legitimising some types of violence (e.g. war, the sports of boxing and wrestling) while outlawing other types (e.g. random violence). Religion smooths modern life to blandness as it tries to ignore and repress the death instinct and the drive towards aggression. Freud sees the culture of modernity as a struggle between Eros, the drive towards sexual objects and the preservation of the species, and or death, the drive towards the destruction of that which stands in the way of the individual. Civilisation tames aggression by turning it inward to take the form of a conscience with an unconscious sense of guilt that manifests itself as anxiety and fear (Freud 1962: 81). It is of course precisely this sense of guilt that Christianity offers redemption from – and it is a sense of guilt that is the source of the discontent of the modern world.

The egoistic drive of the pleasure principle is in tension with the altruistic drive of community, of living together, and the reality principle: '... the two processes of individual and of cultural development must stand in hostile opposition to each other and mutually dispute the ground' (Freud 1962: 88). For Freud, it is the altruistic drive that is winning, with the effect of repressing individual desires in modernity. He has little if anything to say about work, production, wealth or economy – but, like Marx, he is also trying to gain insight into the conditions of unhappiness.

Harvey Ferguson suggests that reading a version of Freud from the very short *Civilization and its Discontents*, rather than the whole of his extensive body of work, leads to a 'vulgar Freudianism' (1996: 220). But even a vulgar version of Freud throws up a series of issues that suggest a different critique of modernity than that offered by Marx. Let me summarise these:

- The individual begins to emerge as traditional society withers away.
- The self or subject of the individual is put in tension with the collective of society.
- In the past this tension was managed by a strict, feudal, agrarian social order, reinforced by religion. In modernity these old structures began to be displaced by enlightenment thought – science and rationality, the

modern state, capitalist economy, urban life and the separation of work from family life through wages and factories.

- Civilisation responds to the tension with cultural regulations (laws, manners, codes of conduct, fashions) which are adaptable and continually in the flow of change.
- The management of aggression and the channelling of sexual energy into work and production is the cultural effect of civilisation. •
- The frustration of the individual's instincts leads to a harmony but a discontented one.

Freud does not propose a revolution or promote a breaking out of sublimated instinct but his critique suggests that civilisation needs to loosen its bonds on the individual if it is not to be broken up by individuals seeking outlets for their desires.

Culture and critique

Freud offers a critique of modern society from the perspective of its impact on the mind and feelings of the individual but there is much from the social perspective that he does not discuss: the division of labour, industrialisation, urbanisation, changes in family structure, class, work, consumption, and so on. His major contribution was with understanding individual development (ontogenesis), but he believed it was closely connected with the development of society (phylogenesis). Marx, on the other hand, does analyse the social dimensions of modernity, with particular emphasis on the dominance of economic relations, but has little to say about the effect on individuals other than that they are alienated. Both Marx and Freud mount a critique of modernity that incorporates a critique of religious understanding; in both cases religion is a discourse that has encouraged tolerance of the impact of modern society on individuals through illusory 'knowledge'. Both critique the effects of society as restricting the life of the individual – through alienation or repression. Both posit a natural state of human being, prior to alienation or repression in modernity, to which individuals might return to live their lives to the full if liberated through a transformation of modern society.

The theoretical criticism that this book will discuss takes the force of Marx's critique of the material exploitation of human beings but finds it too restricted to the field of political economy. Freud offers some insight about the impact of modernity on the individual and hints at the cultural processes by which it can be understood. By the 1940s radical political solutions did not seem to offer a way of transforming societies to reduce unhappiness – the totalitarian developments in Germany, Italy and in the USSR promised to increase happiness but rapidly turned out to have a massive cost in human lives and restrictions on those who were left. These political transformations threatened to hasten modernity towards its logical end; they seemed to fail to take account of the lives of the people who lived within these regimes. What critical theory began to address with the emergence of the Frankfurt School (or at least the phase of the Institut für Sozialforschung when Max Horkheimer took over as director in 1930) was the *cultural* basis of the state of modernity that led to unhappiness. The mode of *cultural critique* did not become the principal object of critical theory until Hitler's regime dismissed Horkheimer and made it impossible for the other members of the Institut to remain in Germany, thus displacing the Frankfurt School. As Jay argues, the Frankfurt School were interested in reinvigorating Marxism through retracing some of its links with Hegelian dialectics. Their aim was to transform society not through direct political means or through a revolution led by the proletariat but through *praxis*, the linking of theory to experience and action (see Chapter 7). The approach of critical theory was not to build up a systematic response or to form alliances or factions with political interests. Critique, of existing ways of understanding the world and of the ways of the world itself, was the way towards changing the world. By the time that the Frankfurt School became established at Columbia University in 1937, Jay suggests that the enthusiasm for Marxism and socialism had shifted to a more modulated perspective influenced by the *Lebensphilosophie* (philosophy of life) of Nietzsche, Dilthey and Bergson that emphasised the role of the individual and took up an anti-systematic stance that would recognise society as a totality (1973: 43–9).

Adorno says, 'The cultural critic is not happy with civilization, to which alone he owes his discontent. He speaks as if he represented either unadulterated nature or a higher historical stage' (1983: 19). He identifies the dilemma that underlies critical theory: unless it claims a transcendent position, such as having access to God's view, then the only tools with which to criticise culture are the ones made available by that very culture. It's a bit like sitting in dirty water trying to wash oneself clean – but we do that every time we take a bath. Adorno's point is that culture must engage with itself, must reflect on its nature and process, question whether the stuff of culture is engaged with the reality of existence. This is what critical theory does; it necessarily stands back from the flow of existence, takes a reflective perspective, looking over the breadth of cultural forms, recognising changes over time, commenting on the distribution of cultural products. As Adorno puts it, 'culture originates in the radical separation of mental and physical work' (1983: 26). If culture is a reflection on the form that society takes, it is also part of the substance of that society. Cultural critique engages with the form of society through a sustained criticism of the substance of culture. And in so doing, it does of course contribute to culture.

The heritage of the Frankfurt School is to treat culture as a substantive part of society as against treating its content as a thing in itself, as, for example, literary criticism or art history usually do. In his remarks on cultural criticism (*Kulturkritik*) Adorno was arguing against criticism that attempts to identify eternal values and reflect on the past. But he was also rejecting a form of cultural criticism that attempts to identify the ideological structure of culture:

> Hence, the task of criticism must be not so much to search for the particular interest-groups to which cultural phenomena are to be assigned, but rather to decipher the general social tendencies which are expressed in these phenomena and through which the most powerful interests realize themselves. Cultural criticism must become social physiognomy. (Adorno 1983: 30)

The idea of social physiognomy sees society as a whole of which certain aspects – the cultural – are more accessible to reflective thought. But the sort of theoretical criticism that Adorno is proposing analyses features with the whole in mind, so that it is the form of society which is subject to critique and the components of substantive culture being referred to are treated as both arising from that form and indicative of it.

Criticism by theory does not lead to direct proposals for social change. It does not give rise to a revolutionary passion to overthrow social institutions and introduce a new political order. Neither does it propose social reforms that might be incorporated by existing political regimes. Cultural critique produces nothing – but texts. It is itself a reproduction of culture, stimulating the process of culture as reflection. What might arise from it, however, is a culture that is constantly questioning itself, resisting the tendency to accept and take for granted. Its impact, if it has any, is on individuals – those who engage with the texts. And if it has any effect, it is to stimulate a constant state of tension between the individual and the culture, to foster a sense of discontent, a sense that things could be better. Criticism by theory tends not to offer either definitive knowledge – as the rhetorical form of science often does – or solutions – as the rhetorical form of political discourse usually does. The rhetorical form of critical theory has much in common with philosophy in that it draws on existing theory, empirical accounts, political positions and historical understanding to produce an *argument*. But the argument is never resolved, there is no *quad erat demonstrandum*, no closing down of the debate. It is an argument against the possibility of a final solution.

Further reading

The critical theory tradition begins with Marx, and while his work is complex and difficult to approach as a whole, there is much to be gained from exploring his *Early Writings* (1975) and the early chapters of Volume One of *Capital* (1976). Freud's later writings that begin to address society are most relevant, especially *Civilization and its Discontents* (1962) and Harvey Ferguson's *Lure of Dreams* (1996) provides a useful and critical background to his comments on modernity. Adorno's writings on critique and culture appear in a number of places, but the first essay, 'Cultural Criticism and Society', in his collection *Prisms* (1983) is a good place to begin.

Notes

1 Of particular interest are a series of feminist authors who explore the links between Marxism, critical theory and feminism, including Barrett (1988), Landry and MacLean (1993) and the contributors to Benhabib and Cornell (1987) and, more recently, O'Neill (1999).

2 I have in mind particularly the work of Alvin Gouldner (1976, 1980).

3 All emphases in this and all future quotations is in the original unless specified.

TWO

Culture as Myth

When Achilles was dipped in the River Styx by Thetis, his sea-goddess mother, she was trying to make him invulnerable. But because the heel by which she held him did not go in the water, it remained as a weak point that was later penetrated by an arrow shot by Paris and resulted in Achilles' death (Bulfinch 1981: 260fn). This story works as a myth because it is a fictitious narrative that gives us a moral: that even those who are apparently incapable of being hurt continue to have a point of vulnerability. This moral remains as a popular idea thousands of years after the narrative was first told, in the phrase 'Achilles' heel', used to refer to the weak point in a person who otherwise seems strong and resistant to harm. There are three characteristics that identify this story as mythical. Firstly its narrative form, in which actions and events have effects with ramifications not envisaged at the initiation of action. Secondly, this narrative form of relations and consequences has a moral effect because they can be transferred to other different but comparable situations in the world of human lives. Thirdly, the narrative is recognisably fictitious but this does not weaken the moral import of the tale. Just because the 'facts' of the story are fantastic and not a literal description of real events does not prevent the story having relevance to real lives and actions. Indeed, the potency of the moral is emphasised by the unlikely events of the story because they show that it does not present the particular circumstances of real lives, of specific people acting in time and place. The story works metaphorically as an allegory, as a narrative that can symbolically resemble other situations to do with people who appear strong, and so it can be applied in a variety of real circumstances.[1]

One of the distinctive features of this type of myth is that it involves supernatural persons and events – the powers of goddesses and a river in the underworld. But the word 'myth' is also used to describe the implicitly moral accounts of the modern world that follow a similar form but refer to natural and believable forces. For example, the idea that eating too much chocolate, chips or pizza causes acne is also a myth. Here the account of causes, actions and ramifications is not couched in terms of a story with characters with names and ascribed powers but is a generalised account of effects caused by ordinary human behaviour. The mythical nature of this second type of myth is in its fundamental fictitiousness – it describes causal relations that are insupportable in experience but that, if true, would not be described as a myth. However, this type of 'myth' is often declared in equivocal terms such as: 'While there is no scientific evidence that diet causes acne, dermatologists have differing opinions on the role of diet.' The advice offered often suggests a compromise such as: 'Some people find that certain foods seem to make their acne worse.' Even as it is declared a myth, it is given some credence and retold yet again, so, despite its mythical character, it continues to provide a popular moral tale that can be applied to the actions of those who eat too much chocolate or fatty food. In the fantastic myth of supernatural forces it is clear that interpretation is required to apply it to ordinary action. In the modern myth of 'natural' forces it appears that no interpretation is required to read the moral meaning from it.

I will call these two types 'type one myths' – historical stories with super-human characters and fantastic events – and 'type two myths' – timeless stories purporting to describe causal relations between human action and nature. Together they suggest what myth means in modern culture: a fictitious story that is commonly told with moral effect. Such stories are indeed the stuff of culture. Myths are narratives of the connections between forces that humans control – those of human action and will – and forces that are superhuman – those of gods or of nature. But whereas myths of the first type describe specific events that are clearly the product of imagination, myths of the second type describe general events in reality as it is actually experienced. From the modern perspective it is easy to see that myths of the second type are the result of being 'debunked' by science: a more potent account of the causes of acne replaces a 'folk' notion that is insupportable by scientific theory, backed by empirical evidence. The power of a non-mythical type of thinking – science – appears to dispel the truth of the myth, but despite this it survives as a popular idea with moral connotations.

Critical theory is interested in how myth has been transformed in modern-ity. On the one hand it seems to recede as a mode of knowledge used to understand the events of the world and the place of human action in the world. Myth appears to be displaced by the instrumental reason of post-enlightenment thinking that both provides a powerful critique of the factual contents of myths and offers alternative narratives of cause and effect. Now scientific thinking may be very powerful in describing the process of the natural or material world but it has proved less effective in the arena of morality: the ways in which human beings *should* act and the effects of those actions on the human condition. What fascinates the critical theorists is how myths have transformed so that they take on qualities of both type one myths and type two myths. The moral tales of modernity are not so much of gods with supernatural powers, fantastic characters and events (though such mythic qualities remain in the capacity of detectives to solve riddles, the superhuman strength of 'bionic' humans and the unpredictable ways of alien beings) as about the way that ordinary life is represented. Modern myths appear much more like type two myths that survive despite their vulnerability to being 'debunked' by other explanations, such as those of history and science. The allegorical effect and moral impact of modern myths, however, is sustained as if they had the form of type one myths as if moral principles could be derived and transferred to real human actions to guide and explain them.

At first glance it might appear that myths can be exposed as such merely by pointing to their fictitious form. But to identify a myth does not remove its potency as a moral tale: just because we know that a dipping in the River Styx could not confer invulnerability on any human does not prevent us continuing to retell the Achilles myth. As Barthes famously writes, 'myth is a type of speech', a system of communicating that adds to the 'pure matter' of the world a 'type of social usage' through a system of signification that represents the world as a message that has meaning (1993a: 109). It is tempting to suggest that myths are simply fictitious whereas science and history are based in 'fact', but myths claim the status of a factual account without devices (excess, jokes, irony) that might subvert those claims. Barthes actually identifies 'statements of fact' as one of the rhetorical figures of myth (1993a: 154). If history and science provide a challenge to myths in modernity (in earlier epochs these forms of speech are much more difficult to disentangle), myths are not simply dissolved by such powerful counter-forms of story telling.

Myth lies at the heart of culture because it involves a linguistically formed account of human relations with the world. Language is not used simply for communicating in the present, for dealing with the practicalities of existence, but is also used to tell stories, the made-up products of human imagination that circulate in the culture, typically by word of mouth but also in written and other forms. Such stories provide the common bond of a shared sensibility, a mode of understanding and a system of values. They guide human actions by providing examples of what is good and what the consequences of the bad might be. Myths survive by being told and retold, despite the fact that they may not be true, because they serve a number of cultural purposes. Firstly, there is likely to be some basis in fact: there may well have been a warrior called Achilles whose apparent invulnerability in battle seemed to set him apart from other men *as if* he had been protected by a mother with super-human powers. While diet may not be *the* cause of acne, it may be a contributing or exacerbating factor in some cases. Secondly, myths provide a way of talking about phenomena that are of interest to humans; they give a story-form to situations and experiences which allows a topic to be engaged with, whether it be heroism or spots. As a metaphor they provide a mode of expressing relationships between humans and their world that can make sense even if it is not literally true. Thirdly, myths provide adequate explanations in the absence of better explanations. How else are we to make sense of exceptional heroism or acne? Though it may be superseded or modified, the structural form of subsequent knowledge can follow that of myth.

The continuing role of myth within society in the face of its constant challenge by factual accounts has been a recurring theme in critical theories of culture. The potency of myth as cultural knowledge is because it survives the metamorphosis of retelling to provide the aesthetic appeal of metaphor and narrative at both the most popular and the most sophisticated levels. It is the multi-faceted character of myth, its resistance to reduction or systematisation, that keeps it at the centre of cultural form. Critical theory shows how myth supports the existing social order, making it and its history appear natural, inevitable and incontestable. On the other hand, myth does provide a metaphorical language and the opportunity for retelling and reinterpretation that particular forms of speech, such as those of science and technology, do not.

Ancient myth in modern culture

Ancient myths – type one myths – are often associated with religion, and the myth systems in Japan and India are related to still extant religions. We can see that in oral cultures, myths serve the purpose of carrying religious, philosophical and cultural ideas. In pre-literate cultures, the stories are told and retold, passed from generation to generation, varying from teller to teller, incorporating the individual teller's embellishments and local history. We can see how such myths work as 'knowledge' for those societies. They answer questions to do with origins: Where did we come from? Where did the earth and its animal and plant species come from? They also answer questions about relations between human beings: they tell of kings and queens, of heroes and heroines, of good people and bad. They even provide information about the proper relationships between social strata and between different cultures. They are a way in which a culture preserves its history, remembering its wars, its leaders and natural disasters such as famines, droughts and floods. As well as entertaining through their imagination-stimulating narrative form, they provide a guide as to how people should act towards each other and in the material world.

Many ancient myths have survived the demise of the societies and religions that they emerged from and have endured being written down, most notably by the poets of ancient Greece – Aeschylus, Homer, Plato, Sappho, Theocritus and many others. The form of the modern novel seems to have its origins in the transcription of myths. By writing down the Odysseus myth, Homer fixed both the content and the narrative style to make it a particular story attributable to a particular author, which Robert Graves refers to as the 'first Greek novel' (1996: 666). The ancient Greek myths were incorporated, often with additions and name changes, into Roman mythology and written down by a new set of poets. Long before Hollywood produced 'epic' versions, these myths were adapted and borrowed by a range of artists who used them for inspiration. While the original myths have no authors – in the oral tradition of telling, the teller should not draw attention to himself and his contribution – as the Graeco-Roman tradition developed, the idea of an author and of creative or imaginative invention emerged. The survival of ancient myths into modern western society has provided a resource for high culture in Europe. Many famous English poets – Alfred Tennyson, John Milton, Lord Byron – were inspired to write poems that retold Greek myths or parts of them. Titian, Blake, Botticelli, Poussin, Van Dyck, Brueghel, Turner, El Greco, Moreau, Odilon Redon, are a few famous names amongst the many painters in the western tradition who have used the characters and events of Greek myths to provide topics for their work. The images and ideas of myths continue to be altered, recycled and reused, finding a place in a variety of contexts. For example, Walter Crane, who is best known as a children's book illustrator and member of the Arts and Crafts movement in England at the end of the nineteenth century, engraved an image of 'The Horses of Neptune' emerging from the crest of breaking waves as they pulled Neptune's chariot. This image in turn inspired a television advertisement for Guinness that used video overlay techniques to re-create the impression of breaking waves turning into the form of the heads and manes of horses.

Not only has Greek mythology had a direct impact on the European traditions of poetry and painting, the study of these myths at school and university level, usually through studying the dead languages of Greek and Latin, has been a key part of the education of the cultural elite until very recently. The study of mythology has been regarded as a good training for being a politician, a military commander, a diplomat and a civil servant. How have ancient or traditional myths survived in this way?

Myth provides an account of fate, of the forces of nature that bring about events over time affecting not only the natural world but the world of human beings as well. The recounting of myth reminds humans of their mortality and their fallibility in the face of the continuity of nature and the irrevocable determination of fate. As Graeme Gilloch explains, Walter Benjamin thinks of myth in this way: 'Myth involves human powerlessness in the face of unalterable natural laws and the subordination of reason before the blind, uncontrollable forces of the natural environment' (1996: 10).

Myth is about the things that are beyond reason that human beings cannot anticipate, predict or properly understand but that they are subject to. These forces of nature are given coherence by attributing them to the omnipotent force of a god or gods whose form and powers can be imagined. It is the connection between the human, experienced and real world and the superhuman, imagined and fantastic world that myth explores. But myths are more than this, serving an allegorical function of symbolising deeper moral or spiritual meanings. This allegorical function of myth suggests that they can be translated or decoded to explain what lies behind their symbolic contents. The use of metaphor and figurative forms gives the listener or reader the pleasure of discovery – and myth can accommodate many different interpretations. There can be a doubling of pleasure when the meaning becomes clear later, after hearing the narrative, and the myth's moral can be adapted to fit a variety of circumstances. A myth may become metaphorical shorthand to explain something complex or explain a range of different practical situations that have core elements in common. Precisely because it is open to interpretation and yet resistant to a single interpretation, the form of myth enables it to return, to be retold, repeated and reused endlessly.

For Benjamin, the idea that modernity was progress, that history was of society developing and leaving its past behind in its wake, was untenable. He saw the work of history as one of redemption that required a continuous reappraisal and reinterpretation of events (see Benjamin 1973a and Chapter 7). His rather gloomy perspective on myth was that its essence was return and that the modern faith in progress 'seems no less to belong to the mythic mode of thought than does the idea of eternal return' (Benjamin 1999: 119). Just as Achilles after his death returned to Odysseus as a shade, so both their myths continue to return in various forms as the history of modernity rolls on. Any idea that progress will take us away from culture's roots is as fictitious as any myth – if only because cultures consistently rediscover the past and rewrite their myths.

Adorno and Horkheimer: Myth versus enlightenment

As Gilloch says, '[m]odernity presents itself as the end of myth', (1996: 10) and it is with the enlightenment of modernity that myth at first seems to be threatened. The legitimation of knowledge as narrative constantly retold is confronted by a form of knowledge grounded in reason, evidence and truth: science. And it is this confrontation between myth and enlightenment thought that Adorno and Horkheimer consider in *Dialectic of Enlightenment* (1979). They trace their notion of enlightenment back to Francis Bacon, who, writing at the beginning of the seventeenth century, began to articulate a new systematic approach to knowledge of the material world which led to what we now call 'technology', by which nature can be dominated and controlled. It is a system of knowledge that we can now recognise as based on scientific method, but to begin with, there was no method of experiment, replication, quantification, and so on. Its origins lie in discovering reason in human action and causes in natural action that would include simply pragmatic knowledge based on experience – much early engineering, building design and agriculture would have been like this. Enlightenment knowledge is grounded in understanding the consequences of actions that provides a basis for *rational* thought. Action is rational when it is based on a reasoned understanding of the outcomes of possible actions so that it can be oriented to achieve particular ends or goals. Reasoning can be abstracted from the practical context of action to become a reflective and imaginative process – a form of knowledge characterised by causal thinking and rationality directed to outcomes or ends.

These hallmarks of what Adorno and Horkheimer treat as enlightenment thought began a process of the displacement of earlier forms of explanation, most importantly animism and other religious beliefs about gods and spiritual forces, which by the end of the eighteenth century was well advanced. Animist thinking is of course implicit in ancient mythical thought in which fantastic things happen because of the supernatural powers of gods and sometimes of men and beasts. Enlightenment thought provides alternative explanations based on what is present to the senses and accords with predictable outcomes. There is, then, a conflict between enlightenment thinking and mythical thinking, although at any one point in history neither will completely dominate all thought. Even before the enlightenment, much everyday human action must have been guided by something like means–ends rationality in order for crops to have been planted, animals domesticated and metal tools to be made. But this did not stop the people who achieved these technologies believing in gods and spirits.

As enlightenment thinking challenges mythical thinking, there is a dialogue and dispute that Adorno and Horkheimer treat as dialectical. The emergence of enlightenment begins with the social organisation of mythical thought by a class of priests and sorcerers who interpret, analyse and write down what is known. Their work achieves a form of power over the natural world of fetishes and totemic animals through the rituals and categories they promote and those they proscribe. Modern religions, even though they are based on belief in supernatural powers, are part of the process of enlightenment. They provide a rationalising of beliefs: firstly through a reduction in the number of gods and a gathering of all their powers into a single omnipotence; and secondly by fitting together belief in the power of God with the power of humans through the notion of *sin*. The human will to act is not controlled by God, but if humans do not do his bidding they are guilty of sin. Modern, non-mythic religions assist in the process of universalising the validity of concepts that claim to represent reality, helping to subordinate the individual to the rationality of the system. What is lost is individual thought and reaction to the world; such individual thought is channelled through systems of thinking – religion, science, art – into an established response.

It is the class of priests and sorcerers who control mythic knowledge, and far from mythical thought simply dying away, it comes to inhabit enlightenment. Over time, the generally accepted ways of understanding and doing change towards enlightenment and away from myth in a process that Adorno and Horkheimer describe, like Weber, as a 'disenchantment' of the world (1979: 5). The magic and wonder of the natural world, of the seeming independence of the world from human action, fades as its workings become known and understood. The hierarchy of gods gives way to logic, to rational thought and instrumental reason. But strangely, science itself becomes a mode of thought that also takes on a mythic form. As a system of signs that enables nature to be subject to calculation, Adorno and Horkheimer talk of mathematics as 'the ritual of thinking' (1979: 25). The effect is to turn thought into a thing, an instrument for the domination of nature. Instead of being free and open, thought follows a process – that of rationality – which is already set for it: 'For enlightenment is as totalitarian as any system. Its untruth does not consist in what its romantic enemies have always reproached it for: analytical method, return to elements, dissolution through reflective thought; but instead in the fact that for enlightenment the process is already decided from the start' (Adorno and Horkheimer 1979: 24). This repetitive and controlled form of thought becomes as restricted and unquestioning as mythic thought. Adorno and Horkheimer argue that enlightenment thought has ceased to think about thinking: it doesn't question the basis of knowledge or the practices of thinking. Science does not confront the issues of ethics and morality, aesthetics and beauty, of what is good and true that are traditionally dealt with in myth. Instead it propounds a limited and closed objectified system of thought which is 'an automatic, self-activating process; an impersonation of the machine that it produces itself so that ultimately the machine can replace it' (Adorno and Horkheimer 1979: 25).

A traditional view of modernity as progress would see a withering away of myth in the face of scientific thinking – as a mode of knowledge that tolerates fiction, myth is no match for one that replaces it with a factual account of reality. But the critical theorists argue that the form of myth actually resurfaces within the adoption of the methods of science and technology as the only adequate mode of knowledge. What appears as rationality, as based in reason, as an account of the facts, begins to operate as myth in the sphere of culture. Enlightenment thinking for practical purposes, especially to do with the material world, may be effective in realising the will of humans, but as a cultural system it becomes mythic through rigidifying the processes of nature, treating them as predetermined and beyond the power of human will. It is the unitary and unbending form of reason in modernity that lends itself to domination, both of nature and of human will.

It seems at times as if the Frankfurt theorists are against science as a mode of thought, but of course they accept it has a way of thinking that is appropriate for understanding the material world and one that can oust metaphysical and theological illusions. Their critique focuses on how the success of scientific methods during the nineteenth century in making sense of the physical world led to them being applied to understanding the human world of history, politics, philosophy and sociology. It seemed as if mathematically based science provided a model of how all human knowledge should be: grounded in sensory experience, observation and deduction. It is particularly the attempt to introduce 'positivism' into the human sciences that they attack consistently (Adorno 1979; Marcuse 1941) for its effective undermining of the critical component in social theory that uses metaphysics, imagination and reason to dare to think differently from what is given. As Held sums up their position: 'Resignation to the given follows from the positivist view that concepts must be grounded in observed facts, and from the notion that the real connection between facts represents an "inexorable order"' (1980: 162). Simply put, the problem is of trying to reduce the 'subject' of the human sciences to an 'object' that can be studied with the techniques and methods of the material sciences. As Adorno points out, lecturing late in his life in 1968 on the nature of the discipline of sociology, society is made up of active, knowing human subjects, so that 'the ideal subject of science is, finally, society as a whole, which performs the act of knowing ... sociology consists essentially of the reflection of science upon itself' (2000: 137). What the positivist, uncritical, human sciences do is ignore the capacity of a society to know itself (and indeed act on that knowledge), and treat it as a mere object to be observed. Adorno accepts that the human individual can be treated as an object (by biological science, by medicine), but the subject of society is irreducible to the status of an object. It is the very thing that generates the knowledge of itself, and no methodology can take up a position outside of society and its lived relations to study it 'objectively'.[2] A positivist methodology removes – or, at least, puts aside – the questions of value, of struggle, of how the world ought to be or could be; precisely the questions that motivate critical theory. Lecturing in 1968 Adorno argues, in a critique of positivist sociology, that natural science developed through a certain degree of fetishistic concern with its own methods that 'becomes an end in itself, without any relation to its subject matter' (2000: 128). It is precisely this insularity that he sees as destructive of sociology and other human sciences that take themselves to be autonomous disciplines that can copy the natural sciences by adopting the practical purpose of addressing the 'facts' and tackling 'social problems'. Social sciences can stand alongside the natural sciences to achieve a domination of nature – human nature – but in doing so they abandon their critical potential and their power to gain insight into the 'essential nature of society' (Adorno 2000: 15) and how history shapes it. It is the fetishising of science and its methods, not only within science but within the culture as a whole, that leads to the mythical character of instrumental reason, to the unquestioning acceptance of a certain mode of rationality that is exemplified by natural science, and whose efficacy is evidenced in technology and the successful domination of nature. If scientific rationality provides the fulfilment of enlightenment thought, positivism becomes one of its mythical forms.

Adorno and Horkheimer show how myth survives as a way of legitimating the world of rationality and enlightenment thinking by taking the Odysseus myth as a lesson in modernity. The various adventures that Odysseus and his companions experience on their journey to Ithaca can be read as a morality tale for the modern world. For Adorno and Horkheimer, Odysseus, in the versions we read and hear, uses *cunning* in the face of adversity, and, rather than succumbing to fate, he manages to overcome the threats of the world. These threats usually come from supernatural forces and gods but Odysseus overcomes them in very practical ways. This focus on the self and its capacity for preservation is a theme of the Odysseus myth and also a theme of modernity. The idea that one is responsible for one's own destiny and doesn't have to give oneself up to what fate has in store comes with a form of reason in which planning and forethought are used instrumentally to dominate and overcome the natural world. Adorno and Horkheimer see Odysseus as the prototype bourgeois individual who is 'compelled to wander' (1979: 43) – our wandering is not across Greek seas but along the paths of what we call 'careers'. He engages in a form of sacrifice as his men are eaten by the Cyclops, lost to the monster Scylla and perish in a shipwreck. The sacrifice is of the collective for the project of the journey, which in modernity means that the individual identity is sacrificed to keeping the system going. Adorno and Horkheimer comment on the class distinction between Odysseus and his men: their fate is to serve him, and while they may follow him faithfully, they get the hard work while he gets the pleasure and excitement. His crew rowed the boat past the Sirens' island with wax stopping up their ears while Odysseus, securely tied to the mast, was able to give himself up to the rapture of their song. Nonetheless, the fate of both is an allegory of modern class society because neither the bourgeois nor the worker is free to enjoy abandonment to the song of the Sirens: 'The stopped ears which the pliable proletarians have retained ever since the time of myth have no advantage over the immobility of the master' (Adorno and Horkheimer 1979: 36). The restrictive management and organisation that manifested in Odysseus as a cunning response to the forewarning by Circe of the effect of the Sirens' song is the same mode of thought that is employed by the modern manager who restricts the lives and imaginations of himself and his workers to sustain efficient production. Adorno and Horkheimer use this allegory to demonstrate the conditions of work in modern societies and its continuity with the experience of culture (see Chapter 3).

The risks and sacrifices that Odysseus and his crew experienced seem to parallel the sacrifices and risks of modernity. We sacrifice the freedom to think and act in ways that suit us to fit in with the requirements of modern life – to follow the education, career path and family life that is prescribed by our culture. Our lives are not a predictable continuation of the lives of our parents and forefathers; they have the pattern of a journey on which there are risks and challenges and on which we have to anticipate fate and apply cunning to get by. As we move from place to place, seeking employment, partnership or pleasure, we threaten or sacrifice the communal bonds with those around us. This is applying rationality to achieve the ends prescribed by capitalism in the modern world. It is equivalent to the sacrifice of what for Freud are our instinctual drives – but Adorno and Horkheimer are more concerned with the sacrifice of our place within nature and the social world. For them, it is the domination of selfhood that is the insanity of modernity and enlightenment: 'Odysseus, too, is the self who always restrains himself and forgets his life and yet recalls it only as wandering' (Adorno and Horkheimer

1979: 55–6). Enlightenment thought is totalitarian in the way it takes over modern people and subjects them to a form of life that sets them against each other and against nature; that is the consequence of the drive to dominate nature. For the critical theorists, myth is a form of thought that emerges out of the life experiences of a society, one that can be continually reinterpreted and reused and so is a cultural resource. But in modernity, myth in the form of enlightenment becomes unitary and stagnant, providing the means of domination but no route to freedom.

Freud: Dreams and myths

There is a parallel between the interpretation of myth and the interpretation of the contents of dreams as developed by Freud. He took dreams seriously but not literally: dreams have to be subject to interpretation before they can tell us anything about our feelings or experiences. His method treats the contents of dreams as symbolic representations of experiences and feelings that connect what might appear to be real events and people in unreal ways. The characters in dreams can change and indeed can be compound: one 'person' in a dream may represent a number of people. In his analysis of his own dream of an encounter with a woman called Irma, the central character is not a representation of one person but a compound of at least five other women, including his own daughter, other patients and potential patients. Freud's conclusion is that the dream is not really about a person but about his skill in treating patients in terms of diagnosing hysterical symptoms and treating them successfully and in competition with other doctors. He says of the dream: *'Thus its content was the fulfilment of a wish and its motive was wish'* (Freud 1976: 196). His wish was to exonerate his actions in offering psychological treatment and exculpate him from the suffering of others from illnesses that he could not or did not treat or for which his treatment was refused.

Dreams, like myths, do not represent the world in a real way. Dreams have the quality of myths type one in that they have the form of an historical story with characters who are superhuman (e.g. more than one person) and strange events (e.g. coincidences, connections). The various characters that Freud calls to mind in his analysis are suggested by features of the Irma character and various effects of treatments are suggested by events in the dream (including an injection of trimethylamin given by his friend Otto). There is also a sense in which dreams are like myths type two in that they purport to describe causal relations (symptoms and illnesses, physical and psychoanalytic treatments, recovery and demise). But Freud does not take dreams as dismissible, as is usually the case with type two myths: just because the 'facts' in the dream are clearly wrong (such as the 'senseless idea' of an injection of trimethylamin as a treatment – Freud 1976: 183) does not mean that the dream is meaningless.

Freud of course famously used myth to understand the sexual development of humans (see Chapter 5). He put forward the contentious account of the Oedipus Complex, in which the different sexualities of male and female children are worked out through a series of transformations of their relations with their parents of different sexes (Freud 1976; 1977). Freud's use of Sophocles' drama treats it as a myth; his argument for the force of the ancient story in modern times is that its audience feel some compelling identification with the experience of incest and patricide: 'It is the fate of all of us, perhaps, to direct our first sexual impulse towards our mother and our first hatred and our first murderous wish against our father. Our dreams convince us that this is so' (Freud 1976: 364). Whether Freud's reading of the Oedipus myth onto the development of human sexuality is persuasive is not so important here;[3] it is an aspect of his theory that is largely overlooked by critical theory (except of course the telling send-up and critique of its social consequences by Deleuze and Guattari 1984). His use of ancient myth to critique a taken-for-granted religious or biological account of sexual development is, however, reminiscent of the way critical theory uses myth as a potent resource for disturbing existing world-views.

Just as Freud takes up a systematic and rigorous analysis of dreams that seem meaningless in terms of the natural sciences, so fifty years or so later, structuralism took up the analysis of myths. It used techniques borrowed from structural phonology, particularly the work of Vladimir Propp (1984) on Russian 'wondertales', to found a rigorous analysis of myths. Claude Lévi-Strauss (1968) developed a method of studying the function of characters rather than the variation in their names and forms. The structure of the stories – the arrangement of characters and the things that happened to them – was a vehicle for meanings and values. This technique showed that structurally the same myths arise in different, unconnected cultures, suggesting that they dealt with problems that were fundamental to any human society – problems like the difficulty of grasping the idea of a person being the product of two people, the enigma of life after death, or the taboo on incest. For Lévi-Strauss, the Oedipus myth, for example, is tied up with achieving a shift from a cosmology that understands humans, like plants, as growing from a single seed (autochthony) to a more modern belief that humans are the product of a union between men and women (bisexual reproduction). The structural analysis should work with any version, and Lévi-Strauss fits events from various versions of the Greek myth into his structural analysis, even pointing out that Freud's version fits too (1968: 217). This idea of myth saw it as not merely popular entertainment but also as a form of communication about the knowledge and values in a culture.

Just because narrative forms such as myths and dreams have no intended meaning or direct connection to the characters, actions and events in the world does not mean that they can be dismissed as nonsense. Freud's technique of dream analysis may not have survived as his most potent contribution to our understanding of the psyche, and the structural analysis of myths, despite its methodological trappings of rigour, convinces few today with its analyses. However, Freud's attention to dreams was successful in pointing to the significance of the unconscious in ontogenetic development of the psychic lives of individuals. The parallel idea that the historical development of societies cannot be understood without reference to the mythic contents of culture has also survived.

Lefebvre: Myth and publicity

The Odysseus myth is one that survives into modernity and retains its appeal to the post-enlightenment imagination, providing the basis for countless reinterpretations and reworkings. James Joyce's *Ulysses* is of course one – which Henri Lefebvre takes as a metaphor for the modern journey of everyday life rather than the epic journey of the ancients (1971: 3–11 – see Chapter 6). Lefebvre has a keen sense of the mythological, drawing on both the Greek myths (e.g. his retelling of the Oedipus myth: 1995: 49–55) and modern myths (e.g. his discussion of Chaplin's tramp: 1991a: 10–13; his analysis of the myth of progress and a utopian 'new life': 1995: 65–94). Rather like Adorno and Horkheimer, Lefebvre also argues that myths are displaced by rationality in the 'bureaucratic society of controlled consumption' (1971 – see Chapter 6), but that they return in the sub-system of 'publicity', as he calls it: the advertising discourse that creates value in the objects and experiences of consumption. From its origins in the nineteenth century, 'publicity' offered a price and description of objects, provoked desire and induced the consumer to buy. By the second half of the twentieth century its impact was rather more extensive, so that Lefebvre claims 'there is *nothing* – whether object, individual or social group – that is *valued* apart from its double, the image that advertises and sanctifies it' (1971: 105). In order to promote consumer goods, the advertising image duplicates not simply the object but also the desire, pleasure and happiness it promises. For Lefebvre, this makes publicity the first of the consumer goods because it creates myths, or more precisely it 'borrows existing myths', putting them to the dual purpose of selling a specific good and offering them for general consumption:

> Thus it salvages and reconditions myths, the Smile Myth (the joy of consuming identified with the imaginary joy of the man or woman depicted consuming the object), the Display Myth (the social activity consisting in putting things on display and, in turn, producing such objects as the 'display unit', for instance). (1971: 106)

In taking apart an after-shave advertisement – showing a half-naked youth hanging from a yacht's rigging and scanning the horizon – Lefebvre reads the caption and the picture together to identify the myths that it recovers: nature, virility and their combination. The effect is to present not just a product but a whole attitude to life that addresses the subject of the reader, inserting him or her into the chain of signs and values that acts as ideology. The television advertisement addresses you directly, in your own home, telling you how to live, dress, decorate the house, 'in short how to exist; you are totally and thoroughly programmed' (Lefebvre 1971: 107). Everyday life in the society of controlled consumption is a potential whirlpool of choice and possibility, and 'culture' draws on the downgraded tools of art and poetry to guide us with a series of signs and symbols ('... all that can be consumed becomes a symbol of consumption and the consumer is fed on symbols' – Lefebvre 1971: 108). The symbols of wealth and dexterity, of happiness and love, are woven into a series of myths that are deployed in the content of publicity: Scientificness, Virility, Femininity, Technology, Youthfulness, Reliability, Beauty, Eroticism, Urbanism, Naturalness, Rationality, Fashion, Sportiveness, and so on (Lefebvre 1971: 109).

Barthes: Myth and ideology

Lefebvre in his evocative but rather chaotic way explores the relationship between signs and signifiers and the nature of language. But it is Roland Barthes who is more famously associated with the mechanics of myths in contemporary culture as he moves from a flirtation with a systematic structuralist method towards using this approach to critical effect. Writing about the mythology of the automobile in 1963, for example, Barthes identifies a tension between the 'domestic' and the 'sporty' as mythic forms that the car can adopt (Barthes 1993c; see Dant 2000). These are not simply the devices of publicity, they are ideological myths, perhaps stimulated by advertisements and magazine articles, that become cultural resources for making sense of the object as it is incorporated into everyday life. The same influence of structuralist linguistics that provoked Lévi-Strauss's (1968) approach to myth provides the impetus for Barthes to break from a tradition of interpretation that reads texts, such as myths, in a simple sequential way. We tend to read texts in terms of the rules of experience which fit with our life experience, that is to say, events and experiences are treated as cumulative and fitted into a time sequence which displays the 'logic' of action. Moreover, we tend to treat characters and their attributes as being of crucial importance in grasping the significance of texts such as myths and dreams. A semiological reading disturbs our usual attention to the linear and sequential consequences of actions. It stops us from taking a 'literal' view of them as representing reality or a realist view that treats them like practical instructions to guide our actions.

Barthes is most famous for a series of essays that were originally published in a number of French journals (*France Observateur, Les Lettres Nouvelles, Esprit*) in the mid-1950s and as a book, *Mythologies*, in 1957, translated into English as two separate volumes. *Mythologies* (Barthes 1993a) and *The Eiffel Tower and*

Other Mythologies (Barthes 1979a). The essays were originally produced monthly as journalism rather than as contributions to an academic project, and yet they have had enormous influence on the development of academic thinking about culture. Barthes admits that the topics he chose to write about – wrestling, striptease, Billy Graham, music-hall song, an exhibition of plastics, toys, steak and chips, soap powders and detergent, and so on – were chosen because of their topicality and what attracted his interest. But for all the variety in the topics there is a consistency between his treatment of them. He says that from the start he was impatient at the '"naturalness" with which newspapers, art and common sense dress up a reality which, even though it is the one we live in, is undoubtedly determined by history' (Barthes 1993a: 11). It was only later that he explored the idea of myth as being a distinct language; to begin with he says that the notion of myth seemed to explain these examples of the 'falsely obvious' (Barthes 1993a: 11). Rather more interesting than the trappings of semiological jargon that he used to analyse myth as language was his aim, inspired by a form of Marxism, to undertake 'an ideological critique bearing on the language of so-called mass-culture' (Barthes 1993a: 9). I will look at a couple of examples before exploring how they work as myth and as ideology.

Barthes writes two pages on the face of the silver screen actress Greta Garbo (Barthes 1993a: 56–7) as it appeared in films and in publicity and news photographs. This is not an account of her as a person but Garbo as a 'star' or a cultural icon. He argues that her face, like that of Valentino before her, produces an 'ecstasy' that is to do with notions of courtly love – literally a face to die for. It is of course a made-up face; these are not 'natural' faces, but are made up for the harsh lighting of early black and white films. He describes the ephemeral quality of the flour-white complexion covered in the 'snowy thickness of a mask' as if it is 'set in plaster', a face that is sculpted. The mask is not hiding a secret but offers 'an archetype of the human face' that bears 'a sort of Platonic Idea of the human creature'. That she is known as *'the Divine'* fits with the idea that she is otherwordly, perfect. It is the eyes ('two faintly tremulous wounds') and the 'relation between the curve of the nostrils and the arch of the eyebrows' that reveal the humanity underneath the mask. It suggests to him that Garbo's face is not simply a perfect mask but represents a transition between the ideal and the real, from the mystical to the mortal: he writes of 'the passage from awe to charm'. This transition in the way that myth represents its characters culminates in the face of Audrey Hepburn, which appears not as a mask but as 'an infinite complexity of morphological functions': 'The face of Garbo is an Idea, that of Hepburn, an Event' (Barthes 1993a: 57). The power of Garbo's image is in its representation of an abstract unreal, almost holy, ideal. The power of Hepburn's image is in its dynamic, modern, realistic form. Barthes is pointing out that cinema's technical capacity to carry detail in images changes how it represents and defines beauty. How images are chosen, constructed and presented forms the mythical values of the culture. His critique shows that this shift in the form of cultural images is neither a natural evolution nor a mere shift in fashion, but is an historical process. From the 'deified face' of Garbo to the face of Hepburn as a face 'of substance', this seemingly trivial aspect of contemporary culture reveals a shift in the nature of modernity from adoration of the ideal to enjoyment of the real.

In *Mythologies* (1993a) Barthes takes specific examples of contemporary culture and subjects them to critique as myths rather than question their representation of 'reality' (which would be to debunk them as type two myths). In doing this he is extending the approach of what is called 'criticism' in the study of literature and art to the contents of mass culture. However, he is not engaging in criticism within a cultural form; he is not a film critic but is trying to understand how film is situated in the culture in general. By treating events, narratives or images such as the face of Garbo as not having an obvious or straightforward meaning – that it is beautiful or not – Barthes is treating it as mythological, as connected to other cultural forms and indicative of the way that the culture communicates values and ideas of beauty. And he is specifically interested in the changes that occur within modernity that disconnect us from previous forms of culture.

In another short piece, Barthes considers the mythic effect of an exhibition of plastics (which were new in the 1950s) as signalling a new form of cultural reproduction. He sees it as a form of alchemy, making one thing turn into another, like turning base metal into gold or water into wine. In at one end go some greenish crystals and out the other end come complete, shaped, smooth objects: bowls, toys, tubes, and so on. This appears as a supernatural event, a miracle that happens in front of the eyes of the visitors although hidden in the depths of the machine. This magical simulation of forms is endless, each object precisely the same as the last, and is the result of the chemical properties of plastic (which comes in a variety of forms with names that sound to Barthes as if they come from Greek mythology: polystyrene, polyvinyl, polyethylene). But the things that are produced lack the granularity and fibre of natural materials because 'plastic keeps a flocculent appearance, something opaque, creamy and curdled, something powerless ever to achieve the triumphant smoothness of Nature' (Barthes 1993a: 98).

The lack of a natural form means that plastic is always a material of 'imitation' for Barthes, but rather than imitating rare substances it is prosaic and basic, aspiring only to usefulness. And this, he argues, is the effect of a change in material production that shifts from the form of myth as the imitation of nature to a myth of the creation of usefulness:

> ... it is no longer the Idea, the pure Substance to be regained or imitated: an artificial Matter ... is about to replace her, and to determine the very invention of forms. ... Plastic is wholly swallowed up in the fact of being used: ultimately, objects will be invented for the sole pleasure of using them. (Barthes 1993a: 98–9)

As with the face of Garbo, it is not the objects, their design, or manufacture that he is subjecting to critique but the cultural impact of transformation in mythical form. Technological rationality produces a shift from the ideal materials of nature to artificial and endlessly malleable objects. Plastic has a similar effect in three dimensions to that which photography has in two, in its potential to reproduce and imitate cheaply, *en masse*. The child's toy, for example, can be moulded in plastic to replicate natural (e.g. an animal) or imaginary (e.g. a cartoon character) forms that are safe and lasting when used in play. The endless identical plastic copies retain their power to precisely represent and miniaturise other forms that are less fragile and precious than the singular carved or shaped toys of earlier materials such as wood or metal.

It is in the final essay, titled 'Myth Today', written later than the small substantive essays, that Barthes relates his critique of myth to the political dimension. At the beginning, he sounds like an enthusiast for the possibility of a systematic method that will render the mythological structure of cultural products easy to unravel. But the substantive essays do not break down myths into signifiers and signifieds, let alone into 'mythemes', as Lévi-Strauss (1976: 211) called the units of myths, and their power owes little if anything to a systematic semiology. Barthes was later to abandon the idea that myth has a structural form analysable like a language, having unsuccessfully attempted to offer a structural analysis of the workings of the 'rhetorical' code in *The Fashion System* (1990). More interestingly, further on in the 'Myth Today' essay he makes explicit the links between myth and ideology in which signs have ideological effects that can be subject to critique. Although he is using the word 'myth' in a way that connects with the myths of ancient societies – myths of type one – he is also bringing the idea of myth up to date. In modernity myths are not stories of human characters who engage with gods and perform supernatural feats. In their place are the technologies of modernity (such as cinema and plastics moulding), which appear to have magical effects in representing the world, presenting what is human history as if it were natural. Modern myths are moral accounts of value and cause (what is beauty and how it is formed, what is useful and how it is made) that shift with technological changes. The messages of value obscure their origins and appear to be timeless and independent of how they are created: beauty does not change between Garbo and Hepburn but the technology with which it is represented does; usefulness does not begin with plastics, but the magic of technology gives it a new value.

What Barthes says of myth is that 'it points out and it notifies, it makes us understand something and it imposes it on us' (1993a: 117). In the collection called *The Eiffel Tower and Other Mythologies* (1979a) he writes about 'Conjugations' – marriages that are reported for public consumption in newspapers. He describes three types of marriage, pointing out that their reporting involves more than the simple denotative meaning that so-and-so has married or will marry so-and-so. Each is mythologised as the marriage is extracted from its original setting (the lives of the people involved) and presented in a newspaper in terms of the social order: the grand marriage; the marriage of the beauty queen and the electrician; the marriage of the film stars. The grand marriage is a lavish spectacle of wealth and power with civic dignitaries, military uniforms and a mass of onlookers. The beauty queen eschews glamour, returning to her petit-bourgeois roots to set up home ('two hearts one hearth' – Barthes 1979a: 25). The film stars' marriage is announced as a prospect, an ideal coupling of astral forces, a coming together of mythical gods in the modern era. The newspaper story uses a series of mythological signifiers to represent the marriages that depend on taking the social order for granted and so reinforce the values of social distinction rather than challenge it. And of course it is the re-circulation of values in social distinction that is the point of reporting the marriage in a national newspaper when few readers have any interest in the lives of the people involved: 'Semiology has taught us that myth has the task of giving an historical intention a natural justification, and making contingency appear eternal. Now this process is exactly that of bourgeois ideology' (Barthes 1973: 142). Ideology smooths over the contradictions between the interests of different classes by treating the existing social order as natural, as beyond question. The readers don't know or really care about the the people getting married but their history is an occasion to reconfirm that the social order is as always, as if it was natural. Myth for Barthes works in a similar way to Marx's account of ideology as the camera obscura that inverts or 'inflects' reality, distorting things rather than creating or hiding them, producing a 'kind of nebula', 'a condensation ... of a certain knowledge' (1993a: 121). The point of his analysis is to critique the mythical form of signification as a device that sustains the French class system.

Myth, Barthes argues, achieves the particular ideological effect of persuading us that a certain order of the world, a certain way of doing things, is given by nature, rather than the result of human action on the world that could have been otherwise. Barthes argues that myth is 'depoliticized speech', by which he means that the political causes or impacts of situations is removed as they become separated from their historical specificity. Myth, he says, achieves its ideological effect by abolishing the complexity of human acts; it 'does away with all dialectics ... organises a world which is without contradictions' (Barthes 1993a: 143). The order of the world represented in modern myth is bourgeois ideology:

> The whole of France is steeped in this anonymous ideology: our press, our films, our theatre, our pulp literature, our rituals, our Justice, our diplomacy, our conversations our remarks about the weather, a murder trial, a touching wedding, the cooking we dream of, the garments we wear, everything, in everyday life, is dependent on the representation which the bourgeoisie *has and makes us* have of the relations between man and the world. (Barthes 1993a: 140)

Bourgeois ideology has become all-pervasive in modernity, incorporating all classes, covering up contradictions between classes and operating as an account of the world that will work for everyone, passing itself off as naturalistic. This is a rather different approach than Adorno and Horkheimer adopt towards the role of myth, but the naturalism of bourgeois ideology is based for Barthes on 'technical, scientific progress, on an unlimited transformation of nature' (1993a: 142) – the same technological rationality and all-pervasive impact of instrumental reason that the Frankfurt critical theorists identified.

Baudrillard: Reality and illusion

Baudrillard's later work identifies the trajectory of late modernity as being towards bringing off the 'perfect crime': the 'murder of reality' that will result in the extermination or disappearance of the 'vital illusion' with which modern culture sustains reality (Baudrillard 1996b, 2000). Baudrillard's strategy is to suggest that we resist:

> Against the extermination of evil, of death, of illusion, against this Perfect Crime, we must fight for the criminal imperfection of the world. Against this artificial paradise of technicity and virtuality, against the attempt to build a world completely positive, rational and true, we must save the traces of the illusory world's definitive opacity and mystery. (2000: 74)

The mythology of a culture is the network of illusions that sustain it, providing a sense of reality to those who live within it, of a world that they inhabit and which is theirs. If the 'perfect crime' were to be achieved, we would of course no longer have any sense of 'reality' as something that could be represented and myths would no longer have any potency. This position is remarkably close to that of the Frankfurt theorists: we must beware the mythification of science (the perfect crime) while recognising the centrality of myth to society and its continuing history.

Baudrillard's work, especially that written after 1976, employs a range of resources from philosophy, social theory, science, technology, literature, history, film, poetry – and myth. Many of his references, like his metaphors, reoccur at different points in his work to produce a mythical structure with its own cast of characters who have recognisable attributes and with whom his readers become familiar and comfortable – just as the readers of any set of myths. Baudrillard's skill is to wield myth to undermine myth, to use the metaphorical devices of writing to turn reality back on itself, to achieve a similar effect in our minds to that of *trompe l'oeil* and the mirror in the material world. Rather than debunking myths type two, as science so often attempts, he retells myths type one in ways that undermine the claims of instrumental reason. For example, the riddle of the Sphinx and Freud's application of the Oedipus myth to a 'complex' are called on to help make sense of the transformation of human social action from production to seduction (Baudrillard 1990b: 137–44).

One of the myths Baudrillard uses is attributed to the ancient Chinese author Zhaung-Zi, who tells how a good butcher wields a knife in such a way that it never blunts:

> Strictly speaking, the joints of the bones have gaps in them and the cutting edge of the knife has no width. Whoever knows how to drive the extremely fine blade into the gaps manages his knife with ease because it is working in empty spaces. That is why I have used my knife for nineteen years and its cutting edge always appears newly sharpened. (Zhuang-Zi, *The Principle of Hygiene III*, quoted in Baudrillard 1993a: 120)

The butcher who tries to cut through bone, cartilage and sinew will blunt his knife, as will the analyst his cutting edge if he proceeds according to a method that progresses from one term in the system to the next in a sequential and linear fashion; the logic of technological rationality rapidly becomes a blunt instrument that will be of little use in grasping the workings of myths in modernity. Just as Barthes seized on semiology as a technique for reading myth against its ordinary reading, Baudrillard is looking for a different approach that 'follows the body beneath the body', like Zhaung-Zi's butcher, and which looks for what 'runs beneath the discourse and traces something (a name, a formula) whose absence haunts the text' (1993a: 121). The myth of Zhaung-Zi's butcher provides Baudrillard with a way of describing the work that he does on the myths of modernity that is not systematic and brutal, does not follow the blunt logic of instrumental reason or 'objective knowledge', and has more in common with the deconstructive analysis of a literary text ('the knife and the body are exchanged, the knife articulates the body's lack and thereby deconstructs it in accordance with its own rhythm' – 1993a: 120).

Baudrillard treats some of his literary sources – particularly his references to Borges and Canetti – as if they were myths. For example, Chamisso's story *Peter Schlemihl* and a film of *The Student of Prague* provide him with metaphors of the alienation to be found in consumer society through their mystical use of mirror images and shadows (Baudrillard 1998: 188). Borges provides a myth of illusion, of the representation of the real, with the 'Rose of Paracelsus' (Baudrillard 1990b: 164–6) and a myth of simulation of the social as a game in 'The Lottery of Babylon' (Baudrillard 1990a: 150–3). The idea that chance is what determines the lives of individuals and that the game cannot be anticipated also occurs in the story of the 'Death in Samarkand' (Baudrillard 1990a: 72–4; 1990b: 136). What these tales do is to suggest that fate has a logic of which we occasionally get a glimpse after the event. But the logic of fate is never constituent of what we take to be reality – it cannot provide us with sufficient information about how we should act, only enough to warn us of the unpredictable nature of fate. These moral tales of the human desire to play and to guess, to attempt to beat chance and fate, provide a device with which Baudrillard discusses the failure of a master strategy, an analytic method such as instrumental reason through which fate might be controlled and reality tamed. He quotes Canetti – 'past a certain point in time, history has not been real' (in Baudrillard 1990a: 14, and in different translation 1994b: 1; 2000: 62) – to provide a starting point for his ruminations on the impossibility of taking control of history, of dominating the real and operating a 'final solution' of bringing evolution to an end (Baudrillard 2000: 3–30).

A theme that recurs throughout Baudrillard's work is how representation both relies on and undermines the existence of the real – it appears like the real, but displays its unreality, rather as the fictitious nature of myths do. But each representation takes on a form of reality at the level of the imaginary that can sometimes be distinguished from the reality of the senses. Baudrillard's curiosity about the seductive effect of mirrors and *trompe l'oeil* comes together with his interest in myth in Pausanias' version of the story of Narcissus, in which 'Narkissos' had a twin sister with whom he was in love till she died; looking in the spring water at his own reflection he imagined he was looking at his sister (1990a: 68–9). Cloning, a recurring theme in Baudrillard's later work, is 'a monstrous parody of the myth of Narcissus' that produces a doubling in which there is no illusion: 'The double is an imaginary figure that, like the soul or one's shadow, or one's image in a mirror, haunts the subject with a faint death that has to be constantly warded off' (Baudrillard 1990a: 168).

For Baudrillard, the form of myths as stories of fantastic possibilities enables him to explore a series of modern myths that test social values and the boundaries of reality in late modernity: cloning, fractals, DNA, war, terrorism, hostage taking, sex, and so on.[4] Whereas instrumental reason might approach these topics as ones that needed to be debunked as type two myths, Baudrillard recognises that by treating them as type one myths that need to be retold slightly differently, they might teach us something about our world. These modern myths are dealt with in the terms in which they circulate within the culture – in the press, television, films, art, science fiction, literature, even sociology and philosophy – rather than in the singular language of science. By describing how they contribute to a circulating set of values with which we orient ourselves in the modern world, Baudrillard undermines these myths without engaging in any technical account of the truth of the matter. This is in contrast to those commentaries that follow the strategy of instrumental rationality that identifies causal relations in the social world as equivalent to causal relations in the material world, and dismisses type one myths as simply stories. The 'impossibility' of what is described in ancient myths denies them any purchase on the lives of moderns, though they may have poetic or other aesthetic qualities that are entertaining. The same application of instrumental rationality exposes type two myths as appearing to represent the world truthfully but actually being based on fiction.

Conclusions

Myth takes on a different quality in modernity when the language of supernatural forces gives way to the language of 'natural' relations: the systematic language of science as it describes the material world. The allegorical function of myth provides a way of describing things that are difficult to imagine or say without giving them a structural form, and it can also represent patterns that recur in different forms at different times. Most powerfully, Adorno and Horkheimer argue that enlightenment thought itself begins to operate as a myth, generating moral precepts from a causal account of the workings of the world. But in the hands of Lefebvre and Barthes we are shown how the everyday world of ordinary culture, of advertisements and newspaper articles, is constructed as a series of myths that encourage us to take the social world as natural and to take for granted its social structure.

The critical theorists do not offer an analytical method[5] capable of revealing the fictitious nature of myths but engage in interpretation and argument, in redescription and retelling that changes how myths are read. The writing of the critical theorists tends towards the essayistic and fragmentary rather than the systematic or analytical; it lends itself to retelling myths that can represent the changing shape of modern culture. Adorno and Horkheimer offer a retelling of the story of Odysseus as the first modern (1979: 43–80), Lefebvre offers a retelling of the myth of Oedipus as one of the desire for social order and boundaries (1995: 49–55), and Freud's retelling of the Oedipus myth has already superseded the potency of the original in modern culture (1976: 363–6, 1977 315–322, 330–343). Barthes's *Mythologies* (1993a) has taken on the weight of a mythical text that provides a moral code for reading modern culture, while Baudrillard's myth of the end of sex and a return to the world inhabited by immortals brings the ancient myths right up to date (2000: 3–30).

Summary

- *Traditional myth* – type one myth – is a fictitious narrative, told and retold, that blends natural and supernatural characters and forces to moral effect.
- *Modern myth* – type two myth – appears to be a description of nature, but is debunked as 'false'. Nonetheless, it continues to be told and retold to moral effect.
- *Adorno and Horkheimer*: Enlightenment is seen as the dispersal of the fantasy of myth with science, but science itself becomes mythical.
- *Freud*: Dreams play a similar role for the individual that myths play for society – although not 'real' or 'factual', they contain an underlying truth.
- *Lefebvre*: 'Publicity' (advertising) is the form of modern myth by which value is attributed to the possibilities for choice in the society of controlled consumption (e.g. Smile Myth, Display Myth).
- *Barthes*: Myth has an ideological impact, connecting cultural objects to everyday life. A semiological reading interrupts the taken-for-grantedness of modern myths, providing a critique of how they obscure history and

treat as 'natural' the values of bourgeois society – that is, beyond question and beyond change.

- *Baudrillard*: Myth has a role in social theory to explain by metaphor and analogy and thereby resist the untenable master strategy of rational, scientific discourse. Myth can help to understand the illusions of reality, including the consequences of science (e.g. cloning).

Further reading

Thomas Bulfinch's *Myths of Greece and Rome* (1981) provides easily accessible versions of the ancient myths and the illustrations remind the reader of the powerful impact they have had on the history of western art. The age of Roland Barthes's *Mythologies* (1993a [1957]) means that many of its references to ordinary culture have become rather obscure for younger readers, but it continues to be a stimulating account of what we might take to be the modern equivalent of the myths of Greece and Rome and it is fun to work out the contemporary equivalents to Barthes's myths.

Notes

1 I am using 'allegory' in a rather loose way here. Walter Benjamin, for example, distinguishes carefully between allegory and symbol – see Gilloch 2002: 80–2.

2 This problem of studying a knowing subject produces what Giddens terms the 'double hermeneutic', which sociology must recognise because it 'deals with a pre-interpreted world, in which the meanings developed by active subjects actually enter into the actual constitution or production of the world' (1976: 146). The social world must not only be interpreted as an object, but the ways in which it is interpreted by social actors as subjects must also be interepreted. The actions of the actors being studied may be altered by what is learnt.

3 For an interesting, scholarly and succinct overview of Freud's theory of sexuality and a neat summary of the problems with the Oedipus Complex, see Weeks 1985: 127–48.

4 Notice that Baudrillard mixes the themes of modern science and technology with those of culture in general; in the tradition of critical theory he treats natural science and its products as myths no more worthy of reverence as 'facts' or 'scientific knowl-edge' than any other cultural product.

5 Barthes's attempt to offer a systematic semiology does have the appearance of an analytical method but it does not produce singular readings.

THREE

Work and Non-Work

'It's home from work we go' – this cheerful line sung by the dwarfs as they return from their day's diamond mining in Disney's *Snow White and the Seven Dwarfs* (1937) sums up much of the modern idea of work: a masculine, physical, activity that is done away from the home for a substantial period of the day. With the housework left for Snow White to do (who, along with assorted benign animals, insists on whistling while she works), the real 'workers' were happy to come home when their period of 'work' was complete. The dwarfs, trumping along in a line, more or less in step to their singing, offer a much lighter face to the sphere of work than Fritz Lang's regimented ranks and lines of workers off to the day-shift, eleven years earlier in *Metropolis* (1926). Lang's workers, their heads bowed, trudge in time but with no tune, all dressed alike in a uniform of jackets and trousers that are worn and faded. When they get to work – also underground – they attend to the machines in a frenetic and driven way. One machine is like a clock that requires the worker to follow its every movement, unceasingly and at its pace: in one memorable scene it takes on the appearance of a face that devours workers. Like Disney's workers, Lang's are male, working away from their homes, engaged in a physical activity for a substantial period of the day. But Lang's rather more dystopian view adds an exploiting leisure class, regulation by a clock, domination by machinery and a sense of the futility of the work.

The distinction between these two representations of work can easily be identified in the economic relations that characterise the situation of the worker. While the dwarfs appear to own their tools, the rights to mine their diamonds and the product of their efforts, the *Metropolis* workers must sell their labour power to the exploiting capitalist class in return for what are clearly meagre wages in conditions not of their own choosing. In the way of filmic representations, these differences in their circumstances are emphasised by the demeanour and attitude of the characters. The dwarfs are happy with their lot and regard the arrival of Snow White with her special charms (and willingness to undertake domestic work) as a bonus. The *Metropolis* workers are wretched and poor and easily led by the robot version of Maria into destroying the machines they work at. Although stereotypical, these representations do give a sense of some of the features of the reality of work.

Time and effort is expended on activity that is neither intrinsically rewarding (satisfying or pleasurable) nor going to bring immediate returns (such as food to take home). The idyll of work in the Disney film is, however, in sharp contrast to Lang's emphasis on the automated machinery that transforms and dehumanises work. The *Metropolis* workers forget the wives, children and homes that they endanger when they flood the subterranean world but the dwarfs support and defend Snow White in her difficulties with witchery.

Critical theory has challenged the view of work that underlies its representation in both of these very different films, not least by pointing to the ways in which symbolic representations, such as those of Disney, encourage an acceptance of the form of work in advanced capitalism. In general, critical theories neither focus on work as a distinct sphere of life, nor provide a detailed empirical account of the organisation of work. What they do is treat work as one component in the totality of modern life so that 'work' is contrasted with what appears to be 'non-work', and what emerges is a critique based neither on the class divisions so starkly presented by Lang nor on the gender divisions central to Disney's vision. Instead, critical theory develops a theory of work as an aspect of modern culture that undermines any presumed distinction between work and the rest of human activity in modernity.

Marx: Work as species-being

It was Marx who, largely through a debate with the political economists, set out a theory of work as estranged labour under capitalism that constitutes a distinct activity and sphere of life. Labour is the selling of the labourer's time and effort to the capitalist as a commodity that is then employed as a means of production: 'In political economy *labour* appears only in the form of *wage-earning activity*' (Marx 1975: 289). Work as an activity becomes the commodity 'labour power' when the form of private property develops into a series of social relations entailed in the accumulation of capital and its investment in production. But the activity of work is for Marx a feature of what it is to be human that distinguishes us from other animals. Whereas non-human animals are at one with their life activity, which includes making things such as nests, the human animal makes 'his life activity itself an object of his will and consciousness' (Marx 1975: 328). Animals only produce to meet their immediate needs but the human 'truly produces only in freedom from such need', that is, when he creates something apart from himself 'in accordance with the laws of beauty' (Marx 1975: 329). There is something about the work of transforming nature that is of essence to what it is to be human: 'It is therefore in his fashioning of the objective that man really proves himself to be a *species-being*. Such production is his active species-life' (Marx 1975: 329).

The 'purposeful activity' of fashioning the natural, objective world is something that humans do naturally, expressing the relationship between human consciousness and action beyond mere animal necessity (Marx 1976: 284). Marx's analysis is based on an individualist model of human existence ('man'), in whom life activity is controlled by consciousness: 'A *being* sees himself as independent only when he stands on his own feet, and he only stands on his own feet when he owes his *existence* to himself' (Marx 1992: 356). This 'natural' form of work as free and spontaneous activity is transformed under capitalism to be nothing more than a means to an end, once labour is alienated from its product. Labour is the capacity to engage in work activities that may be offered on the labour market as labour power (Marx 1976: 270). The labour process involves a mixture of intellectual and physical effort that Marx famously describes as

> a process by which man, through his own actions, mediates, regulates and controls the metabolism between himself and nature. He confronts the materials of nature as a force of nature. He sets in motion the natural forces which belong to his own body, his arms, legs, head and hands, in order to appropriate the materials of nature in a form adapted to his own needs. Through this movement he acts upon external nature and changes it, and in this way he simultaneously changes his own nature. (1976: 283)

It's not difficult to see why those working dwarfs were transformed into singing dwarfs when their labour took on this noble character of transforming nature – into diamonds too! But then Marx argues that the commodification of labour power under capitalism leads to alienation, to the estrangement of the worker from his product, from his species-being, from his fellow workers and from the process of production (1992: 324). Estranged labour is work undertaken for wages paid by the non-worker, the owner of private property – the capitalist. This is what leads to the experience of the drones in *Metropolis*. Marx's critique of the mode of capitalist production hangs on his critique of work as transformed into labour: the emancipation of workers would reunite them with their species-being by making their work truly theirs, rather than a mere means to existence. Crude communism would simply reproduce on a more general level the relation of the worker to private property, but his own version of communism, Marx tells us, 'is the genuine resolution of the conflict between man and nature, between man and man ... between existence and being, between objectification and self-affirmation, between freedom and necessity, between individual and species' (1992: 348). But we do not learn about what forms work will take, or how the meeting of individual needs and the work of self-reproduction will be socially organised. What would be the status of domestic work and leisure beyond capitalism?

In Marx's analysis the worker owns her or his own labour power and is free to sell it in order to reproduce her- or himself. He allows that the reproduction of labour power requires not only food, clothing, fuel and housing for the worker, but also human reproduction and nurturing, including education, which contribute to the total cost of subsistence of the life-process of the worker. What he does not explore is work that is done on behalf of others (such as family, friends, neighbours, community) outside of the labour process in capitalist production. What is the status of the work that is simply involved in the reproduction of labour: the labour of birth, the housework, childrearing (Snow White's share)? What is the status of work that is simply unproductive: those days when no diamonds are unearthed, or when the labourer is incompetent or lazy? Marx's economistic outlook allows him to get around these problems by talking about the 'average' or 'general' character of labour and claiming it as productive if it 'produces or reproduces capital' (1973: 306fn). Another way of putting this problem is that Marx does not distinguish between different social actions which could be construed as 'work' but which seem merely ancillary to the labour process. Can all such activity be subsumed under the category of reproducing labour power for capital, or do these non-work activities constitute the realisation of species-being?

Some activities may be construed either as work or as pleasure depending on the emotional tone and motivation: playing with children or meeting friends cannot be simply reduced to the reproduction of labour power. The work done as a 'hobby' or 'pastime' is taken on by choice and for pleasure but it may be productive (working on the allotment) or creative (making a model boat or a hand-knitted scarf). Many non-work activities such as taking a walk involve 'work' in the sense of an expenditure of effort, but these uses of the body for pleasure and satisfaction are not negated because they refresh and revitalise the wage labourer's body. Sometimes this sort of work may create 'products' (the model boat, the scarf) that have value in themselves even though they do not contribute directly to the circulation and exchange of values. This is not the sort of work that we return home from; it is work we return home for, for the pleasure in self-creation that we find in the activity. And it is precisely these pleasures and satisfactions that many find in at least some aspects of their paid employment – as the conditions of work have improved under capitalism, the 'labour process' and even the concept of 'alienation' have become formal, technical descriptors of economic relations rather than experienced or felt relations for many who sell their labour power.

Arendt: Toil and trouble

Hannah Arendt intervenes in Marx's account of work and labour by recovering a distinction derived from Greek culture in which *labour* is the necessary, cyclical toil of everyday life that in pre-modern cultures slaves were assigned to undertake. *Work*, on the other hand, refers to the production of things, 'works', that endure beyond any labour process – exactly that activity which Marx describes as the labour process, the process of producing things.[1] She points out that it is nature, not capitalism, that imposes on humans the requirement to labour to meet physical needs, which gets in the way of the species-being activity of working to create 'works' (Arendt 1958: 104). Emancipation from the drudgery of the routine work of *re*-production is not possible according to Arendt; labour, including such pain and toil as it involves, must be accepted as part of the human condition, which would cease without it. But she argues that humans could be free of alienated labour, the labour of the *Metropolis* workers, in the way that the dwarfs (if not Snow White) are. There are of course people – the very rich, the severely disabled – whose every need is met by assistance from others. But this is not a particularly enviable situation. Arendt says that '[f]or mortals, "the easy life of the gods" would be a lifeless life' (1958: 120) – she could be describing the joyless, profligate life of the owning class that Lang depicts in *Metropolis*.

Arendt's argument begins to have some critical edge when she points out that in modern society we have come to love labour and to disregard works. The industrial revolution replaced *workmanship* with *labour* so that what are produced are merely things to be consumed. Work is activity that, initially through violent action on material forms, creates something of permanence, something that endures, something that has solidity and is the fabrication of its maker. This type of activity has a beginning and an end: the completion of an object that was first simply an image in the mind of its maker. Labour, on the other hand, is effort that is continuous and without end; it needs to be repeated, and is often carried on without any sense of a final product, other than to reach the end of a period of time (the shift, or the need to attend to something else). Work produces things to be *used,* and in the industrial age this only refers to that work which produces original models from which the mass-produced series is generated by a mixture of machines and labour. For Arendt, the shift from tools to machines that is characteristic of industrialisation not only transforms the work of building the world into the labour of production but also transforms the worker: 'Unlike the tools of workmanship, which at every given moment in the work process remain the servants of the hand, the machines demand that the laborer serve them, that he adjust the natural rhythm of his body to their mechanical movement' (1958: 147). This is exactly the distinction between Disney's cheerful dwarfs with their hand tools and the workers dominated by Lang's symbolic clock machine. Arendt's distinction between work and labour emphasises the autonomy of the worker, who retains control over the material world (tools, work) and can use that control to realise the contents of imagination (creation), and the subjection of the labourer to control by the masters, who specify what he shall do. In the industrial age, machines that control the speed and detail of the work often represent those masters. Arendt clearly approves of autonomous 'work' as an essential aspect of the human condition – it is one of the ways that humans establish themselves in the world – though not all humans may engage equally in the activity. Industrialisation, mechanisation and automation are central to the critical theorists' analysis of work in modern societies. But, as we shall see, unlike Arendt, many critical theorists recognise that the impact of instrumental activity, based on the machine, extends beyond the sphere of productive work into the non-work lives of modern individuals.

Adorno and Horkheimer: Work and culture

For Max Horkheimer, the work of human beings creates the material and social world around us (1972: 200–2 – see Chapter 7, p. 134). This is true of our material environment: but also of our immaterial environment: the ideas and values, the tastes and significances that we perceive are given to us by the works – including the works of sociology and philosophy – through which we are able to perceive things and make sense of the world. Just as the work we do shapes the world, the work that others have done shapes us. However, the critical theory of Adorno and Horkheimer does not address 'work' as a distinct theme but treats it as a medium through which instrumental reason affects modern life.

> Technology is the essence of this knowledge. It does not work by concepts and images, by the fortunate insight, but refers to method, the exploitation of others' work, and capital. ... What men want to learn from nature is how to use it in order wholly to dominate it and other men. (Adorno and Horheimer 1979: 4)

As enlightenment has taken hold of modernity, technology has led to a systematic organisation of work that employs tools and machinery in the domination of nature. That systematicity has extended to the domination of workers, whose work life – just as in Lang's movie – is driven by the rhythms and demands of machines. What the critical theorists argue is that these processes extend into the cultural life of modern society. Just as the worker is dominated at work, so (s)he is at home and in leisure, which leads to a restriction of the life of the individual, a state of unfreedom, even within the sphere of private life outside the process of production.

In treating the mythical encounter between Odysseus' sailors and the Sirens as a pre-echo of the conditions of late modernity, Adorno and Horkheimer use it to emphasise the continuity of work and leisure conditions in late modernity:

> The oarsmen, who cannot speak to one another, are each of them yoked in the same rhythm as the modern worker in the factory, movie theater and collective. The actual working conditions in society compel conformism – not the conscious influences which also made the suppressed men dumb and separated them from truth. The impotence of the worker is not merely a stratagem of the rules, but the logical consequence of the industrial society into which the ancient Fate – in the very course of the effort to escape it – has finally changed. (1979: 37)

This dulling of sensibilities, of critical faculties, of a sense of individuality, is precisely the effect that the *Metropolis* workers demonstrate when they forget about the consequences of their actions on their families. For Adorno and Horkheimer, it is precisely the 'movie theater' – the place where one sees a Disney film and maybe *Metropolis* – that exemplifies the way in which the pattern of the capitalist labour process is reproduced in the non-work life of the worker. It is the 'culture industry' (see Chapter 4) that replicates outside of work the mechanistic domination of the worker that he or she experiences when toiling at a machine. The culture industry also requires subservience to the machine repetitively as it endlessly produces movies, radio broadcasts and television programmes that are, in their turn, spewed out by machines and that produce these consumers as so many automatons, all thinking and acting in the same way:

> Amusement under late capitalism is the prolongation of work. It is sought after as an escape from the mechanized work process, and to recruit strength in order to be able to cope with it again. But at the same time mechanization has such power over a man's leisure and happiness, and so profoundly determines the manufacture of amusement goods, that his experiences are inevitably after-images of the work process itself. (Adorno and Horkheimer 1979: 137)

This depressing view of late modernity begins to spell out exactly how labour power is reproduced; how the worker is prepared for selling her or his labour to capital. But there is always the potential for developing a critical response that may disturb the link between work and non-work. Disney may provide a myth of the happy worker, smoothing over the contradictions of ownership of the means of production and the gendered nature of work. But Lang – and he may have been an original but not the only film-maker to do this – is not prevented by the form of the culture industry from producing a movie that is critical of the conditions of industrial, waged work. Adorno and Horkheimer argue powerfully that the means of cultural production under late capitalism have the *potential* to transform the individual into a mass by dominating the free time in which humans could work creatively or imaginatively for themselves. But this does not mean that all individuals will be so transformed or that the culture industry will operate in the uniform way that they describe.

Marcuse: One-dimensional society

In a paper originally published in 1941, Marcuse (1998) develops an argument about the cultural impact of mechanisation and rationalisation, which favoured large corporations producing large quantities of goods. These large economic organisations created a cultural form based on efficiency and profitability that shaped future capitalist production. This industrial 'apparatus' transformed the individualistic rationality of early capitalism, which had been focused on self-interest, into the form of technological rationality that 'establishes standards of judgement and fosters attitudes which make men ready to accept and even to introcept the dictates of the apparatus' (Marcuse 1998: 44). The effect was not to disregard individuality but rather to subordinate the individual to criteria external to her- or himself: those specified by and rewarded by the apparatus. The lives of those who work within the apparatus become directed towards efficient production by having to follow machines but also by the bureaucratic and administrative processes controlling work. Within employing organisations and the culture at large, motivations and goals become 'matters of fact', expressible in quantities of money, outputs and time.

Marcuse recognises that the technical development of production has the potential to liberate human workers from toil and drudgery. But the system of technological rationality is more than using machines to replace unrewarding labour because it extends its mechanistic principles of control to the social arrangements of ordinary lives. The apparatus produces the 'modern masses' according to the principles of standardisation and efficiency but at the same time fosters people as individuals through bureaucratic strategies such as vocational training and managerialism. The mass is neither a 'class' in Marx's sense of being capable of collectively becoming conscious of common self-interest, nor is it a 'crowd' in which individuals give up their autonomy. As Marcuse puts it, '[t]he members of the masses are individuals' (1998: 54) because they uniformly accept a career of self-interest and self-preservation within the criteria established by the apparatus.

Marcuse does not explore the distinction between work and labour because his account of work in modernity is that it is in general *alienated*. This alienation may have its roots in the capitalist process of production but has become endemic to the human condition in late capitalism. Work is a dominant feature of people's lives, but the form of social relations found in employment also shapes people's non-work lives. Marcuse develops Marx's account of an alienated labour process by linking it with Freud's concept of the pleasure principle:

> Work has now become *general* , and so have the restrictions placed upon the libido: labor time, which is the largest part of the individual's time, is painful time, for alienated labor is absence of gratification, negation of the pleasure principle. Libido is diverted for socially useful performances in which the individual works for himself only in so far as he works for the apparatus, engaged in activities that mostly do not coincide with his own faculties and desires. (Marcuse 1972a: 48)

Labour is not simply an interruption of the species-being of human beings; as all work is alienated, it deprives people of the capacity to realise their species-being for themselves. Drained by the demands of work in advanced capitalist societies, workers' non-work lives are also transformed so that their capacity to derive pleasure becomes caught up with their work life. But even the pleasure many take in their work is at the expense of other aspects of their lives. The pleasure to be found in free expression by humans has been absorbed into the process of work, directed to the interests of others; no longer is it simply the expenditure of time and effort that is bought with the labourer's wage. Work in advanced capitalism ties individuals into a social system that transforms their instinctual drives, subordinating them to the system and diminishing their capacity for realising themselves as individuals.

The reality principle dominates the process of waged labour, work which is undertaken in return for money. The pain or unpleasure of work is tolerated in order to gain the scarce resources necessary for existence, and, of course, the unpleasure of work is not equally distributed but reflects and reinforces the social order. But Marcuse identifies another orientation to work using Freud's 'Nirvana principle': the desire for non-work, to do nothing, to seek out the warm comfortable, undemanding atmosphere of the foetus in the womb. It is the search for peace, for tranquillity, that we can recognise in some spiritual searching, including meditation. But it is also the drive for ease and relaxation, to make our homes comfortable, that means individuals will forgo pleasure at work to enable them to consume in ways that will satisfy the Nirvana principle outside work. The Nirvana principle is the point at which the tension between the sex and death instincts is resolved; the search for sexual happiness and the aggression against threats or barriers are dissolved in a state of peace. But it is a move towards death and an essentially conservative or regressive principle; the passivity of the Nirvana state is like a prelude to death.

For Marx, the alienation of labour results from the formal separation of the worker from his product and the means of production, but for Marcuse it is a result of the mechanical routine of work and the diversion of libido. It is the organisation of the production line around repetitive tasks – in factory, office or even school – that makes work alienating. The instrumental rationality governing life at work spreads into non-work life with the effect that 'from the working day, alienation and regimentation spread into the free time' (Marcuse 1972a: 49). It is automation that ultimately transforms human work into a dominated, mechanistic and alienating activity in advanced capitalism. In place of straightforward work that requires physical effort, the partially automated line gives workers the stress of responsibility combined with the requirement to use mental effort and imagination as part of the work. For example, the high-pressure saleswoman has both to learn a prepared script and be alert and responsive to the situation, ready to invest her mind and imagination in it. The work is standardised according to a 'system' that workers must follow, but they are judged on results which derive from what extra they add to the system in terms of enthusiasm or spark – or simply persistence.

Automation brings about changes in the organisation of work that are linked to the 'total administration' of society, in which the distinction between workers and employers become lost. In place of a conflict of interest between real social groupings of 'labour' and 'capital', Marcuse sees workers caught up in a social system or apparatus that is faceless and impersonal. As blue-collar work declines and white-collar work increases, trade unions increasingly negotiate with employers rather than confronting them; their radical political agenda gives way to accepting some responsibility for managing workers. The traditional dialectic between capital and labour disappears and is replaced by what Marcuse calls a 'vicious circle which encloses both the Master and the Servant' (1972b: 40). Any distinction between the owning classes and the working classes fades as those who manage the automated workforce become themselves part of an automated system, working to performance standards. The result is domination by a system rather than by a class as the effect of automation becomes one of workers participating in their own alienation.

However, automation does offer the possibility for escape: 'Complete automation in the realm of necessity would open the dimension of free time as the one in which man's private *and* social existence would constitute itself. This would be the historical transcendence towards a new civilization' (Marcuse 1972b: 43). Automation could free workers to enjoy more non-work time, but, in Marcuse's analysis, the organisation of labour under the 'performance principle' channels the energy of both the libido and the aggression and destructive instincts of the death drive into work activities. The apparently rational incitements to compete against production targets, to demonstrate commitment and to be ruthless are applied universally throughout the work sphere, dominating workers' lives. Of course workers are rewarded in advanced capitalist societies with high wages, but instead of doing what they want in their free time, they spend the money on the goods and activities that capitalism provides. The symbolic goods from the culture industries combined with the desire for more commodities – goods and gadgets – keeps workers working rather than enjoying their free time. The products of the culture industry, combined with a formal administrative language that presents the system as rational, lull workers into a state of 'Happy Consciousness' in which they believe that 'the real is rational and that the system delivers the goods' (Marcuse 1972b: 78). This continuous cultural form of work and non-work inhibits individuals from recognising that they could both work less and determine their own needs and satisfactions.

Not all workers in advanced capitalism experience work in the same way, and Marcuse recognises that not all work is equally painful. The autonomy of artistic work in which workers produce 'work' that they can sell as their own, provides a model of what unalienated work might be like (see Chapter 5). However, even creative work becomes caught up in a system of agents, dealers, galleries, curators and critics who seek to direct and control production, nonetheless autonomous, creative production shows how work activities could be unalienated. Marcuse's critical analysis of advanced industrial society ends by suggesting that the only response is *refusal*: to comply with the system and with the circulation of values that in one-dimensional society have come to characterise the social relations of work and non-work. Marcuse gives us a negative basis for going into the future:

The critical theory of society possesses no concepts which could bridge the gap between the present and its future; holding no promise and showing no success, it remains negative. Thus it wants to remain loyal to those who, without hope, have given and give their life to the Great Refusal. (1972b: 200)

Marcuse's development of Marx's analysis of labour explores the development of the logic of mechanisation and automation into the organisation of all types of work, not just factory work. Like Adorno and Horkheimer, Marcuse identifies how the impact of the technological rationality applied to making productive machines is extended firstly to the organisation of human work and then to the values and orientation of non-work lives. Together, the Frankfurt critical theorists move beyond Marx in understanding the way that work and the alienation of work are not simply economic but also cultural phenomena. The ways in which work is transformed to increase the domination of workers under advanced capitalism provides the model for their domination through the cultural sphere in all aspects of their lives.

Gorz: The dual society

The Frankfurt theorists do not explore the nature of work and its relation to non-work in any detail but before discussing Gorz, for whom it is a central theme, it is useful to note the difference between more traditional Marxist and critical theoretical perspectives. Harry Braverman (1974), for example, argues that human labourers, even as they rent out their labour power, retain some control over their skills, abilities and willingness. Braverman, however does describe how 'scientific management' systematically organises the workplace of both the factory and the office in such a way as to minimise the autonomy of the worker. His account of the workplace is much more detailed than Marcuse's and also differs in that Braverman does not subscribe to critical theory's analysis of technological rationality and a one-dimensional society, believing instead that the worker is able to retain some freedom outside of the sphere of work. Unlike the critical theorists, he does not link the impact of advanced industrialisation on the workplace to cultural processes such as consumption and the private sphere. Henri Lefebvre, on the other hand, extends Marx's critique of work under capitalism as alienating to include the everyday life of the worker. It is the necessity of earning a living that turns work from a 'vital and human need' into 'a mysterious punishment' under capitalism (Lefebvre 1991a: 166). The worker, whose experience of the world is in individual terms, does not know that her or his efforts are contributing to a form of social labour that enables surplus value to be extracted. It is within the context of alienation that human beings create objects and human products, including institutions and ideologies, that appear 'real' and independent of human existence, but for Lefebvre 'it is man himself they are creating' (1991a: 168). Liberation, for Lefebvre, cannot be achieved by transforming the relations of production under which work takes place, but requires a dialectical analysis of the relations between appearance and essence, reality and unreality, that will bring alienation to consciousness.

André Gorz's critique accepts the loss of autonomy in work that Braverman spells out, but emphasises the potential for freedom from alienation in the sphere of non-work. His account of a dual society distinguishes the *heterono-mous* sphere of work, in which the life of the individual is controlled from outside, from the *autonomous* sphere of non-work, where the individual has control over her or his life. Advanced capitalism has led to increased control over work through a scientifically managed, automated work process in which workers have less and less control, even as a collective. What they produce is of no interest or direct use to them – 'all that matters is the wage packet at the end of the week or month' (Gorz 1997: 38). As they look to society in the form of the state and business to meet their needs, the demands of the 'atomised, serialised mass' of the working class become consumerist demands (Gorz 1997: 40). However, workers do retain a measure of autonomy outside their working lives through the 'marginal zones of autonomy formed by tiny allotments or back-yards of workers' houses' (Gorz 1997: 35). Gorz finds a zone of activity beyond the mass culture of consumption in which ordinary people aspire to autonomy over what they do: to buy their own business or set up in small-scale production, for example. This sphere of *autonomy* is somewhere between alienated work and leisure, a sphere beyond control and systematic manage-ment and largely beyond the sphere of industrial politics.

Like Marcuse, Gorz recognises that automation could potentially free work-ers from most if not all of the drudgery and toil of labour because it has reduced the labour time necessary to produce what the society needs. But Gorz is willing to accept a Faustian deal of selling labour power in the alien-ated heteronomous sphere of industrialised production in order to produce enough as a society, and earn enough as individuals, to maximise access to the autonomous sphere. He does not look to the proletariat as an historical class subject that can act as a political force to transform the relations of pro-duction, but identifies a category of people who do have the capacity to change the system: the 'non-class of post-industrial proletarians' who are underemployed (Gorz 1997: 68). These are the people who work for wages not career or community because of the mind-numbing nature of automated work (in the call-centre as much as the factory) or the lack of security of their short-term, temporary or part-time employment. These are the people who will lead the way in engaging with the heteronomous sphere of work just enough to enable them autonomy in their lives beyond work.

Gorz sees the demand for autonomy as attempting to meet human needs within the 'private niche' of 'family life, a home of one's own, a back garden, a do-it-yourself workshop, a boat, a country cottage, a collection of antiques, music, gastronomy, sport, love, etc.' (1997: 80). He argues that the sphere of individual sovereignty

> is based … upon activities unrelated to any economic goal which are an end in themselves: communication, giving, creating and aesthetic enjoyment, the production and reproduction of life, tenderness, the realisation of physical, sensuous and intellectual capacities, the creation of non-commodity use-values (shared goods or services) that could not be produced as commodities because of their unprofitability – in short, the whole range of activities that make up the fabric of existence and therefore occupy a primordial rather than a subordinate place. (Gorz 1997: 81)

Unpaid work (domestic work, community work, child rearing, personal caring, and so on) is crucial to sustaining social lives and individual identities and it takes place in the autonomous sphere. The boundaries between work done for an employer and work done within the domestic sphere clearly have social, political and economic consequences, on which some feminist accounts of work have focused. For example, Christine Delphy explores the difficulty of distinguishing housework from other work undertaken by women on agricultural smallholdings, all of which is productive and can be treated as a 'package' of work done for 'self-consumption' (1984: 87). And Dorothy Smith explores the ideological and power relationships around the domestic work of helping children with their homework: 'When does a child's learning become the business of "the home" rather than the school?' (1988: 194).[2] Like Delphy, Gorz argues against wages for housework, but he commends Marcuse's comments (and quotes Touraine) on the feminisation of industrial socialism, which, in challenging the ethics of competition and accumulation, has brought the values of reciprocity, tenderness, spontaneity and love of life to the fore (Gorz 1997: 85). Gorz suggests that mutual aid, cooperation and sharing can meet many of the needs that we currently look to the state to meet – although it will still be necessary for the management of society as a material system (distribution of work, training, transport, communications; information).

Touraine: The programmed society

Alain Touraine, writing in France in 1969, followed the critical approach to advanced capitalism as he began to describe the 'programmed society', in which the principles of planning and organisation applied in the workplace spread to all spheres of life: 'The production process imposes a life-style that matches its objectives and its power system. The individual is pressured into participating – not only in terms of his work but equally in terms of consumption and education – in the systems of social organizations and power which further the aims of production' (1974: 7). This sounds very close to Marcuse's analysis, but for Touraine, the worker is left a measure of autonomy, despite being alienated through what he calls 'dependent participation'. The worker depends on the programmed society for sociality, belonging to a social group, as well as for material needs, but Touraine remains optimistic that social relations can be transformed through some form of negotiation rather than the negation of a Great Refusal. The programmed society produces a degree of conformism – much as in Marcuse's one-dimensional society and Lefebvre's 'bureaucratic society of controlled consumption' – through the system of propaganda, advertising and financial stimulants that 'seduces, manipulates, and enforces conformism' (Touraine 1974: 9). Whereas for the Frankfurt theorists the analysis of the class structure gives way to an analysis of a culture as a whole, Touraine identifies a class of *technocrats* who programme society through their management of major areas of investment, planning, administration, education, research, transport, cities, housing programmes and even cultural life (1974: 50). This new class, armed with knowledge and a certain level of education, takes political control of areas of social life largely in the hands of the state or big business and replaces an early capitalist class that controlled through ownership and the accumulation of capital.

Touraine argues that the 'living standards' of ordinary people have replaced the 'ways of life' that used to be associated with sections of the working classes who lived in a community and worked in the same industry (e.g. the mining, fishing or shipbuilding communities). His concern over the loss of 'ways of life' shows a typically French concern for the 'everyday' existence that is reminiscent of the *Annales* historians and Lefebvre (see Chapter 6). However, rather than advanced capitalism producing a mass culture, Touraine sees it as becoming more individualistic, with a fluid set of values outwardly visible to all – the values of consumption both of consumer goods and of services such as health and education. Touraine takes account of the programming effect of mass consumption, but unlike the Frankfurt critical theorists, he does not see the whole field of non-work activities, of leisure, as totally dominated by the programmed society. He argues that cultural life itself is stratified, so that the relationship with the contents of mass culture vary – the young, for example, will have very different cultural demands to the old, and the rich will dominate consumer culture in a way that the poor cannot. But leisure time is also characterised by 'freedom from rules and from accepted or socially imposed models of behavior' (Touraine 1974: 212) and is available for deliberate, unregulated activity. It is in the sphere of non-work that cultural activities can be 'desocialized' so that the individual can discover the 'autonomy of personality' (Touraine 1974: 220).

In post-industrial society cultural identity is less determined by profession and more time is spent in non-work, so there is greater possibility for meeting the demands and creativity of the individual. For Touraine, this non-work, form of cultural identity generates political activity through social movements rather than work-defined classes (1974: 226). The autonomous individual is able to participate in the cultural criticism of 'socialized consumption' – the mass media, mass consumption – and Touraine identifies an alliance of scientists, artists and the young against the 'forces of social integration and cultural manipulation' (1974: 224). The programmed society threatens domination by technocrats who will drive society according to a logic that overlooks the variety and complexity of individuals. But through its tendency towards the circulation of information and enhanced communication it also offers opportunities that can be taken up by individuals and used to resist that domination.

Like the Frankfurt School, Touraine does not propose revolution as the route to societal transformation, but he is more optimistic than they are about the democratic process and the political impact of new social movements. These coalesce around non-work interests that do not 'affect the division of labor or forms of economic organization, but, more deeply, cultural values' (Touraine 1988: 150). Such social movements, and for Touraine the women's movement is the principal example, criticise not the social use of progress, but progress itself. They offer a critique of industrial values, those that inform the programming of society, through the reactions of those cultural actors who are trying to keep or recover control over their own lives. There is in Marcuse's later writings (1969, 1989) an interest in the emergence of social movements – particularly the civil rights and student movements – but critical theory retains a philosophical mode of critique based on negation that does not resolve so easily into political action as does Touraine's critical sociology.

Both Gorz and Touraine begin from the same Marxist analysis as Lefebvre and the Frankfurt School, of work under capitalism as alienating. But while the Frankfurt School see the alienation of work becoming characteristic of cultural life in general, Gorz and Touraine see the potential for human autonomy and social transformation in the sphere of non-work. For both there is a re-articulation of the idea of work as constitutive of social being; but it is through 'work' undertaken in the name of leisure, family, community and personal expression that individuals can assert their freedom in the 'programmed' or 'dual' society. Such work may be 'labour' in Arendt's sense, but because it is done for others in a collective spirit, it is more than mere toil. Both Gorz and Touraine recognise the risk to individual autonomy of the mass culture of advanced capitalism, but neither sees any reason why the individual should succumb to it. They argue for non-revolutionary ways of taking over politics through the assertion of autonomous life beyond the control of the state or business.

Baudrillard: The end of production

Jean Baudrillard (1998), writing just a year later than Touraine, in 1970, is suspicious of 'leisure' as a creation of consumer society; to treat time as an object that you can 'have' as 'free' is already to accept the cultural domination of time in general that comes with the selling of labour power. The freedom to 'waste one's time' or even 'kill it' during the holidays is a form of private property that is the direct result of having 'earned' time through work during the rest of the year. For Baudrillard, the consumption of leisure involves 'the very ideology of alienated labour' and is subject to the same 'ethics of pressured performance' (1998: 155), although he is not including the range of activities that Gorz and Touraine consider outside capitalist production. However, Baudrillard argues (1993a: 6–49), the process of production as the exploitation of labour power by capital, has come to an end.

In his *Grundrisse* (1973), Marx shows that the strength and skill of the worker's labour power is progressively transformed into a form of fixed capital as machines, 'dead labour', that become the essential ingredient in the capitalist production of value. With automated machinery the worker becomes a subsidiary ingredient who 'merely transmits the machine's work, the machine's action, on to the raw material – supervises it and guards against interruptions' (Marx 1973: 692). But Baudrillard interprets this transformation as merely demonstrating that the mode of production could never be understood as a real process of exploitation of living labour. While Marx took his analysis to be true because it was determined by 'real' relations at the level of material existence between workers and capitalists, Baudrillard argues that these were never more than a set of structural relations that can and have been transformed. He offers a series of inversions of Marx's analysis that disconnect labour power from the realm of determinate relations and the real, recasting it as a system of indeterminate relations that exist as a *code* in place of Marx's analysis of the *mode* of production: 'With the hegemony of dead labour over living labour, the whole dialectic of production collapses. ... Everything within production and the economy becomes commutable, reversible and exchangeable according to the same indeterminate specularity as we find in politics, fashion or the media' (Baudrillard 1993a: 16).

Baudrillard is not simply dispensing with Marx's analysis – rather, from his close critique he develops his own account of the emerging social relations in late modern societies (Baudrillard 1975, 1981). While he argues that production has ceased to be central to understanding social formations, he shows that capitalism has not. He replaces Marx's realist account of the labour theory of value with the code of the 'structural law of value', which sustains value in a society of machinic production. This replaces exploitation as the extraction of a surplus from the expenditure of labour power with a 'mode of domination' (Baudrillard 1993a: 10) that operates not through bodily violence or bloodshed, but through the circulation of a code of values as signs that achieve a symbolic violence. With the end of the centrality of labour power in production, exploitation under capitalism shifts from the sphere of work to the sphere of non-work; to the practices of consumption, including that of leisure.

Labour, of course, does not disappear immediately, but has become a sign amongst many, exchangeable against, for example, non-labour. The work of labour is no longer production, but *re*production, and specifically the reproduction of the code, the structural law of values characteristic of the mode of dominance. A key sign in the code is that of labour itself, so there is a 'ritual of the signs of labour' that socialises society's members into the network of signs that are the 'model of social simulation' (Baudrillard 1993a: 11). In a mode of domination in which productive work has been substantially taken over by machines, what we find is a model of labour as service-oriented rather than directly productive. Even the labour of work with machines is a form of service in which commodified work is no longer a process but a signification of labour – a ritual of the engagement of the worker in the circulation of values of the society. It is the very substitutability of every act of labour for every other act of labour that means that the labour process has 'become indifferent to every object and even to labour itself' (1993a: 13). Again, Baudrillard finds support for his argument from Marx, quoting the *Grundrisse* on how labour as a productive force, as skill and knowledge, becomes absorbed into fixed capital, Instead of an opposition between labour and capital, labour as a productive process is merged into capital, and as a social relation it becomes dispersed through the various means by which people are socialised:

> Labour ... pervades every aspect of life in the form of a control, a permanent occupation of spaces and times, regulated according to an omnipresent code. Wherever there are people they must be *fixed*, whether in schools, factories, on the beach, in front of the TV, or being retrained. ... Such labour is not, however, productive in the sense of 'original': it is nothing more than the mirror of society, its imaginary, its fantastic reality principle. Perhaps its death drive. (Baudrillard 1993a: 14)

Because of its removal from the sphere of production, the labour process that underpins Marx's analysis of the mode of production has collapsed into the sphere of consumption; everything that contributes to the circulation of signs constitutes labour in the sense of supporting the mode of dominance that is late capitalism. Labour is not productive in Marx's sense but as the giving of service, which Baudrillard calls 'prestation', in which it 'conjoins the body, time, space and grey matter' (1993a: 17). In a development of Adorno and Horkheimer's analysis that free time is filled by the culture industry to prepare people for work, Baudrillard argues that work and free time can no longer be seen as opposed. Free time, non-work, requires the same commitment of the member of society to the circulation of values, and the worker's free time is consumed in a form of 'complex labour' that Baudrillard links to Marcuse's critique of the impact of automation (Baudrillard 1993a: 18fn8).

The implosion of production and of the labour/capital relationship does not stop society continuing to emphasise the social value of work and rewarding work with wages. But the significance of wages is no longer as a payment for the commodity of work, as if the worker can use the wages in her or his own way to reproduce labour power. Baudrillard argues that wages are a form of 'investment' that capital makes in the worker as a way of controlling her or him, and he even claims that trade unions are a way of sustaining the pretence of a link between wage levels and labour (1993a: 19). It is the traditional labour movement he argues, who, sustain the 'illusion of productive labour' and 'experience their leisure under the illusion of freedom' (1993a: 30). But if Baudrillard is right that political economy acts as an alibi, an 'imaginary-real' (1993: 31), that is after all nothing but a simulacrum, where does he locate the real real? As he seems to jettison every common-sense understanding of the mechanics of our society, what foundations does he have to offer in place of those solid principles of production, labour and the experience of work that we derive from Marx?

Firstly, he does not dispense with the category of capital, which, he contends, has not only 'set men to work' but has also 'impelled them to culture', which includes, as well as political economy, the languages of needs, information, communication, rights, liberty, sexuality, preservation and even the death instinct (Baudrillard 1993a: 34). Secondly, the experience of humans is founded not on these indifferent discursive structures, in which values endlessly circulate as signs in a code, but in the realm of the symbolic. Baudrillard displays a nostalgia for primitive, pre-capitalist culture, the days when symbols really meant something and the bottom line was not money but death (1993a: 36). He is not promoting personal violence or death as a solution, but we must not forget that machines represent 'dead labour'; in place of the political strategy of confronting capital from the perspective of labour, Baudrillard is arguing for a cultural strategy that will lead to the collapse and death of the system.

In marked contrast to André Gorz, Baudrillard argues that renegotiating the relation between labour and free time, or non-work, is futile. Instead, what is required to stall the code is to refuse the slow, deferred death that capital gives as the gift of work to labour: 'To refuse labour, to dispute wages is thus to put the process of the gift, expiation and economic compensation back into question, and therefore to expose the fundamental symbolic process' (Baudrillard 1993a: 41). The power of capital is not confronted in the labour process, Baudrillard warns, and it cannot be seen as merely exercised in the work-for-wages that is labour. It is in a symbolically violent form that the dispersed power of capital can be seen to operate and a refusal to participate is the only response: 'This is the only absolute weapon, and the mere collective threat of it can make power collapse. Power, faced with this symbolic "blackmail" (the barricades of '68, hostage-taking), loses its footing: since it thrives on slow death, I will oppose it with my violent death' (Baudrillard 1993a: 43).

This refusal is reminiscent of Marcuse's 'Great Refusal', and indeed with the very risky response of the *Metropolis* workers to their situation, which exchanged the slow death of their work for the life-threatening violence of flooding their underground workplace. However, Baudrillard is suggesting that the symbolic violence of public demonstration (which might include the often violent, risky and dramatic actions of green activists, roads protesters and anti-capitalist demonstrators that have become more familiar since he was writing) is much more appropriate than simply refusing to participate in circulating the code.

Lazzarato: Immaterial labour

The traditional idea of labour is that it leads to production of some *thing*, something material such as the bolt of cloth or the pig iron that Marx refers to in the opening chapter of *Capital* (1976). While Baudrillard argues that the shift to automated machine production spells the end of production in this sense, Maurizio Lazzarato argues that it is linked to a shift towards immaterial labour 'that produces the informational and cultural content of the commodity' (1996: 132). Rather than seeing the replacement of labour power as the source of value by a circulation of signs, the notion of immaterial labour highlights the work that goes into the production of those signs.

The first form of immaterial labour is the passing on to the worker of the work of organising production. The post-Taylorist techniques of 'participative management' have passed much of the responsibility for managing the process of production, traditionally undertaken by the agent of the entrepreneur (the foreman or manager), on to the workers, who have become, as Lazzarato puts it, 'active subjects'. Immaterial labour includes the activities of workers who participate in quality circles, team-building exercises and preparing mission statements, and who fill in suggestion forms and contribute to 'away days' and other activities that reflect on and redesign the nature of their work. These activities, which are not directly productive but designed to increase productivity, seduce the subjectivity of the worker into seeing her or his interests as commensurate with those of the capitalist entrepreneur. The threat of losing one's job, combined with bonus and other incentive schemes, means that the worker is willing to undertake the communicative and reflective work of immaterial labour on behalf of capital. Work of this first type of immaterial labour involves the workers taking up a position in a 'circulation of information' and taking responsibility for self-control and motivation.

The second form of immaterial labour is when the productive work is of something in itself immaterial – language, images, ideas. The making of films such as *Snow White* or *Metropolis* is an example this form of immaterial labour, and it is the communications industries that Lazzarato calls the 'classic forms of "immaterial" production: audiovisual production, advertising, fashion, the production of software, photography, cultural activities and so forth' (1996: 136). The production of immaterial goods is hardly new (all cultural products are immaterial in the sense that they are not dependent on a specific material form to be consumed – the same story may be a novel, a play, a film or a TV programme). In addition to the creators of communicative products (not only 'artists' but 'hacks' too) we could add many of the professions (lawyer, accountant, surveyor, banker, and so on). Even where professionals are apparently engaged in the process of material production (engineer, architect), *they* actually *produce* something that is immaterial (drawings, plans, instructions, advice, collaboration) which exists only as communicative content.

As Lazzarato tells us: 'This immaterial labor constitutes itself in forms that are immediately collective, and we might say that it exists only in the form of networks and flows' (1996: 136). Immaterial labour is characterised by a lack of constraint within a material site – the four walls of the factory or office – because it flows between workers (in documents, reports, diagrams, plans on paper, in meetings, on the telephone and increasingly in emails and websites). The work of immaterial production can be done just about anywhere (at home, in the car, in distributed offices) – hence the tremendous growth in the amount of travelling, use of mobile telephones, portable computers. As the technologies for producing communications become more flexible and independent of fixed sites, then only one determinant of the location and space of work remains: the face-to-face interaction. The co-presence of actors (classically in the 'business meeting') brings about a particular form of immaterial production because what is communicated cannot be refuted or ignored. Lazzarato points out that many of the workers involved in communication flows are self-employed and that their experience of work often blurs into leisure because the communicative activities of their work are so similar to the communicative activities of non-work: consuming texts, commenting on them, socializing, and so on.

The third form of immaterial labour that Lazzarato discusses is the work that we all do outside of the production process but which is necessary to initiate production. As he says 'immaterial labor finds itself at the crossroads (or rather, it is the interface) or a new relationship between production and consumption' (Lazzarato 1996: 138). This is the work that we do as consumers in choosing, in creating a demand or a need for a given product. This dispersed labour, at some distance from the centre of production (the firm), is traditionally seen as an autonomous sphere (that of private life). But as the distinctions between the public and private spaces of labour and domestic life (including work) are broken down along with the distinction between the factory/office as the place of work and the home as the place of rest, we need to recognise how consumption is also a form of work: 'Consumption is then first of all a consumption of information. Consumption is no longer only the "realization" of a product, but a real and proper social process that for the moment is defined with the term communication' (Lazzarato 1996: 140).

Instead of work being understood as a social relation that as labour produces commodities, Lazzarato, like Baudrillard, is setting out the social conditions of late modern societies in which the distinction between work and non-work is becoming blurred. All activities, including those of communication and engagement with the culture, are 'labour' in that they contribute to the creation of value on which the hegemony of capitalism depends.

Like Lazzarato, Hardt and Negri (2000) retain the concept of 'labour' to specify the nature of work that contributes to the circulation of values within the global late capitalism that they call 'Empire'. To the proliferation of immaterial labour achieved through communication, especially through new computer-based technology, they add the category of 'affective labor', of human contact and interaction (Hardt and Negri 2000: 292). The 'repressive desublimation' that Marcuse saw (see Chapter 5) as the way human qualities were reinvested in the sphere of work, enlivening the process of selling and providing service, is a key component in the 'work' of late capitalist societies. This is the work of offering of a human, caring face, which is essential in most service industries but is at the core of health, social care and entertainment work. It is the willingness to cooperate with other people, both workers and 'clients' or 'customers', to show care and interest in their lives and feelings. But in this development, Hardt and Negri see a nascent communism; rather than a critique that leads to the refusal proposed by Marcuse and Baudrillard, they are optimistic that as work is humanised with affect, what is produced is not things but sociality: 'Today productivity, wealth, and the creation of social surpluses take the form of cooperative interactivity through linguistic, communicational, and affective networks. In the expression of its own creative energies, immaterial labor thus seems to provide the potential for a kind of spontaneous and elementary communism' (Hardt and Negri 2000: 294).

Conclusions

Work continues to be a key theme in the critique of capitalist social relations at the beginning of the twenty-first century. But whereas for Marx, the taking of work out of the home, into the factory, created a distinctively capitalist mode of production, by the end of the twentieth century work had taken on a very different role. Instead of 'work' being transformed into commodified labour, critical theory has developed a critique of work as a cultural form that has moved out of the sphere of production to affect all aspects of modern life. Marx's analysis identified the economic sphere of production as the defining social relation, and he focused on the accumulation of wealth through the exploitation of labour as the principal determinant of the form of modern societies. But early critical theorists, most importantly Marcuse, showed how the techniques developed in advanced capitalism to control the productive sphere also dominated the sphere of non-work: leisure and private life. It was Marcuse who showed that alienation was the result not so much of wage labour as of participation in modern society: industrialisation changed the whole of people's lives under capitalism, including their sense of identity, their emotional and their sexual being.

Marcuse and, later, Gorz recognised that the productive capacity of modern industrial society meant that the burden of labour could be reduced for workers. For Marcuse, this created the possibility for autonomous creative life that might lead to social transformation through a refusal of the performance principle. His solution of revolution at the level of human existence rather than simply the level of the economy has often been seen as utopian (see, for example, contributions to Pippin et al. 1988), but his optimism laid the ground for a form of critique that could see in simply threatening to opt out a fundamental challenge to the hegemony of capitalism. Gorz embraced the much less transformatory possibility of an autonomous sphere in which the individual could develop an unalienated existence, while tolerating a continuing role for the administrative state and corporate capitalism.

Alain Touraine is optimistic that the seeds for a transformation of the programmed society are already present in the way that social movements respond not only to the alienation of commodified productive work but also to the broader cultural environment. Unlike the early critical theorists, he does not see the penetration of the administrative principles of industrial society into every aspect of individual life, nor does he see the need for compromise in the way Gorz implies. The new politics of social movements bring to the fore the tensions between work and non-work but promise the possibility of negotiating new forms of social life not determined by the mode of production.

It is Baudrillard who takes to the extreme the penetration of non-work life by the dictates of capital, arguing that we continue to do the work of capitalism as we consume and take our leisure. No longer can 'work' be grounded in the action and effort of production because it is indistinguishable from the continuous work of reproduction, circulating the signs of a code. Like Baudrillard, Lazzarato argues that the work of consumption is itself an immaterial labour and Hardt and Negri reprise Marcuse's arguments about the confusion between work life and the personal expression of emotion, affection and attraction. The effect of these critical theories is to overthrow the distinction between work and non-work, between alienated labour as the human function in capitalist production and the potential for the human being to act freely 'in his animal functions – eating, drinking and procreating, or at most in his dwelling and adornment' (Marx 1975: 327).

It may seem odd to suggest that the smile with which Snow White met the dwarfs on their return was just as much 'work' as the work they had undertaken with pickaxes at the mine. But then, it was not very long ago that the 'housework' she had undertaken with a broom and duster would also not have seemed to be serious work – it is through a sustained feminist critique of the analysis of work within the social sciences that domestic work has come to be seen as just as much a part of production as waged labour itself. Whistling at work and even casting spells now appear to be immaterial labour under late capitalism...

Summary:

- *Marx*: Work as the species-being of humankind becomes alienated labour under the capitalist mode of production – separated from home, organised in the factory.
- *Arendt*: Under industrialisation, labour as the repetitive, unavoidable toil of everyday life becomes characteristic of human work for machines.
- *Adorno and Horkheimer*: Domination of work life spreads into home life in late capitalism – leisure and non-work follow the rhythm and rationality of the workplace, amusement becomes the prolongation of work.
- *Marcuse*: The industrial apparatus promotes 'individuals' who follow the work patterns of machines and the cultural values of the system as if they were their own. The seeking of pleasure and the drives of the libido are drawn into work life so non-work life becomes shaped by the desire for comfort, peace and a 'Happy Consciousness' (the Nirvana principle). Alienation is extended to 'free' time in which consumption follows the dictates of capitalism – the negative response of 'refusal' rejects the dictates of the apparatus.
- *Marcuse and Gorz*: As mechanisation becomes automation, there is the potential for freeing workers from the drudgery of labour.
- *Gorz*: The 'heteronomous' sphere of wage labour could be reduced and the 'autonomous' sphere of work for self and community could be increased. Work not undertaken for a wage, for an employer, need not be alienating and can allow the assertion of individuality.
- *Delphy and Smith*: The 'non-work' of domestic labour, seen by Marx as a dimension of the reproduction of labour power, short-circuits capitalist production as 'self-consumption' but may be seen as undertaken on behalf of the state, even at its direction.
- *Touraine*: Control of the mass culture 'programmed society' by the class of 'technocrats' nonetheless leaves individuals with some autonomy and fluid values of personality and creativity. Social movements can offer a critique of industrialised values and an opportunity for unalienated expression.
- *Baudrillard*: 'Production' as a determinant of social relations comes to an end as skill and effort is transferred from workers to machines and 'work' becomes a service relation. The domination of consumers under late capitalism is through a code of sign values – including those of 'work' and 'leisure' – that are endlessly circulated. A symbolically violent rejection of the code is the only response possible that does not contribute to the circuit of signs.
- *Lazzarato*: In late modernity, the emphasis of production shifts from material goods to the 'immaterial' goods of culture, communication, profession and emotion.
- *Hardt and Negri*: The communicative and affective form of immaterial labour makes new forms of politicised social relations possible.

Further Reading

Harry Braverman's *Labour and Monopoly Capital* (1974) continues to be a good way to follow the logic of Marx's writing on work in the *Grundrisse* (1973) into the age of mass production in the factory and the office. Tony Watson's *Sociology, Work and Industry* (1995), Graeme Salaman's *Working* (1986) and Keith Grint's *The Sociology of Work* (1998) provide a useful overview of themes in the sociology of work.

Notes

1 Agnes Heller finds a middle path by first following Marx's distinction between work and labour, in which work has a 'species essential quality' while labour is that which produces exchange value, but she goes on to reject it in favour of an 'everyday understanding' of work as 'what has to be done' (Heller 1984: 61–2).

2 The work of writers such as Delphy and Smith has much in common with the tradition of critical theory that is being argued for in this book; it is lack of space that has prevented this theme from being properly explored here.

FOUR

The Critique of Everyday Life

For Trotsky, writing a series of articles for *Pravda* in the 1920s after the October Revolution, the real socialist revolution was going to be cultural and would only be achieved by bringing about changes in the ordinary life of the Soviet people. As well as new economic and political relations, the material contradictions of everyday life that had sustained the old order had to be confronted if the contradictions of capitalism were to be dispersed:

> The whole problem lies in the contradiction [between] the basis that everyday life has in material production and the new tasks, needs, and functions which have also become a part of everyday life and play a huge role, at least for the proletarian vanguard. ... A critical disclosure of the contradictions in everyday life is precisely what distinguishes Marx's method. (Trotsky 1973: 59–60)

Trotsky wrote about the ordinary things that needed to be changed after the socialist revolution: vodka drinking; the cinema; morality; the church, the family, communal living and working; spitting and leaving cigarette butts; bad language; civility and manners. He wanted to persuade the masses that everyday life, despite its difficulties, was theirs and that they should take responsibility for it.

Trotsky's call to the Soviet people to throw aside practices that sustained social divisions, promoted individualism and tolerated poor conditions seems, with hindsight, rather bourgeois and high-minded. It sounds as if he was encouraging the citizens of the Soviet Republic to adopt as part of socialist culture the mutual respect and concern with the details of everyday life that characterised the European bourgeoisie. But his recognition that socialist liberation could only be achieved when people took control of their ordinary lives foreshadowed a concern that is to be found in a future generation of critical theorists. They also saw in the way that capitalist society shaped and modified everyday life a threat to the ability of ordinary people to live their lives in their own interests. However, the critique of the European critical theorists does not attempt to admonish ordinary people for their ways of living as Trotsky did. Rather than seize on the cinema as the way to change lives for the better ('the best instrument for propaganda' – Trotsky 1973: 33), some have argued, as we will see in Chapter 6, that the mass media have had a malign influence on the shape of ordinary lives. The critical theory tradition shares Trotsky's critique of the privatising, individualist, acquisitive habits promoted by capitalist culture and agrees with him that relying on state bureaucratic regulation is not enough to ensure equality between people. The state, they have argued, in collusion with the centralising tendency of modern consumer culture, restricts the capacity of people to shape their own lives while giving them the illusion of 'choice' and individuality. The cultural critique that I shall discuss in this chapter is directed to aspects of ordinary life that are shaped or at least affected by the dynamics of modern, advanced capitalist societies. The sorts of topics that will crop up are: the articulation of individuality; the distinctions of gender; consumption (often typified in the object of the car); ways of moving through space; and the uses of language.

Everyone has an 'everyday life', most of the time. The phrase refers to the ordinary, routine nature of human existence in which tasks are repeated more or less every day and those tasks are linked to keeping the person going – meeting biological or animal needs and meeting social needs that are distinctively human. Agnes Heller defines everyday life as 'the aggregate of those individual reproduction factors which, *pari passu*, make social reproduction possible' (1984: 3). Everyday life can be contrasted with the exceptional times of war, disaster, revolution or famine, when undertaking such tasks is suspended, or modified in some way. During the twentieth century the activities and the material of everyday life came to be recognised as of enormous significance in understanding human existence. For a number of historians, philosophers, social theorists and sociologists, the realm of the everyday has become the focus of attention. Indeed, there is an American tradition of sociology that takes as its field of concern 'everyday life', but it is not associated with critique. For Erving Goffman (1971), Jack Douglas (1971), Peter Berger and Thomas Luckmann (1966) and others who follow their thinking, the attention turned on everyday life is purely sociological; they wish to describe it in its richness (see also the early collection edited by Truzzi 1968 and the more recent textbook by Weigert 1981). To generalise, this sociological tradition rejects macro-social processes as determining the form of social life and regards social actors as collectively and collaboratively responsible for creating the social worlds they live in. The systematic study of everyday life then provides '[t]he only valid and reliable (or hard, scientific) evidence concerning socially meaningful phenomena we can possibly have' (Douglas 1971: 12). The American tradition takes almost the reverse view from the critical theorists' claim that the institutions of advanced capitalist economic systems determine everyday life in modern societies. What is central to the American 'everyday life' sociologists is the empirical study of the processes of ordinary life. But this close study of practices is almost absent from the critical tradition – although there are striking exceptions, such as the work of Michel de Certeau, which is discussed below.

Adorno and Horkheimer: The loss of individuality

Adorno and Horkheimer treat everyday life as a residue of existence that has been sullied by the development of modern capitalism. In *Dialectic of Enlightenment* (1979) they see the dominating effects of the regime of instrumental reason spill over from the sphere of work into the personal lives of individuals, who are 'forced back to anthropologically more primitive stages [as] the persistence of domination brings about a fixation of the instincts by means of heavier repression' (Adorno and Horkheimer 1979: 35). They seem to despair of the ordinary lives of individual people, who have become progressively powerless as their income has risen because they have become part of the mass and so succumbed to the 'administered life, which preforms every sector of modern existence including language and perception' (Adorno and Horkheimer 1979: 38). While they don't discuss the minutiae of everyday activities, what they do comment on is the way that individuality becomes displaced in modern societies. Individuals become isolated from each other and lose their personality: 'Men travel on rubber tires in complete isolation from each other', and even if they do manage to travel together, their conversations are 'always identical and regulated by practical interests' (Adorno and Horkheimer 1979: 221–2). In their rather lugubrious and depressing view of the ordinary life of individuals Adorno and Horkheimer sound like a pair of sad-faced clowns entertaining the crowd with an excess of woe, always looking on the dark side of life. As they describe life in the modernity of instrumental reason, the individual progresses towards 'cretinism' and gives up the biographical trajectory through which a cumulative independent identity would develop under other circumstances: 'One might almost say that the notion of human life as the unity in the history of an individual has been abolished: the life of the individual is defined only by its opposite, destruction, but all harmony and all continuity of conscious and involuntary memory have lost their meaning' (Adorno and Horkheimer 1979: 216).

This theme of the loss of individual identity that can be sustained in ordinary life is in contrast to the bourgeois life of early capitalism, in which individuals, those rich enough to avoid the toil of work and to have an education, could be free to shape their own lives. Adorno's witty, ironic and beautifully turned fragments in *Minima Moralia* (1974) remark on the fall of the life of men and women under modernity while hinting that the dialectic can be reignited. As he begins to address the good life and how it might be recognised if not achieved, he seeks to inspire some form of resistance to the penetration of the mode of production into every aspect of every life. What must be resisted is the pressure of society that threatens to crush individuals into 'an amorphous and malleable mass' (Adorno 1974: 139). For Adorno, admittedly trapped in intellectual solitude by his exile, the attempt to discover individuality lies in *thought*, in making judgements on the world around him and identifying the traps that lie in wait in a world organised instrumentally and driven by consumption. The strategies of thought that he explores require a 'morality of thinking' and involve retaining habits and postures of mind that can escape the imposition of an external pattern (Adorno 1974: 73). But in modern society everyone is restless, and rather than with thought or critique they attempt to fill their lives and assert their individuality through '[p]seudo activity', often seeking the assistance of 'the monstrous machinery of amusement', which 'constantly grows bigger without a single person being amused by it' (Adorno 1974: 139).

Adorno bemoans the way that the sensibility of the workplace and of the market impregnates ordinary life to produce a breed of person who is 'clever, witty, full of sensitive reactions', because they have 'refurbished the tradesman's mentality with the day before yesterday's psychological discoveries' (1974: 24). The result is that 'the entire private domain is being engulfed by a mysterious activity that bears all the features of commercial life without there being actually any business to transact' (Adorno 1974: 23). One of the ways that people become caught up in a pre-formed individual life is through the material culture of modernity. For example, as Adorno complains about the impact of functional design on modern homes ('factory sites that have strayed into the consumption sphere') and the development of interest in furniture design and interior decoration ('arty crafty sensibilities'), he suggests that complete resistance is impossible, so the only strategy is an 'uncommitted, suspended one' of a private life that meets the expectations of the social order (Adorno 1974: 39). Such a form of everyday life may enable a person to fit in and keep up appearances, but for Adorno they should be under no illusion that this is the life of a free subject or a true means for establishing individual identity. This very weak form of resistance allows his vituperative criticism of the administered life still to cut while he offers no alternative other than an attenuated nostalgia.

Horkheimer also describes the change from a bourgeois, semi-liberal social order at the beginning of the twentieth century, to the domination of social life by industrial power by its middle. Writing in 1957 on 'the concept of man' (Horkheimer 1974a), he notes the changing role of the family: from sustaining continuity of status and profession between generations, towards producing people who will fit in with the administered society. The family, he argues, has 'surrendered many of its remaining functions to other institutions or to society at large' (Horkheimer 1974a: 11) – he notes that mothers are more likely to go out to work and that there has been a shortening of the period when young people stay in the home. He also notes that there is a decline in the way that marriage and the family can provide a sphere of escape for the individual from the pressures of society. Returning to this theme in 1966, Horkheimer argues that there is less 'breathing space' in individual life for the development of friendship within marriage. The potential for fostering individuality becomes limited in the face of a culture of 'mounting uniformization' in which 'the upcoming generation become simply functions in an increasingly planned and managed society' (Horkheimer 1974b: 95).

For Horkheimer, the way that the car is used provides an exemplar of the way that modern life becomes organised for the individual, drawing people into a pattern of movement and action that is dominated by the material apparatus of modernity. The car is faster, more efficient and requires less care than the horse as a mode of transport but presents the individual with a whole new set of constraints on freedom:

> It is as if the innumerable laws, regulations, and directions with which we must comply were driving the car, not we. There are speed limits, warnings to drive slowly, to stop, to stay within certain lanes, and even diagrams showing the shape of the curve ahead. We must keep our eyes on the road and be ready at each instant to react with the right motion. Our spontaneity has been replaced by a frame of mind which compels us to discard every emotion or idea that might impair our alertness to the impersonal demands assailing us. (Horkheimer 1947b: 98)

Just as incorporating technology such as the car into everyday life constrains the individual's spontaneity, so does their ordinary cultural life. The amusements and leisure-time activities of modern culture are regimented and stripped of the pleasure of engaging with the world in the spirit of objective reason. Hobbies, for example, illustrate for Horkheimer the way that leisure activities are stereotyped and devoid of emotional engagement or depth: 'The idea of the hobby, of a "good time", or "fun" expresses no regret whatsoever for the vanishing of objective reason and the stripping from reality of any inherent "sense"' (1947a: 38). Through our use of cars, the hobbies we take up and the leisure activities we pursue we allow our everyday lives to be administered and pre-formed. These activities seem to offer possible respites from the imposition of instrumental reason; but while they may appear to retain the capacity for individual spontaneity, they have in fact already been shaped and determined.

The reflections of Adorno and Horkheimer on the culture of everyday life are eerily conservative: the days of bourgeois, liberal values are applauded over the decline of individuality into mass mediocrity. Their view of private life seems to be from their perspective as white, middle-class, male intellectuals, and is difficult to construe as an account of 'everyday life' in the sense of experiences shared regardless of gender, class or age. What is most depressing is Adorno and Horkheimer's resignation to the half-hearted and limited strategy of what we might call a 'minimal resistance' to the penetration of everyday life by administered culture. They seem to abandon any action in ordinary life that might resist or respond to the pressure to conform within everyday culture – as Adorno puts it, 'Wrong life cannot be lived rightly' (1974: 39).

Marcuse: False needs of consumption

We have seen how for Adorno and Horkheimer the material stuff with which everyday life is surrounded can be a way in which the patterns of lives are

69

shaped by their society. It is Marcuse who begins to spell this out as being a process of the consumption of commodities that accompanies a rising standard of living, and general liberalism: 'The people recognize themselves in their commodities; they find their soul in their automobile, hi-fi set, split-level home, kitchen equipment. The very mechanism which ties the individual to his society has changed, and social control is anchored in the new needs which it has produced' (1972b: 22). Everyday individuals' identity and activities are shaped through the commodities that they purchase and use. It is not just people's work lives but also their home lives that are then shaped by the processes of scientific management and organisation, because the system for mass distribution and marketing has to match that of mass production. By linking commodities to people's inner lives – their thoughts and desires – the needs of the individual and society can be treated as synonymous. Advertising, product placement, feature articles and specialist magazines on what to buy create a culture through which one-dimensional society 'introjects' society's needs onto the individual. As individual identity is whittled away through systems of work and mass culture, people see themselves not as distinct individuals but as a mimetic reflection of the society as a whole. Marcuse argues that advanced capitalism imposes illusory 'false needs' that it would be neurotic for the individual to reject or criticise: 'The result is euphoria in unhappiness. Most of the prevailing needs to relax, to have fun, to behave and consume in accordance with the advertisements, to love and hate what others love and hate belong to this category of false needs' (1972b: 19).

'True' needs are the vital ones of nourishment, clothing, lodging, although Marcuse does not deal with the distinction between false and true needs in any fine detail. The boundary is difficult to specify – when does a meal cease to be nourishment and suddenly become a 'false' need? When its contents have been advertised? When it is more complicated than is required for satisfying hunger? When there is too much of it? Perhaps Marcuse's distinction between true and false needs should not be taken as other than dialectical; the distinction enables us to question the idea of 'needs' and ask whose they are. The distribution of commodities throughout society suggests the possibility of a classless society – both boss and worker can enjoy the same TV programme, even a 'Negro' can own a Cadillac (Marcuse 1972b: 21). But this homogenisation of individual needs simply serves to show that each has the same needs as those of the whole of society. Needs emerge within a society through history, but under the repressive administration of advanced society the individual is not free to choose – choice is only within a range that is presented as possible and always within the context of the society's need for production and consumption.

Commodities become incorporated into the ordinary lives of individuals more deeply than through being experienced as a need. Marcuse argues that human instincts – desire, energy, libido – are channelled to fit in with those of technological rationality, and the 'mechanical contrivances' of modern commodities are part of this process:

> The average man hardly cares for any living being with the intensity and persistence he shows for his automobile. The machine that is adored is no longer dead matter but becomes something like a human being. And it gives back to man what it possesses: the life of the social apparatus to which it belongs. (1998: 47)

In a similar way to Horkheimer, Marcuse sees the relationship between the person and the car as symbolic of the relationship between the modern individual and the social system. It is the system of roads, signs and roadside businesses that pre-form the driver's path, not the terrain or the spontaneity of the driver, so that '[b]usiness, technics, human needs and nature are welded together into one rational and expedient mechanism' (Marcuse 1998: 46).

Marcuse argues that it is not only the commercial world of commodities and advertisements that shapes everyday lives. The welfare state has developed in collaboration with industrialised capitalism and it codifies, calculates and assesses individual needs through an administrative system that operates standards while maintaining inequality and difference. Rather than question the process, individuals acquiesce and accept the benefits of the system: '... there is no reason to insist on self-determination if the administered life is the comfortable and even the "good" life. This is the rational and material ground for the unification of opposites, for one-dimensional political behaviour' (Marcuse 1972b: 52).

The social system of advanced capitalism produces a form of mass society that Marcuse sees as highly centralised and systematically managed from above (2001: 83). He is clear that modern, everyday lives are administered through the mechanisms of the state and the mass media that have largely taken over the roles of the family in terms of socialisation and mediating between the individual and her or his society. What Marcuse shares with Adorno and Horkheimer is a critical approach to everyday life that sees it as dominated by the social systems produced according to the principles of instrumental reason or technological rationality. What the Frankfurt critical theorists pay little, if any, attention to are the habits, routines and practices of everyday life that may provide the potential of resistance to domination.

Lefebvre: Alienation and disalienation

The French tradition of concern about 'everyday life' came to the fore in the work of the historians associated with the journal *Annales* (including Lucien Febvre, Robert Mandrou, Fernand Braudel and Guy Thuillier). They wrote about the historical continuity of experiences, customs and traditions that were largely private and, until the twentieth century, changed gradually and by hardly perceptible degrees (Roche 2000: 5). But the impact of modernity – industrialisation, urbanisation, the growth of the money economy and capitalism – has led to dramatic and continual change in everyday life. Braudel comments that 'in the world of ideas, the people of the eighteenth century are our contemporaries', and that in 'habits of mind and feelings' we would have much in common with Voltaire and his contemporaries (1992: 27). But in terms of the details of everyday life the difference would be enormous and shocking: 'Between his world and ours, a great gulf would open up: lighting at night, heating, transport, food, illness, medicine' (Braudel 1992: 28). The change in the material conditions of ordinary existence has accelerated in modernity, and historians like Roche and Braudel have carefully documented the social impacts on everyday life (for example, of changes in housing – Braudel 1992: 266–311; Roche 2000: 81–105). It is this tradition that is continued by French critical theorists such as Henri Lefebvre.

The Frankfurt critical theorists do not generally use the term 'alienation' to describe the domination of the individual's everyday life in advanced capitalism (with the exception, of course, of Erich Fromm – see, for example, 1963: 120–52[1]). But for Lefebvre, who blended a radical Marxist political critique with imaginative and creative philosophical reflection, it was alienation that characterised everyday life in industrialised, capitalist society. He approved of the materialism in Marx's approach to alienation in the *1844 Manuscripts* – as opposed to the idealistic form of alienation in Hegel's phenomenology – but he was critical of Marx's focus on work and the division of labour as the site of alienation. What about leisure and private life? What about the everyday, ordinary aspects of people's lives under capitalism? Rather than waiting for a revolution in the economic arrangements of work and production, Lefebvre argues that everyday life can itself be a 'disalienating' process. From Marx, he derives the concept of 'total man', who is determined by the wholeness of his everyday life, which includes not only work but also self-reproduction: 'Man appropriates his integral essence in an integral way' (Marx quoted in Lefebvre 1991a: 65). But unlike Marx, who sees both the problem of alienation and its solution in the organisation of the relations of production, Lefebvre sees the problem in the contradiction between work and a person's whole life.

For Lefebvre, 'total man' is an ideal concept of what unalienated human being is, but under capitalism the components of work, leisure and private and family life have become segregated and differentiated. In leisure, for example, we seek a break from work, an opportunity to unwind, to relax, to get away from it all, including getting away from day-to-day family life. It is 'distraction', entertainment and relaxation that are sought out in leisure time – not education or even art (Lefebvre 1991a: 33). Reading books and watching films will be for escapism and excitement and their content (action thrillers, romance, science fiction/fantasy) will be as far away as possible from 'real life'. But whereas the Frankfurt theorists see this as demonstrating the penetration of the administered society into ordinary lives, Lefebvre argues that the pursuit of leisure shows that people are not succumbing to alienation; they wish to assert their individual identity and pursue their own interests. Leisure activities are an attempt to recover something of free human being, and through practices such as sports, hobbies and pastimes, people are attempting to get closer to an understanding of what it might be to be a 'total man'. For Lefebvre, critique must begin with these activities of everyday life that are not work, but there is a double-bind because leisure has only one meaning: to get away from work: 'They *are* critique in so far as they are *other* than everyday life, and yet they are *in everyday life*, they are *alienation*' (Lefebvre 1991a: 40).

Unlike Horkheimer, Lefebvre sees hobbies and other leisure activities as practices that can potentially express individuality. But he agrees with Marcuse's view of material life under commodity capitalism: 'The *devaluation* of the human world grows in direct proportion to the *increase in value* of the world of things' (Lefevbre 1991a: 59). For Lefebvre, 'style' was the material form of ordinary life before its displacement by 'culture' at the end of the nineteenth century, the period when mass-produced material goods gave substance to an emerging form of everyday life. The sense of style and a ludic spirit became lost in the dreariness of the everyday world, in which rational production and consumption aimed at producing a temporary satisfaction that would always be closely followed by a state of dissatisfaction in which new needs could be stimulated (Lefebvre 1971: 79). The social system that developed to manage the culture of needs he calls the 'Bureaucratic Society of Controlled Consumption' (BSCC) (1971: 75). It has replaced the extremes of famine and poverty still experienced in unmodernised societies, but it does not produce pleasure and happiness and the result is a continuous feeling of unrest. The BSCC is both a material process of producing and consuming goods, and a discursive or cultural process that deadens real, individual motivations while stimulating desire for new products. Lefebvre writes, for example, about the way women's magazines link the worlds of experience and make-believe by mixing precise and detailed information about where to buy and at how much with 'a form of rhetoric that invests clothes and other objects with an aura of unreality' (1971: 86). The magazines describe and present images of dresses, dishes, furniture, houses and gardens that are beyond the capacity of the ordinary individual to buy or make, mixing them with items that we *can* buy or make for ourselves. Lefebvre's critique is more than a weary complaint about the trivial nature of the media, because he points out how the material substance and practical activity of our everyday lives becomes mingled with fantasy. The impossible is projected onto the ordinary to disguise the compulsion to consume and our limited capacity to adapt: '... practical texts on make-believe fashions and ... make-believe sections ... on practical fashions' (Lefebvre 1971: 86). The bodily, lived experience of everyday life is of course a disappointment when compared to the images and ideals we are presented with. But consumption is not simply about the objects that might be bought; it is also an act of imagination, of consuming the signs that work as metaphors and metonyms for the joy of consuming in general.

Just as the car is an exemplar of the domination of human nature for Horkheimer and Marcuse, for Lefebvre the motor-car is the 'Leading-Object' of the BSCC that shapes both individual behaviour and a series of social systems from economics to speech (1971: 101). The size, power, cost and performance of the motor-car provides a system of social distinction. Space, especially in cities, is conceived of in terms of the traffic system, which takes priority over accommodation and provides the opportunity for interaction and simultaneity of presence without exchange. The car has practical significance as a means of communication and transport, but as it conquers the realm of everyday life it restores risk and hazard, providing 'all that remains of adventure in everyday life' (Lefebvre 1971: 101). But as Lefebvre points out, the car as a subsystem of the BSCC is also an 'absurd' object that destroys everything and then itself; the car as a means of communication fails when the traffic system becomes gridlocked ('the automobile is the arch-symbol of autodestruction' – 1971: 104). Fashion and tourism manage the same feat: fashion destroys its compulsion when everyone is fashionable, and the delight in the exoticism of the tourist attraction dissolves when everyone has been there.

Rather as Marcuse does, Lefebvre describes the modern state as contributing to the BSCC by a kind of 'programming' of consumption through the myriad regulations that control personal financial matters, activities of buying and selling as well as the uses of public spaces and services. A particular example of this programming of everyday life by the state is the new town, which is 'strangely reminiscent of colonial or semi-colonial towns with their straight roads criss-crossing at right angles and their frequent police patrols' (Lefebvre 1971: 59). Control is achieved by the bureaucratic arrangements that determine where you can go and at what times, how fast you may travel (public transport systems, parking restrictions), where your house may be, what design it will have, what recreation facilities are available, and so on. The new town development corporations act in the absence of a sufficiently comprehensive local administration; there can be no representation of residents until the residents are there, so someone else plans the place they will eventually move to.

Lefebvre is a frustratingly vague and rambling writer. He only occasionally refers to other writers' work, he does not build up a systematic argument, and it is difficult to see to what extent his ideas are original – much of what he writes is very similar to the Frankfurt critical theorists, although he only occasionally makes reference to Marcuse. He shares with them concerns about the loss of individuality, the shift from production to consumption, and the penetration of the interests of the consumer society into the private lives and activities of ordinary people. But he goes further than seeing alienation as the result of the system of thought that pervades modernity – instrumental reason – by describing everyday life as in itself alienated. His focus on everyday life is, however, rather more optimistic: he argues that we can chose to live it differently and thereby confront alienation and so change the world we live in. He wants a cultural revolution, but not one based on art or on aesthetics or on transforming work and the relations of production: 'Let every technical means be employed for the transformation of everyday life!' (Lefebvre 1971: 204). The praxis that he proposes for this cultural revolution reasserts individuality on three fronts (Lefebvre 1971: 204–5). Firstly, through removing the institutional repression of sexuality as well as giving juridical and political equality to the sexes. Secondly, through reform of city spaces away from the focus on industrial production and towards the control of space for everyday life, including play and art. Thirdly, through a rediscovery of the festival, not simply as a break from everyday life, but as a form of enter-tainment controlled by those who will enjoy it.

Certeau: Strategies and tactics

Like Lefebvre, Michel de Certeau (1984; Certeau et al. 1998) is also interested in recovering the realm of everyday existence for those who live it, both through theoretical discussion and through attempting to describe it. His is not grand theory in the sense of attempting to describe the structure or dynamics of society as a whole; instead he tries to summarise how ordinary existence is lived in modernity. Certeau's critique draws on the ideas of Pierre Bourdieu and Michel Foucault rather than the critical theory tradition, but, as Michael Gardiner points out, his work emerged in the context of an 'ongoing preoccupation within Western societies concerning the deleterious effects of modernity and mass culture' (2000: 159 – he goes on to explore the continu-ities between Certeau, Adorno and Horkheimer, and Levebvre). Certeau is critical of the impact of consumer society but, unlike the Frankfurt theorists' view of individuality as dominated by instrumental reason, he identifies how individuals manage to maintain some control of their everyday lives despite the impact of mass culture.

One example of how ordinary people assert their wishes and needs in the face of those prescribed by consumer culture is what Certeau calls *la perruque* ('the wig') – the work done by the worker for him or herself that is disguised as work for the employer (1984: 25). The examples he gives are of the secre-tary writing a love letter on company time and the cabinet maker 'borrowing' a lathe to make some furniture. In today's work culture the examples would more likely be sending emails to friends and browsing websites at the office that are not related to the employer's work. Not only is it subversive of the values and practices of late modernity, it is *disalienating* for the worker, who is recovering control over the time and effort expended:

In the very place where the machine he serves reigns supreme, he cun-ningly takes pleasure in finding a way to create gratuitous products whose sole purpose is to signify his own capabilities through his *work* and to confirm his solidarity with other workers or his family through *spend-ing* his time in this way. (Certeau 1984: 26)

75

Nothing of material value is stolen and the worker remains officially on the job, but, in using the employer's time, premises and equipment, the worker undertakes something that is not productive work, but neither is it leisure time either. Certeau was interested in the practices, including those of language, by which ordinary people resist the dictates of the 'programmed' or 'managed' society and claim a measure of control over their ordinary lives. The example of *la perruque* illustrates the subversion of both language and practice: a wig dissembles (appearing as hair) as does the worker (pretending to work for the employer but actually working for himself), as does the unofficial use of the word (the slang use does not appear in ordinary dictionaries as a meaning). In English the word 'foreigner' (as in 'doing a foreigner') works in a very similar way to refer to a job done not for the employer (i.e. that is outside his jurisdiction), and is also a slang use that does not get reported in the standard dictionaries.[2]

Rather than take his philosophical origins from Hegel or even Marx, Certeau is attracted to Wittgenstein's intention 'to bring words back from their metaphysical to their everyday use' (Wittgenstein 1978: 48, quoted in Certeau 1984: 9). He rejects the claims of traditional philosophy to be 'expert' and able to assert what is the case universally and to explain things in general as if from the outside. What appeals to Certeau about Wittgenstein's approach is that rather than attempt to establish a mastery over the form of language, he continues to work within ordinary language to understand its form. Certeau was attempting to do the same sort of thing with culture: to identify the ordinary ways of speaking or acting that are recognisable as 'practices' of the everyday. By 'practices' he is referring to the way the term is used both by Wittgenstein and by Bourdieu to identify how people make their language and make their everyday social lives. In other words he is distinguishing 'practices' both from the idiosyncratic or personal ways that an individual may have, and from the rule-governed, dominating ways that are prescribed by institutions and ideologies.

Rather like Lefebvre, Certeau addresses the practices by which space becomes a dimension of the everyday world. For Lefebvre, social space has a duality that makes it dynamic rather than fixed and stable: always both a 'field of action' and a 'basis for action', a site of the 'actual' and of the 'potential', a collection of objects and things and a set of tools and procedures (Lefebvre 1991b: 191). But Certeau is more directly interested in how space is appropriated through everyday practices such as walking through a city, which he contrasts to looking down over it, reading it, as from a tower like those of the World Trade Center (1984: 91–3). The overview of the city is equivalent to the aloof, theoretical perspective of the planner or cartographer who is not part of the flow of activity that is the city. Since 11 September 2001 when those towers were brought horrifically down to earth, we have come to recognise that they were indeed part of the city with thousands of people coming and going, engaged in ordinary activities. But Certeau's account of the towers as a viewing platform for tourists emphasises the distance and disengagement from the life of the city beneath, which reveals the city as a whole, as a 'Concept-city' that is the creation of modern rationality in the form of scientific and political technology. The functionalist administration of such a city attempts to eliminate those aspects that do not fit with the concept – abnormality, deviance, illness, death, etc. In 1980, over two decades before the towers were brought down by terrorists, Certeau was writing of the decay of the Concept-city and of the limits of the techniques of planning and rationality; rather than the catastrophic event, he saw its destruction through the 'microbe-like' practices of 'swarming activity' that produce 'everyday regulations and surreptitious creativities' (Certeau 1984: 96).

For Certeau, neither the practices of language nor those of walking have been dominated or reduced to a pre-determined system within modernity. The practice of walking is how the lived, everyday character of the city is constituted as each individual follows her or his own path, perhaps taking an habitual route, perhaps making an unusual expedition. There is no overall plan or pattern, no prescription of the myriad actions that make up the regularity of the living whole. As Certeau says, it is possible to track and map these paths, even to count and predict, but such methods do not catch the quality of the practice itself: the act of passing by (Certeau 1984: 97). The act of walking is equivalent in the city to the speech act in language and achieves the 'appropriation' of the space by the walker, whose actions in turn situate 'place' within space. Places are both connected and differentiated as the walker chooses a path, takes a detour or short-cut, or avoids a particular route. This articulation by the individual walker achieves for Certeau an 'enunciatory' form, equivalent to the way a speaker takes the words and grammatical possibilities of the language but produces her or his own particularised utterance. In both walking and speech things can be done differently and the rules broken. But for both language and walking in the city to work, the behaviour of individuals must follow the regularity of a practice. There can be transgression and experiment, but without recognition of the rules, speech will not enable speakers to express meaning and walking will not provide walkers with paths that will get them where they are going.

Walking is expressive of meaning because of the range of individual styles that make up the practice Certeau refers to as being a 'forest of gestures' (1984: 102 – the phrase derives from Rilke's 'trees of gestures'). The gestures cannot be translated into text, and the textuality of walking, the street and place names, do not add up to meaning except in so far as they are part of the walk: '*Saints-Pères, Corentin Celton, Red Square* ... these names make themselves available to the diverse meanings given them by passers-by; they detach themselves from the places they were supposed to define and serve as imaginary meeting points on itineraries' (Certeau 1984: 104). For Certeau, the itinerary, a series of relations between places, provides a narrative in the everyday experience of people moving through space, expressing actions and indicating what will be seen. The map, in contrast, suggests no action or particularity but dominates space with the calculative rationality and unemotional distance of science.

Certeau notes that personalised map making has given way to the autonomous form of the modern geographical map that erases itineraries to provide a 'totalizing stage' or 'tableau of a "state" of geographical knowledge' (1984: 121). But Barthes, writing in 1967, recovers the map for its users as something that can be 'read' semiologically, like an ideogram, so that the city's centre point can be seen as its 'gathering point', the location of exchange, eroticism and play (1988: 199–200). Barthes (1982) revisited the same idea later when he wrote about Tokyo, where the official map shows a city form with a centre that is in fact an empty and forbidden place – the walled and leafy residence of the emperor who is never seen. But he reproduces some impromptu maps sketched by inhabitants that excel in their gestural quality against the textuality of geometrically precise printed maps. He delights not only in the gestures of those who create an impromptu map – including a rather un-Japanese reversal of a pencil to employ an eraser – but also in the way that the city requires you to orient yourself 'by walking, by sight, by habit, by experience' (Barthes 1982: 36).

For Barthes, then, the itinerary and the map become merged when they are used for practical purposes: to find streets or distinguish places for activity or identify the absence of activity, as in the centre of Tokyo. Certeau's account of walking in the city is rather sentimental: walkers never hop on a bus or retrieve their cars from an underground car park. His walker manages to avoid the barriers, bridges, underpasses and controlled crossings of the modern city, which are the result of rational planning. The routes for cars and buses are rather more planned and administered than those for the pedestrian, as we have seen both Horkheimer and Marcuse point out. But car drivers too get to know their own routes and itineraries, mixing street names with visible landmarks much like a pedestrian. The search for the 'best' route is a regular topic for discussion, and a range of driving practices identify short-cuts and 'rat runs'. U-turns, jumping lights, lane swapping, breaking speed limits, driving over kerbs and cutting in are in the repertoire of transgressions that drivers use to achieve their route. Such driving practices, oriented to arriving as soon as possible and overcoming the city's constraints on the vehicle's capacity, resist the hegemony of the planned and policed route. Of course, drivers will also take detours for scenery, to drop someone off and even just to see where a road leads. As they pass by they will note buildings or places of interest to which they might return another day, and will respond to the aesthetics of their environment: buildings, billboards and other vehicles.

A binary distinction between 'strategies' and 'tactics' is a key feature of Certeau's account of the everyday that distinguishes its practices from the ideology of institutions and societies. A 'strategy' is the circumscribed, 'proper' relationship between spatial and institutional forms, such as 'a proprietor, an enterprise, a city, a scientific institution', and exterior subjects, such as 'competitors, adversaries, "clienteles", "targets" or "objects" of research' (Certeau 1984: xix). The tactic, on the other hand, is characteristic of the everyday practice that 'insinuates itself into the other's place, fragmentarily, without taking it over in its entirety', and, being without place, is dependent on time, watching for opportunities, manipulating events (Certeau 1984: xix). The sorts of everyday practice that Certeau is referring to include talking, reading, moving about, shopping, cooking, and so on. He is interested in the way that, in getting through ordinary life, people employ clever tricks, cunning, practical knowledge of how things work. While critical theory has tended to bemoan the way that consumption has come to dominate cultural life, Certeau sees in the practices of consumption occasions for the employment of 'tactics':

> The analysis of the images broadcast by television (representation) and of the time spent watching television (behavior) should be complemented by a study of what the cultural consumer 'makes' or 'does' during this time and with these images. The same goes for the use of urban space, the products purchased in the supermarket, the stories and legends distributed by the newspaper, and so on. (Certeau 1984: xii)

In the second volume of *The Practice of Everyday Life*, Certeau and a group of colleagues undertook detailed micro studies of dwelling and cooking that began the study of the practices of consumption and the use of space (Certeau et al. 1998). Their close study of a family's life in a local district builds up a picture of activities and relationships that constitute the substance of everyday life. The way that the tactics of everyday practices transform space into place are explored to show how a neighbourhood is realised by lived relationships rather than by zoning on a map.

For example, Pierre Mayol discusses how the individual dweller achieves an identity and becomes 'well thought of' within their neighbourhood through actions that demonstrate respect for the standards of 'propriety', including just how close one should be to people: 'Neither too far, nor too close, so as not to be bothered and also not to lose the expected benefits of a good relationship with the neighbors.' (Certeau et al., 1998: 15). Mayol shows how sexuality is a component of propriety that is open to discursive management. Modesty and reserve may provide a position of secure distance, but double meaning, ambiguity and wordplay are tactics by which social space can be crossed – with nothing really at stake but one's character and good standing. The real practice of sex occurs in private, but effects are felt at the level of language – comments about a rumour of adultery, for example – which is able to maintain an ambiguity amenable to variation. Innuendo is the way that erotic speech can be managed within the bounds of propriety and to meet the immediate social context; it is toned down in the presence of children or young women or 'respectable' elderly people. Mayol tells of a street vendor who risked propriety to attract attention and customers, specifically women, to his stall with his manner of speaking:

... when women bought vegetables from him, it went from 'mounds of lettuce' to 'well-hung' onions, and moving on to carrots 'that, when squeezed enough, the juice comes out' ... one day a deeply shocked customer publicly slapped him, to the amazement of everyone around – a supreme insult that the vendor succeeded in parrying by coming out with a superb curse ...: 'Death to virtue, for Christ's sake!'. (Certeau et al., 1998: 28)

The practice of consumption here is not just buying things, for it involves a complexity of modulated behaviour: the vendor utilises an eroticised discourse to promote his goods, and, even when he seems to be losing a customer, manages to employ a tactic that will retain his neighbourhood standing as a man of pleasant good humour.

This discussion of 'dwelling' nicely reinforces the way that physical and embodied space is also social and cultural space, and at the level of everyday life they cannot be separated as they might in a discussion of physics or art. There is in the work of Certeau and his colleagues something of the American tradition of studying the everyday empirically to draw out its fullness and complexity. But what is very different from the American tradition is the attempt to draw a critical distinction between the social strategies that constrain local and individual identity and action and the tactics by which everyday life can be recovered for those who live it.

Baudrillard: Objects and consumption

While Jean Baudrillard does not address everyday life directly, he does explore the shift of emphasis in modern capitalist societies from industrial production to the development of mass consumption and material life. The topic of consumption is a feature of Lefebvre's concept of everyday life, and present in Marcuse's account of the impact of advanced capitalism on the members of society as well as Certeau's interest in ordinary lives. Baudrillard's first book originally published in 1968, *The System of Objects* (1996a), initiates a theme that remains throughout his work: the relation between the subject and the object. Here the object is the material object available for consumption that is transformed as it is drawn into social relations such as those that create the atmosphere of domestic interiors and the fascination of collectors with similar objects. Rather than simply see the object as socially constructed, Baudrillard allows that there is something in the object that acts on the subject. The objects of everyday life, practical objects, are 'constantly in flight' from their technical and functional meanings towards their cultural meanings (Baudrillard 1996a: 8). This is because objects are drawn into use to meet needs in everyday life, needs that are defined and specified within the culture. So, to use Baudrillard's example, a coffee mill has elements that are objective and functional: the electric motor and the system for delivering electricity to it. But the coffee-grinding function becomes specific to the use of the object (how the coffee gets ground) and the outward appearance is, he argues, purely a subjective matter. It is the subject of the user who interacts with the object in terms of how fine the coffee is ground and how the shape and colour of the grinder fit in with the rest of the kitchen. It is tempting to think of such mundane artefacts as specified in their technical objectivity, but in fact the culture affects the technology as the practices of use constantly feed back on the system of techniques.

Rather than seeing technological reason as a system that imposes itself on the lives of people through the materiality of life, as Marcuse implies, Baudrillard is arguing that objects are drawn into social relations of need and use and they participate in a system of relationships with other objects: a system of objects. The system of objects is not technological or functional but is, at least in part, shaped by the significance that the object has within everyday life. In modernity, in the consumer society, symbolic relationships between objects become signs in a system of meaning. The 'naturalness' of wooden furniture, for example, becomes a sign rather than a lived symbolic relationship as furniture becomes organised in a system of functionality. Functionality here is a property of objects in relation to the uses made of them in a given society. The colour and texture of wood in modern societies is not there because that is how furniture has to be made; it is there because it signifies 'naturalness'. As such it competes with other materials (leather, fabric, chromium, plastics, foams) that within the system of functionality will generate a different 'atmosphere'. Wood can also be substituted for by imitations (plastic fakes, veneers) that, as signs, connote naturalness but have no material relation with the world of nature.

While much of the system of objects that define everyday life is to be found within the home (including the fixtures and fittings – though Baudrillard avoids discussing architecture), the motor car is an object that stands both as an object in itself and as an object that is also a home. Just as the car is the 'Leading-Object' for Lefebvre, for Baudrillard it epitomises the object in the system of objects – it is a 'sublime object' because of the way that it opens up relations of space-time. The car provides a domestic context and yet an escape from the routine and mundane:

> The car achieves an extraordinary compromise, for it makes it possible to be simultaneously at home and further and further away from home. It is thus the centre of a new kind of subjectivity, but a centre bounded by no circumference, whereas the subjectivity of the domestic world is strictly circumscribed. (Baudrillard 1996a: 67)

The way that objects are located within the system of objects in modern societies is to do with their status within the categorial distinction between models and series. In the era of craft production, each object was a model: individual and distinct, fit for purpose or, for the wealthy, decorated and enhanced to signify social distinction. But in the industrial era, most objects are predominantly machine-produced from a line such that each is indistinguishable. Of course the rich continue to own singular 'models' from which serial production derives copies, but, as Baudrillard points out, things are more complicated because we find ways of imbuing the serial object with the qualities of distinction of the model. Most obviously this is through the 'personalisation' of the object, in which it is made to take on subjective characteristics. Objects are produced and marketed to make them distinct from the others in the series – to have a different shape or colour, slightly enhanced functionality or specification. This is what constitutes fashion (Baudrillard 1996a: 142). Even the most singular object in industrial society is usually one of a production series, so what becomes important is the 'idea of the model', which is 'the idea of absolute difference'.

Baudrillard's interest in the system of objects makes his approach to consumer societies rather different from that of Lefebvre or Marcuse, who see the process of consumption as realising the destiny of a system of production. Baudrillard shifts attention from production to consumption, recognising that there is no system of relationship with objects that can be treated as prior to social and cultural organisation. For both Marx and Marcuse, a system of primary needs lies behind human relationships with objects because the biological body has minimal needs for sustenance and shelter (although see Sahlins's discussion of Marx's view of human needs – 1976: 148–61). What such approaches suggest is that an economic system such as capitalism creates needs that are not 'real', in the sense that human bodies would survive even if such needs (for cars or electric coffee grinders, perhaps) were not met. But Baudrillard resists such a biological reduction and understands 'need' as a relation between subject and object that emerges within the culture through a system of sign exchange. As he points out, in all societies the urgency to demonstrate excess (the divine or sacrificial share, sumptuous discharge, economic profit) is key to the survival of the society, if not of its poorest members (Baudrillard 1981: 80–1). What counts as 'need' for an individual is culturally defined so that 'the threshold of *obligatory* consumption can be set well above the strictly necessary – always as a function of the production of surplus value: this is the case in our societies, where no one is free to live on raw roots and fresh water' (Baudrillard 1981: 81).

It is in *The Consumer Society* (1998, first published in 1970,) that Baudrillard argues that the myth of Galbraith's (1962) 'affluent society' lies in measuring an individual's happiness by the visible goods and services that she or he consumes. This measure of 'the accumulation of the *signs* of happiness' is no measure of a real, underlying quality of happiness because the state of inner happiness actually experienced by people is not susceptible to external measurement (Baudrillard 1998: 31). The affluent society may apparently meet basic needs for more members of society – reducing hunger, for example. But for Baudrillard this is nothing to do with reducing social segregation and increasing overall happiness. New modes of distinction emerge in the form of environmental disbenefits so that shortages of space, time, fresh air, greenery, water and silence replace the shortages of food and shelter. However, it is not a shortage of goods to consume but a shortage of knowing *how* to consume that sustains class distinctions: 'Knowledge and power are, or are going to become, the two great scarce commodities of our affluent society' (Baudrillard 1998: 57). Far from saying farewell to class, Baudrillard reminds us that consumption signals class status: in consumer society the lower and middle classes 'prove themselves by objects' and achieve 'salvation by consumption' (Baudrillard 1998: 60).

American theorists such as David Riesman (1950) saw the emergence of a dynamic new affluent society in which 'other-directedness' would lead to a democratic form of social integration based on the sharing of new social values through the mass media. But Baudrillard argues that while the mass media claim to offer us the 'truth' – real images, immediate reports – all this serves to obscure our distance from what is reported. Their truth is precisely that 'I was not there', and so it is for me fantasy; it is not my experience 'but the dizzying whirl of reality' (Baudrillard 1998: 34). Baudrillard sees the inhabitants of consumer society only saved from the intolerable tedium of their own limited lives by the illusion of engagement in the exterior world through the media. The problems of social distinction and poverty that for Galbraith and Riesman were matters for social engineering or tinkering with the system are for Baudrillard fundamentally embedded in capitalist society. He argues that the major flaw in the theories such as those of Galbraith and Riesman is their belief in *'homo œconomicus'*, the individual who makes rational economic choices based on seeking out those objects that provide the greatest personal satisfaction and happiness. These theorists presume that *homo œ-conomicus* is prior to the affluent society – 'a Man "endowed" with wants or needs which "lead" him towards objects which "give" him satisfaction' (Baudrillard 1998: 69) – and do seem not to recognise him as a creature produced by the consumer society.

Baudrillard argues that we can take nothing as given to the operation of modern society except the linguistic capacity of humans, which enables them to engage in signifying with codes that have social meanings. It is an illusion of psychologists and economists to presume to know what the properties and propensities of individuals would be prior to the society in which they live. However, Baudrillard does not reject the idea of the individual; indeed, his critique recognises a role for individual variation and sensitivity that is absent in the social science he is criticising. Although he makes no reference to the work of Lefebvre or Certeau, his critique of consumerism is a defence of the variability of everyday, individual consumption against the presumption of a 'standardised', rational individual who might be understood as making up a mass of like individuals.

Baudrillard's critique of the *homo œconomicus* does involve a substantial departure from Marcuse's analysis of false needs as a production of capitalist culture but true, vital needs as providing a standard against which others can be judged. For Baudrillard, there is no true or natural state to return to because all needs are produced within the circulation of signs, which is as much a characteristic of late capitalism as is the investment of capital by the entrepreneur. Late capitalism has moved beyond a situation in which one class directly exploits another – all classes are engaged in the process of what Baudrillard calls 'consummativity', in which individuals express needs induced by 'the internal logic of the system' (1981: 82). What Baudrillard describes in his early work is the emergence of a consumer society in which 'consumption is *social labour*' (1998: 84), and alienated labour at that (see Chapter 3, p. 56). The irony of 'consumer society' is that it is a profound contradiction in terms because when we are all construed as consumers and are encouraged to express individual choice, we do not think and act collectively as a society. The result, Baudrillard argues, is that such a society requires an intensification of bureaucratic control to maintain the freedom of the individual to be a consumer. Consumer society then has no collective solidarity and so has to compensate with increased tolerance towards individual variation. The system seems to be anomic and the individual is increasingly encouraged towards the private sphere. In that private sphere, the consumer is obliged to be happy, to seek pleasure and sensation, and to be curious about new things and experiences: 'It is no longer desire, or even "taste", or a specific inclination that are at stake, but a generalized curiosity, driven by a vague sense of unease – it is the "fun morality" or the imperative to enjoy oneself, to exploit to the full one's potential for thrills, pleasure or gratification' (Baudrillard 1998: 80).

Conclusions

The Frankfurt theorists describe the emergence of an administered society in which instrumental rationality spills over into the sphere of private life and individual action. They see the alienation of consumption as entailed in the capitalist mode of production and pay only passing attention to the sphere of everyday life. In the Gallic tradition, however, this sphere becomes a focus of theoretical interest (e.g. Lefebvre) and some empirical study (e.g. Certeau). Although everyday life is alienated in itself, it begins to be described as a sphere for recovering a lived rather than a programmed identity. Consumption is not treated as determined by the demands of a mode of production but becomes a sphere of ordinary social action in its own right – a sphere in which alienation and domination can be resisted through choosing certain practices over others. While for Lefebvre, Certeau and even Barthes such a recovery of everyday life seems a possibility resonant with political effects, Baudrillard warns of the delusion of 'choice' and individuality that become caught up in the system of 'consummativity'. Nonetheless, going against the grain, resisting the pattern, including the way that we are hailed as individuals by the consumer society, may subvert the domination to which we are subject.

Summary

- *Everyday life*: It is the ordinary, routine existence of repeated tasks necessary for individual reproduction, meeting biological and social needs.
- *Adorno and Horkheimer*: Instrumental reason dominates everyday life as well as work life: displacing true individuality, restricting the private domain of family life, constraining through material apparatuses (e.g. the car driver), hobbies and leisure.
- *Marcuse*: Domination operates through the creation of false needs (commodities, cars, entertainment), manufactured desires and managed means of meeting them so that sated consumers fall into a 'Happy Consciousness'.
- *Lefebvre*: Everyday life is alienated but a sphere in which the being of 'total man' can be recovered. Leisure is an escape from work but possibly also a route to free, autonomous action. The consumption of goods, ideas, values and the use of space is shaped by a bureaucratic society but we could choose to live it differently (e.g. sexual equality, play, recovery of the festival).
- *Certeau*: Through tactics (e.g. *la perruque*) individuals can circumvent the programming of everyday life to assert individual and local identity through practices (e.g. of language, walking and shopping) that resist society's strategies of domination.
- *Baudrillard*: The 'system of objects' is a means by which the dominant culture intrudes into the individual practices of everyday life; function is culturally specified not simply material. Consumer society circulates commodities as signs in a code – a system of consummativity – to which the individual succumbs and contributes under the illusion of choice.

Further reading

Amongst Lefebvre's many discussions of 'everyday life', it is *Everyday Life in the Modern World* (1971) that is most accessible and interesting. Michael Gardiner's *Critiques of Everyday Life* (2000) provides a clear account of the way that the theme of everyday life has been discussed by a number of different authors. Certeau's *The Practice of Everyday Life* (1984) is quite challenging to read but worth persevering with as it contains ideas that have still had little impact on the English-speaking study of society and culture. David Chaney's recent volume *Cultural Change and Everyday Life* (2002) brings the concept of everyday life up to date in relation to the changing culture and society of late modernity.

Notes

1 I have chosen not to explore Fromm's work as part of the work of the Frankfurt School because of his complex relationship with the work of critical theory (see Jay 1973: 88–106; Wiggershaus 1994: 265–73). There is insufficient space in the present book to discuss Fromm but his work does clearly incorporate many of the themes taken as 'critical theory'.

2 Checking the precise usage of such words then of course becomes very difficult. Are they regional? Do they endure?

FIVE

Sex and Sexuality

Within the writing of the critical theorists there is a sense of the centrality of sex and sexuality for human beings that begins to emerge from its obscurity in traditional social theory. The domain of sexuality is one that is potentially not alienated, a sphere of human life in which individuals can be themselves, freely and completely. Human sexuality is at least originally grounded in the animal nature of *Homo sapiens*. Like eating and excreting, movement and posture, sexuality – the desire to engage in sexual intercourse with others – is something we share with other animals that reproduce by sex. Of course, culture has shaped sexuality over millennia, just as it has eating and excreting, and it is no longer possible to be sure what is animal and what is cultural. The natural response of disgust can be stimulated by foods which other people or other cultures desire as delicacies. The same response of disgust can be provoked by the thought of sexual practices that are to others not only desired but are their only route to sexual satisfaction and happiness.

How culture shapes sexuality is clearly a complex matter that is tied up with the development of kinship patterns, the restrictions on incestuous relationships, rules surrounding birth and childcare, the sexual division of labour and notions of gender identity. But civilisation, as Freud argues, has developed in such a way that the individual is constrained from seeking fulfilment and happiness through sexual activity (see Chapter 1, pp. 10–14). This idea of a particular period of cultural development shaping sexuality beyond the constraints necessary for the survival of the species or the culture is what lies behind the critical theorists' interest in sexuality. The period of cultural development that they are concerned with is that of modern capitalism; what Freud described so loosely as *kultur* or civilisation is for critical theory that period in which the capitalist mode of production begins to have cultural consequences which perpetuate alienation. If the individual is to be liberated from the restrictions of late capitalism, freed from the alienation of modern culture, one sphere of life in which that freedom will be realised is sexuality. Indeed since sexuality is so closely linked to the feelings and experiences of happiness, it could be argued to be a key indicator of how liberated or alienated the individual is. But, as we will see, simply extending sexual expression is not the same thing as sexual liberation.

Freud: Sex and death

Behind the critique of sexuality in modern societies lies Sigmund Freud's account of individual repression, which could also be seen as a manifestation of alienation in modernity. He presents a theory of sexual development within the individual, of the tension between the drive to seek bodily pleasure and the impact of societal constraint on that pleasure. Freud's discussion of instinctual drives, specifically that of life, Eros, and the death instinct, also provides a basic scheme for understanding how individual sexuality is open to be channelled by cultural forms in modernity. As the individual develops in a social context, things can go wrong, producing the effects of repression and neurosis.

Instead of construing human instincts as simply animal, Freud's account connects individuals to their social surroundings through the mind: psychoanalysis describes a mental life of ideas and perceptions and experiences that modify and transform instinctual processes. The individual develops a sexuality which does not follow a biologically determined path that can be read off from the state of the reproductive organs. What is to become the adult form of sexuality is a product of the child's interaction with other people and with his or her own body; it happens alongside and as part of the individual's coming to consciousness and awareness of self. It is Freud who leaves behind a traditional perspective of sexuality as biological predetermination to be heterosexual, reproductive in aim and an animal impulse. Instead, he suggests that sexuality is shaped by, and manifest in, the higher human faculties of consciousness and mind. Psychoanalysis recognises sexuality as a bundle of possibilities (including childhood sexuality, inversion, or homosexuality, and a range of perverse orientations and responses) that are shaped and moulded as the individual develops. Society will respond in sexual discourse to these possibilities in ways that will affect what is permissible and acceptable, but psychoanalysis marks a departure from judging acts as sinful or taboo based on what is presumed to be 'natural'.

The perceptions and impressions that individuals receive of how the world is and how they are situated in it are worked on in the mind without necessarily taking on a conscious or linguistic form. They are, however, accessible, according to Freud, through the techniques of psychoanalysis, a talking therapy which enables the workings of the unconscious mind to be brought into the open. Images, language and ideas are then of crucial importance in the development of individual beings and all are manifestations of the link between human individuals and the social context in which they live. For Freud, it is interpersonal relationships, most importantly with parents, which provide the prime social context of the developing individual. But it is not difficult to extrapolate to the more general influence of images and ideas from the culture at large as intervening to shape not only the development of the individual but also her or his psychic and sexual life. Freud's interest in poetry and art is either as a source of metaphors with which to develop his theory or for the insights into the work of artistic production which psychoanalysis might offer. He is not concerned with the impact of cultural products on the psychic and sexual life of people in general, or even of his patients in particular, but it is precisely in this direction that critical theory makes most potent use of his theories.

Sexuality, in Freud's theory, is not a single drive to a predetermined sexual object such as the genitals of the other sex but begins in infancy as polymorphous and perverse: potentially able to be satisfied through a number of parts of the body in a number of ways. He describes the development of the infant through a series of stages of sexuality in which the impact of culture shapes and limits her or his desires, turning them from autoerotic pleasures to focus on objects outside the body (Freud 1977: 88–126). This theory of development later incorporated the Oedipus theory of the impact of sexual attraction between children and their parents (see Chapter 2), but more pertinent to the link between individual subjectivity, sexuality and the world outside the individual is Freud's theory of the libido and sexual instinct. He explains that libido is a force within the individual that is directed towards sexual excitation but is not derived from the sexual parts alone but 'from all the bodily organs' (Freud 1977: 130). The libido is a form of psychic energy that is distinct from the need for food and from other mental processes. The force of the libido is within the person and exists somewhere between the mind and the body, so Freud talks of an 'ego-libido', in which the energy is directed towards the self, and an 'object-libido', when the energy is directed to objects outside the self. The ego-libido forms a 'reservoir' from which the energy of object-libido draws. But the object-libido also draws energy and interest from outside to add to the reservoir and modify the libido within the developing person. For Freud, sexual excitation – which includes both bodily excitation and the tension of mental excitation (1977: 129) – results in pleasure. Sexual pleasure includes thumb sucking in the infant along with all sorts of other bodily sensations, not just those directed towards orgasm or genital activity. Sexual instinct and libido in Freud's account are more than simply biological drives that effect the reproduction of the species.

The seeking out of pleasure may be most obviously represented by the drive to achieve sexual pleasure, but the 'pleasure principle' described in Freud's later metapsychology includes the reverse: the avoidance of unpleasure. Within the process of sex, Freud saw the tension created by sexual desire as an unpleasure, even when it was accompanied by the pleasure of bodily excitation. The pleasure of orgasm is enhanced by the removal of that unpleasurable tension: 'We have all experienced how the greatest pleasure attainable by us, that of the sexual act, is associated with a momentary extinction of a highly intensified excitation'. (Freud 1991: 336–7).

The seeking of pleasure and the avoidance of unpleasure happen in an environmental context, of course, and the 'pleasure principle' is modified by the 'reality principle'. The reality which bears upon a human being is not simply a physical reality but also a social reality which has its effects on the mind and emotions. Identifying what gives pleasure is part of the childhood development process in which some things which give bodily pleasure also produce unpleasure in the ego. In the adult form of pleasure seeking, the higher mental processes 'bind' the instinctual excitation, so that the ego-libido has mastery over what will be responded to as pleasurable. To be sure, the seeking of sexual pleasure is not the only influence on sexuality, and the ego has an instinct for self-preservation that manifests itself as the reality principle, which 'does not abandon the intention of ultimately obtaining pleasure, but it nevertheless demands and carries into effect the postponement of satisfaction, the abandonment of a number of possibilities of gaining satisfaction and the temporary toleration of unpleasure as a step on the long indirect road to pleasure' (Freud 1991: 278).

The reality principle is the adult modification of behaviour that might otherwise be directed to satisfy the libido. Unpleasure is not simply the experience of pain; it is often perceptual: the anticipation of danger or distress. Freud sees, however, that it is not enough, that there are tendencies operating in the self that lie behind the pleasure principle. There are instinctual forces that work alongside the libido that shape the way the ego is formed and indeed the way it can live in society. One of these is the desire for repetition, which may follow the pleasure principle, as when a child wishes to repeat the same game, but which may also go against that principle, as when a patient is compelled to repeat the events of childhood in analysis. Freud finds here an instinctual process that is related to the compulsion to repeat: '*It seems, then, that an instinct is an urge inherent in organic life to restore an earlier state of things* which the living entity has been obliged to abandon under the pressure of external disturbing forces' (Freud 1991: 308–9). This instinctual drive that Freud discovers beyond the pleasure principle is a conservative force, an inertia, that is overcome through external disturbance – the impact of culture on the individual. This is, as Freud recognises, paradoxical: progress and development are not then driven by instinct but in fact occur despite the instinctual drive to return to things as they were. What is more surprising is that this conservative instinct drives towards a time when there was no external influence. It is an instinctual drive towards death that, as life becomes more complex, takes ever more circuitous paths.

Freud recognises that this discovery of a death instinct in the compulsion to repetition seems to contradict the instinct for self-preservation, for self-assertion and mastery. But his solution is to treat them as component instincts that ensure the organism 'follows its own path to death' (Freud 1991: 311) rather than have its life shortened by some other intervention. The result is a tension between two groups of instincts: those driving towards life – the sexual instincts – and those driving towards death. This makes life a journey in which this tension is played out with first one group dominating and then the other. What is important is the balance between these two groups of instincts and the recognition that there is no prime or original instinct which explains the process of life. Freud points out, for example, that there is no instinct to progress, to achieve at a higher level, to become more perfect. Instead he explains the presence of an impulse towards perfection as a repression which is precious to civilisation: '... there is no alternative but to advance in the direction in which growth is still free – though with no prospect of bringing the process to a conclusion or of being able to reach the goal' (Freud 1991: 315).

These are theoretical speculations by Freud, who was not intending to engage in cultural critique. However, he does provide a mechanism that links the individual to society, that sees the drive for pleasure shaped and restricted by the form of civilisation. It also points to the limitations of a logic of progress which is inherent in modernity and in enlightenment thought. His speculations are based on a mixture of the interpretation of some scientific evidence, both zoological and biological, with his clinical experience as an analyst. It is safer to treat this later work as closer to philosophy, even poetry, than science, but it provides a resource utilised by critical theory as a tool for mounting a critique of modern society.

Levebvre: Dissatisfaction

Writing in 1958, Lefebvre notices '[t]he sudden eruption of sexuality in the domain of the image – and more generally in leisure' (1991a: 34) which takes sexuality out of the domain of private life and brings it into a more public arena. But he does not see this as a freeing of morals, a liberating of desires: 'With "modern" eroticism we step outside of the everyday, without actually leaving it: it shocks, it seems brutal, and yet this effect is superficial, pure appearance, leading us back towards the secret of the everyday – dissatisfaction' (Lefebvre 1991a: 35).

These comments represent rather well the main approach of critical theory to the sphere of sexuality: that the private everyday practices of people are subject, under commodity capitalism, to the intrusion of a public form of sexuality which is likely to increase alienation (dissatisfaction) rather than reduce it. Lefebvre's account of the history of everyday life recognises that repression has a part to play in maintaining the balance of sexuality and fecundity, often channelled by religious institutions and practices. As population growth needs to be restricted, so practices are promoted to limit its growth (enforced celibacy, sacrificial prostitution, the encouragement of prostitution, homosexuality and onanism). When populations require stimulation to grow, then sexuality is disconnected from pleasure and becomes a social duty (Lefebvre 1971: 145). But society may become *over*-repressive, he argues, as in those Protestant societies where repression is internalised through ideological means – everyone is her or his own mentor – and violence is held in reserve. The logical development of such over-repressive societies is the 'terrorist society' in which violence is latent:

> ... terror cannot be located, for it comes from everywhere and from every specific thing: the 'system' (in so far as it can be called a 'system') has a hold on every member separately and submits every member to the whole, that is to a strategy, a hidden end, objectives unknown to all but those in power, and that no one questions. (Lefebvre 1971: 147)

Lefebvre offers no historical evidence to support his social theory of repression but his notion of the terrorist society is close to the totalitarian society that the Frankfurt School's critique warns against.[1] The terrorist society is characterised by a series of contradictory forms of everyday life which include writing, art, youth, fashion. One of these contradictory forms is the domination of sexuality by what Levebvre calls an 'eros cult', by which he means the 'proliferation of writings on such themes as sex, sexuality, sexual intercourse' and 'the use of such themes to promote publicity and trade' (1971: 172). Sexuality, he argues, becomes abstract and essentialised, separated from desire, and gives rise to an entity that he calls 'Femininity' – an idealised form of womanhood towards which consumption is directed and which provides a symbol, often sexualised, utilised in advertising. Femininity is a mythical form of human being that exists at the centre of a series of other 'pseudo-natures, products of culture, pure forms draped in artifacts' that include: the Spontaneous, the Natural, the Cultured, the Happy and the Loving (Lefebvre 1971: 173 – see Chapter 2).

Adorno and Horkheimer: Sex and rationality

There is common ground between Adorno and Horkheimer and Lefebvre in that they offer a similar critique of modern capitalism as producing a form of public sexuality that is exploitative rather than satisfying. The way that cultural images encourage a sexuality separated from the natural, straightforward or everyday is characteristic of the culture industry: 'To offer and to deprive [the victims of the culture industry] of something is one and the same. This is what happens in erotic films. Precisely because it must never take place, everything centers upon copulation' (Adorno and Horkheimer 1979: 141). This truncated form of cultural experience works as a hook to trap an audience into continuing to watch and listen to see if the end – satisfaction – will ever be achieved. The titillating promise and denial of sexual possibility produces an unsatisfying public form of sexuality that relieves the culture industry of ever having to present sexuality as integrated into the fullness of life, or of having to question the general condition of human existence.

For Adorno and Horkheimer, enjoyment and pleasure become cultural instruments in certain hands. They read the Marquis de Sade's *Juliette* (1797) as a moral tale, a myth that warns of the dangers of enlightenment thought, depending as it does on dividing the sexes, on separating mind from body and on separating sex from love. The church has had a hand in such separations by oppressing women as witches and then revering them as Madonna, by distinguishing the intellectual and ritualistic love of God from the more mundane love of people for each other. It is Juliette's efficient and systematic approach to sacrilege, her proficient manipulation of rationality, her self-control and her careful planning that enable her to 'demonize Catholicism as the most up-to-date mythology and with it civilization as a whole' (Adorno and Horkheimer 1979: 94). But the character of Sade's Juliette drives this logic of separation towards its conclusions and provides a model of the modern mentality, of one who is a 'proficient manipulator of the organ of rational thought' (Adorno and Horkeimer 1979: 95). Juliette takes the logic of modernity to the point where it becomes intolerably anti-social and indulges in 'the plea-sure of attacking civilization with its own weapons' (Adorno and Horkheimer 1979: 94). The regime of 'libertinage' that she lives by involves men in a 'rational, calculating relation to their own kind' which is of course the same principle of human relations that critical theory sees as characteristic of late modernity (Adorno and Horkheimer 1979: 107). The libertine depends on a metaphysical separation of thought and life in which consciousness can plan and imagine the acts that will bring bodily satisfactions. This is a form of 'progress' in which culture is brought to bear on what might be seen as a process that does not need culture:

> The rake without illusion (whom Juliette stands for) transforms himself with the assistance of sex educators, psychoanalysts, and hormone physiologists into the open and practical man who extends his attitude to sport and hygiene to his sexual life. Juliette's critique is discordant, like the Enlightenment itself. In so far as the flagrant violation of the taboo, which was once allied to the bourgeois revolution, has not adjusted pro-ficiently to the new reality, it lives on with sublime love as faith in that now proximate utopia which makes sexual pleasure free for all. (Adorno and Horkheimer 1979: 109)

The rationality of the libertine appears to lead to freedom but it is utopian and, simply because it flaunts taboo, does not free sexuality, let alone any-thing else. By the same token as we take Sade's 'liberationist' philosophy of the bedroom as a tortured irony, we have to take Adorno and Horkheimer's critique as one based on a belief in some sort of 'true' sexuality. Sexuality has been perverted by modern culture, used by the 'system', 'the culture industry', to sell more goods and to repress and constrain some pre-modern, everyday life form of sexuality – which itself begins to take on a mythical quality.

In a much later radio broadcast, first published in 1963, Adorno sustains the implicit idea of a true, acultural sexuality as he discusses the contradiction between a liberality in certain aspects of sexuality and the legal and moral restrictions on sexual practice (1998). He argues forcefully against the repression of prostitution, homosexuality and childhood sexuality as forms of sexual expression in contemporary societies. This repression through taboo, reinforced by law, shows that 'sexual liberation in contemporary society is mere illusion' that channels and administers only certain acceptable forms of sexuality (Adorno 1998: 72). It is precisely the rationality of enlightened thought, as it is adopted within the regime of modern societies, that leads to a 'desexualization of sexuality itself' in which the liberatory potential of sexuality is disarmed as it becomes defined as 'sex', 'as though it were a kind of sport, and whatever is different about it still causes allergic reactions' (Adorno 1998: 73).

Marcuse: The 'performance principle'

Marcuse (1972a) re-reads Freud very closely in the light of the critique of the dialectic of enlightenment and the culture industry to arrive at a more sociologically sophisticated development of Freud's thesis in *Civilization and its Discontents* (1962 – see Chapter 1). He argues that the interaction of the pleasure and reality principles involves a change in the nature of the pleasure that is sought: it is a restrained and assured pleasure rather than destructive, momentary pleasure. The development of a process within the individual in which pleasure, the sought-for end, is checked in terms of reality, the means to that end, is one that leads to rationality. The means have to be assessed not only for their capacity to achieve pleasure but also for the unintended goals, such as unpleasure, that they may also lead to. It is through the tension between the two principles that 'man acquires the faculties of attention, memory, and judgement. He becomes a conscious, thinking *subject*, geared to a rationality which is imposed upon him from the outside' (Marcuse 1972a: 30).

Reality is outside the individual and can be found in the social conditions of existence manifest in a series of institutions: the family, the school, workshop or office, the state, the law, and the prevailing philosophy and morality. For Marcuse, these social conditions of existence are historically emergent, constituted not merely by the trajectory of civilisation but also by the mode of production. The super-ego, the internalisation of society's rules and constraints, is modified by past reality and by experience of the historical world. So, as the institutions of civilisation change and develop, the internalised constraints on the individual also change. As the culture becomes more complex, so the individual has to be aware of many more details of transgression, of what is permitted and what is not. The reality principle becomes shaped less by physical environment and more by social environment.

As we saw in Chapter 1, for Freud this trajectory of civilisation produces a repressive effect on individuals that weakens the life instincts and strengthens those of destruction. But Marcuse goes further to argue that the effect of history is to change the very nature of the reality principle so that the 'organised domination' in which individuals or groups strive to maintain their dominance leads to a 'surplus repression' that individuals experience (1972a: 43). The interests behind domination take on a distinctive form under capitalism – private property, seeking profit, sustaining the market economy – so that additional controls are needed beyond those required simply to sustain civilisation. Marcuse coins the term 'performance principle' to describe the mode of organisation in capitalist modernity which is 'stratified according to the performance of its members' (1972a: 47). We can imagine that more traditional forms of civilisation would have been organised according to the position in the social hierarchy to which one is born, the operation of a 'birth principle'. But in capitalist modernity it is an achieved class status that provides the basis for domination and individuals learn that their relative freedom from constraints is dependent on what they do – how they 'perform' within the society. Those who labour follow the requirements of the system rather than their own individual needs and are as a result alienated (Marcuse 1972a: 48).

This is a powerful conjunction of Marx's analysis of the mode of production and Freud's analysis of the effect of modernity on the individual. Where Marx tells us little about the experience of alienation, Marcuse draws on Freud to spell out how the modern individual is affected. He argues that it is the sex instincts that suffer most under this historically developing reality principle. The repression of modernity leads to the 'unification' of the various objects of desire into the libidinal object of the opposite sex with its focus on genital sexuality. The effect is to desexualise the body – apart from the genitals – and to promote reproductive sex at the expense of other forms of sexual expression. Under the conditions of an acquisitive and antagonistic society, the energy of the sex drive has to be channelled towards productive work. Nongenital sexuality becomes taboo and a series of 'perversions' are identified and outlawed, not the least of which is homosexuality.

Marcuse accepts that overall, 'general unhappiness' will have decreased as a result of the advances in modernity that reduce pain and suffering. Nonetheless, individual happiness is constrained and the individual's level of awareness is limited through the effects of education and the entertainment industry. As Marcuse puts it, these institutions of socialisation leave the individual in a state of 'anaesthesia from which all detrimental ideas tend to be excluded' (1972a: 82). Happiness for Marcuse is not simply the absence of pain and suffering, nor is it realisable in the individual through bodily experience, the mere feeling of satisfaction. It is linked to both knowledge and freedom; without knowledge and awareness the individual cannot know what freedom could be like.

The idealist tradition of philosophy that seeks freedom from alienation in ideas, knowledge, remembrance and historical understanding is inadequate to the task of pointing towards liberation because it does not address the embodied sexuality of the individual. Western philosophy shares with modern capitalist organisation a tendency towards reason and the performance principle, both of which lead to the domination of nature and the domination of some people by an elite group. And although Marcuse uses Marx's analysis of capitalism to understand the nature of modern civilisation, the account of human being underlying historical materialism is also inadequate to provide an appropriate response. Freud offers some useful clues about the effects of modernity on the individual but has a limited account of the social development of civilisation in modernity and fails to offer anything like a route to cultural liberation. It is to the sensualism of Nietzsche, who identifies the realisation of will as the route to experience for its own sake, to joy and enjoyment, that Marcuse turns. For Marcuse, this suggests that the essence of being is not Logos (reason) but Eros (life). Logos has led to defining the quality of life in terms of 'automobiles, television sets, airplanes and tractors [which] is that of the perfomance principle itself' (Marcuse 1972a: 115). Increasing performance and its rewards becomes redundant once the society produces sufficient for everyone; everyone could be treated equally in a 'non-repressive civilization' (Marcuse 1972a: 107). Marcuse wants to see quality of life judged instead on a set of criteria based on Eros – but an increase in sexual freedoms does not of itself indicate a loosening of repression.

In *One-Dimensional Man* (1972b) Marcuse argues that the apparent extension of possibilities and choices available for individuals is one of the ways in which domination in advanced capitalist societies is sustained. But as mechanisation has progressively de-eroticised the range of human activity, it has narrowed the variety of ways in which the human can obtain pleasure towards sexual experience and satisfaction. The result is an intensification of sexual energy which goes hand in hand with a 'desublimation' of sexuality, an apparent increase in sexual freedom. In the context of both productive work and consumption practices, the body becomes a site of sexual focus:

> This is one of the unique achievements of industrial society – rendered possible by the reduction of dirty and heavy physical labour; by the availability of cheap, attractive clothing, beauty culture, and physical hygiene; by the requirements of the advertising industry, etc. The sexy office and sales girls, the handsome and virile, junior executive and floor walker are highly marketable commodities, and the possession of suitable mistresses – once the prerogative of kings, princes, and lords – facilitates the career of even the less exalted in the business community. (Marcuse 1972b: 70–1)

This liberalisation extends to the individual expression of sexuality, so there is a weakening of taboos and a liberalisation of morality – but in the context of a repressive society this liberty is illusory. In a later paper Marcuse describes how the taboos on virginity, pre- and extra-marital relations, dress and the exhibition of the body are removed at the same time as sex is used as 'a saleable commodity, as a publicity stunt, as even a status symbol' (2001: 90). In a non-repressive society, similar changes might be welcomed as the desublimation and freeing of what are for Marcuse true life instincts that are associated with quiet and tenderness, peace and humanity. But in the society characterised by technological rationality, sexuality is repressively channelled towards societal aims with an aggressive and destructive energy to produce a 'repressive desublimation'.

For Marcuse, human life is not about the development of reason or the domination of nature; these are historical forms that while useful are neither natural nor necessary. What is natural and prior to reason, domination and civilisation is Eros: 'The sex instincts are *life* instincts: the impulse to preserve and enrich life by mastering nature in accordance with the developing vital needs is originally an erotic impulse' (Marcuse 1972a: 95). In looking for the route to liberation Marcuse finds in mythology two figures that suggest an alternative to reality under the performance principle (which he associates with Prometheus): Narcissus and Orpheus. He treats these two characters as symbols of the revolt against toil and domination and of 'the non-repressive erotic attitude toward reality' (Marcuse 1972a: 123). Narcissus fell in love with his own image (not strictly with himself, because he didn't know it was his image) and Orpheus was attracted by his own sex – both symbolise non-productive sexuality and a rejection of the performance principle.

However, liberation requires more than a different approach to sexuality; it requires a response to the reality principle. Here Marcuse turns to aesthetics as the meeting of reason and sensuousness. Aesthetics depends on the making of a judgement, but it is also about pleasure and gives rise to a play impulse in people that reacts against compulsion – pleasure in play and aesthetics displaces the reality principle that dominates the activities of labour: 'Play and display, as the principles of civilization, imply not the transformation of labour but its complete subordination to the freely evolving potentialities of man and nature' (Marcuse 1972a: 140). If civilization could be transformed by a shift towards the play impulse and the aesthetic dimension, sexuality could develop towards a polymorphous eroticism of non-productive sexuality as represented by the figures of Narcissus and Orpheus. Marcuse sees this as a re-sexualisation of the body, a reactivation of all the erotogenic zones: 'The body in its entirety would become an object of cathexis, a thing to be enjoyed – an instrument of pleasure' (1972a: 145). This would of course lead to a change in the institutional form of society, especially through a reorientation of monogamy and the patriarchal family. Work, Marcuse argues, following Fourier, could become pleasure work, the sort of pleasure that is taken now in hobbies and other work done outside of alienated labour.

It is easy to see why Marcuse's theory of liberation through Eros provided a source for many of the political ideas of the 1960s of the counter-culture and hippie movements. We can hear in his emphasis on play, the idea of 'dropping out' and his discussion of sexuality the ideas of 'free love', tolerance of homosexuality and at least the beginnings of feminist questioning of patri-archy. For Marcuse, not only does civilisation threaten to suppress, repress or reshape our sexuality, it does so in ways that will make us subject to the social process. Our sexual desire becomes sublimated into work, into the desire for consumer objects, into the adoration of stars of the media and into the pursuit of a pleasure that only advanced capitalism seems to be able to provide: the pleasures of indulgence, of excess, of absorption. But Marcuse displays an optimisim that civilisation does not have to be this way and that an expanded polymorphous, whole person sexuality, a true Eros, will be part of the route to human and cultural liberation.

Barthes: Sex as love

Like Adorno and Horkheimer, Roland Barthes (1976) finds in the work of the Marquis de Sade an excessive form of sexuality linked to the operation of rationality and social control. In Sade's bizarre utopia of libertinage he describes an enclosed, rigidly ordered 'ideal' society complete with routines for everyday life (food, clothing, communication), a strict social hierarchy and the regulation of vice and debauchery. The order of this Sadian society may be founded on reason but libertinage is far from liberated. It is based on the operation of rationality and the consequent imposition of a regimen that defines, controls and specifies 'pleasure'. Power, Barthes discovers, lies not so much in the relations of bodies – all categories of persons are subject to all forms of degradation – but in speech and imagination. It is through discourse, the power to speak what has been imagined and what will subsequently be enacted, that the control over those within this society is maintained: 'In the Sadian city, speech is perhaps the sole Caste Privilege that cannot be curtailed' (Barthes 1976: 31).

Despite the excess and exhaustion of possibilities, pleasure is subject to definition and control rather than arising from the desires of free individuals. Sade makes what Barthes calls 'pornograms', in which the erotic practices of bodies become fused with discourse so that writing 'regulates the exchange of Logos and Eros' (1976: 159). Discourse is the means by which the control of pleasure is maintained in the libertine's world, and in Barthes's analysis Sadian society sounds like the logical end of a strategy of 'repressive desublimation'.

Marcuse's liberationist aim is to reawaken the dormant Eros, to release it from the repression of the 'performance principle', but Barthes does not seem to share this optimism. In A Lover's Discourse (1979b), a series of fragments that are arranged alphabetically to destroy any idea that there is a narrative or thesis, Barthes explores how discourse is the sphere in which sexual drives come to nothing. This is not failure resulting from societal repression, from taboos or systematic constraints, merely the failure of love to be reciprocated. It seems from Barthes's fragments that erotic love is doomed, not because of the Logos of the mode of production but because once it emerges into culture, love loses its way. The figures or fragments in his text are about the perspective of the person who loves – 'the amorous subject'. What is striking is that Barthes's construction of a 'lover's discourse' is one-sided, a monologue expressing the feelings of the amorous subject that gropes to make sense of the second person, the love object. The second person never becomes the first, never speaks for her/himself, and the fragments are often precisely about failed communication and the limits of understanding in lovers' discourse. The sad part of Barthes's discourse is that we never find an answer to why love fails. He shows us, with painful clarity, the dimensions of the experience of one who loves but does not know if he is loved in return.

There is a figure of agony: 'The amorous subject, according to one contingency or another, feels swept away by the fear of danger, an injury, an abandonment, a revulsion – a sentiment he expresses under the name of *anxiety*' (Barthes 1979: 29). But there is no figure of ecstasy. There is a figure that praises tears (Barthes 1979b: 180). But there is none for laughter. Barthes at one point describes the trajectory of the experience of love:

> ... first comes the instantaneous capture (I am ravished by an image); then a series of encounters (dates, telephone calls, letters, brief trips), during which I ecstatically 'explore' the perfection of the loved being, i.e., the unhoped for correspondence between an object and my desire: this is the sweetness of the beginning, the interval proper to the idyll. ... the 'sequel' is the long train of sufferings, wounds, anxieties, distresses, resentments, despairs, embarrassments and deceptions to which I fall prey, ceaselessly living under the threat of a downfall. (1979: 197–8)

So there is ecstasy as the love object takes form under the subject's exploration, but it seems destined to end in suffering. The amorous subject is 'ravished' by the idea of love but is vulnerable to jealousy, to separation, to absence, to aloneness, to the failure of love to be a discourse that is satisfying, fulfilling and complete. The subject and the object are never merged – which might be the possibility of a sexual expression of love.

The idea of 'ravishment'[2] as something perpetrated by an image is strange and compelling; it is something that is done to the subject of love but not by the object. At many points in the book Barthes refers to the 'Image-repertoire', by which he means the stock of images that are held in the memory of the amorous subject. These are images specifically of the love object, images that constitute an ideal, a form that is not rooted in the physical form of the love object but exists in the mind of the amorous subject. The image is vulnerable to the vagaries of life, not so much that of the love object but the ups and downs of the amorous subject's engagement with the ideal. Emotion is not fuelled by discourse, but discourse emerges from emotion. Barthes tells us that 'ravishment' is an enchantment, a capturing of the amorous subject, a hypnosis – love at first sight (1979: 188–9). He recognises that this is a turnabout from the more familiar form in which the victim, traditionally a passive woman, is captured or conquered. What we have is a modern form: rape by an image. Barthes's amorous subject is fascinated by the voice, the line of the shoulders, the warmth of a hand, the curve of a smile, the slenderness of a silhouette (1979: 191). The ravishment is an aesthetic seduction of the subject in which the object is passive and yet becomes implicated in the human relation that takes on the form of love. Enchantment, the magic of becoming entranced, is not a physical or sexual experience but an entrapment by an idea, an image that is constructed but which has only a slight attachment to sensuous experience. The ideal of love is abstract and not something that can be shared. It is not a social image like the enchantment of religious experience but a personal engagement that is secular and isolating. The image is of course produced in the mind, stimulated by the experience of culture – Barthes's culture is the rarified culture of literature and aesthetic sensibility – but ultimately private and internal. This is sexuality as ego-libido that is refuelled by object-libido but does not lead to pleasure or satisfaction. Desire is felt for an image that is insubstantial and immaterial as the subject becomes seduced by the object, but the play of aesthetics does not produce liberation for Barthes's lover.

A reading of autobiographical essays (1992) published after Barthes's death suggests that the amorous subject of *A Lover's Discourse* is indeed Barthes. In the essays he describes the seductiveness of young Moroccans and the loneliness of nights in Paris. His many friends and admirers do not relieve the loneliness of his lifestyle, especially after the death of his mother. He is constantly seduced not by a person but by the image that that person presents. This might seem to be the fate of the single person who has not established a long-term relationship founded on love or found fulfilment in the reproductive outcome of love. But it might also be the result of a modernity that offers all of us a cultural context in which ravishment by the image has become the way of life. It does not seem that Barthes is attempting in *A Lover's Discourse* to mount a critique of the sexual culture of modernity, but that is one of the effects his set of unhappy 'figures' have. He presents us with the impossibility and the futility of love at the same time as its inexorability. It is not repression that he describes; it is the fate of the modern lover: isolated, disappointed, anxious, waiting, wounded.

Baudrillard: Seduction and the death of sex

The emotional sensibility of Barthes's amorous subject emerges into discourse, moved by the proximity but lack of engagement with the object of love. He reveals the dynamic of the individual's engagement with another, albeit an idealised other; the tension between subject and object that is fundamental to the possibility of freedom but which is always embedded in a discursive and therefore social context. This account of sexual love suggests that the liberation that Freud and Marcuse envisage for the drive of Eros is impossible; only in the enclosed, idealised anti-utopia of Sade's 'pornograms' can

Eros and Logos be successfully brought together. The lover's discourse is always irrational, driven by emotion rather than objective reason, and it is precisely the potential for this as a form of social relation that Baudrillard explores with his concept of 'seduction'.

In his earlier work, Baudrillard argues that in modernity the signs of sex are progressively disconnected from the body, thereby breaking the cultural link between sex and gender, gender and power. He distinguishes between the traditional symbolic significance of tattooing and costume, in which the body is something that is disguised with signs, and the modern fashion system, in which clothing, adornment and make-up are inscribed on the body in a signifying system whose dynamic is sexuality. In primitive cultures, symbolic exchange fixed signs irreversibly to their referents in the material world: the sexual distinction of male and female bodies. But in modernity, the sign has no referent other than the sign system of fashion, so, for example, nudity, as opposed to nakedness, becomes a sign of sexuality that loses its referent to anything of essence in the actions of women's and men's bodies: 'Abandoned to the signs of fashion, the body is sexually disenchanted, it becomes a *mannequin*, a term whose lack of sexual discrimination suits its meaning well. ... it is in fashion that sex is lost as difference but is generalised as reference (as simulation)' (Baudrillard 1993a: 97).

The sign system of the body and its coverings is itself a sexualised system of the exchange of meaning based on what Baudrillard calls the 'phallic exchange standard'. In this system, it is the signs on the surface of the body that make it 'erectile', that is, take on the cultural significance of the phallus as a marker of potent sexuality. In his own endnote Baudrillard makes it clear that there is no natural or biological basis for this: 'We can imagine a culture where the terms are reversed: a male strip-tease in a matriarchal culture' (1993a: 122fn). But in modern culture it is the nude female body that takes on the role of a 'diaphanous, smooth, depilated substance of a glorious and unsexed body' and provides a volatile and provocative surface that can be erotically marked (Baudrillard 1993a: 105). This is the flawless body presented on the catwalks, in soft-pornography and 'genre' films, in advertisements, in striptease and lap-dancing. It is invariably 'sexualised' by a mixture of signs: some smooth the surface of the body (the second skin of body hugging tights, girdles, g-strings, stockings, gloves, dresses, sun-tans, depilation, hair covering ears, fitness and slimming regimes); others break up its surface to emphasise the continuity underneath (straps, high heels, belts, chokers, half-removed clothes). This work of material adjustment Baudrillard calls 'vitrification' because it involves a cleaning up and protection of the body, keeping it flawless so that it can do the work of signifying sexuality while being neither a body that takes pleasure nor one that works: 'neither an erogenous body nor a broken body' (1993a: 106).

The transformation of sex into the play of signs of modern sexuality is a shift from sex as the reproduction of the species, to the formation of the social subject under the conditions of 'neo-capitalism' – an *'economy of the subject'* (Baudrillard 1990a: 115). This modern form of sexual subjectivity is dislocated from the balancing force of the death drive as the possibilities of liberation under the sign of Eros are explored in the pursuit of the pleasure principle. But this is no more than capitalism at work and no route to human liberation: 'When one uncovers in the body's secret places an "unbound" libidinal energy opposed to the "bound" energy of the productive body, when one uncovers in desire the truth of the body's phantasms and drives, one is still only disinterring the psychic metaphor of capital' (Baudrillard 1990a: 39). Baudrillard is spelling out the signifiying practices of Marcuse's 'repressive desublimation': the play of the signs of sexuality is illusory, a *staging* of desire rather than its realisation, and has little bearing on the state of real sexual relations. The latter half of the twentieth century saw the detachment of signs of sexuality from gender as cross-dressing fashions were taken up, especially in pop culture.

Like Barthes's idea of ravishment, Baudrillard's idea of seduction is not reducible to rationality, has its roots in the drive of the libido and is stimulated by an image. In Kierkegaard's *Diary of a Seducer* (1843), it is an image reflected in a mirror that stimulates the sensibility of the seducer (Baudrillard 1990a: 105–13). The play of seduction may seem to be about the inequality of bodily sexual relations, but in Baudrillard's hands it becomes a reversible strategy in which the seducer is always also vulnerable to being seduced – by the object, by the image. In modern culture the play of signs of sexuality for Baudrillard is never determined by the body but seduction is a dynamic that carries the force of sexuality and is a point of engagement between the cultural and the real. Operating at the level of the symbolic, seduction is the force that draws a person into a form of relationship; it is an exercise of power that is immaterial and independent of institutions: '... *seduction represents mastery over the symbolic universe, while power represents only mastery of the real universe'* (Baudrillard 1990a: 8).

Baudrillard was provocatively critical of the women's movement in his *Seduction* (1990a), first published in 1979 (see Plant 1993). He argued that its critique of the operation of power in the field of sex and gender was too tied to anatomy, to the physicality of the sexual body. The problem with a critique centred on bodily sexuality was that it was too embedded in a phallic economy, articulated by Freud but inherent in the very tradition of western civilisation. What Baudrillard suggests is that the field of seduction offers the possibility of a series of reversible appearances that would confound the operation of power. Because 'meaning is vulnerable only to enchantment' (Baudrillard 1990a: 8), the strategies of seduction would be far more effective in disturbing the masculine circuits of power in the discourses of the body. The fluid, reversible form of seduction leads to the possibility of a 'transsexuality' which threatens any established order of gender and sex. Unlike Freud's interpretative system, Baudrillard's concept of seduction does not ground the symbolic in the sex of real bodies. It operates at the level of the sign rather than the real, fixed, social ground of lived hierarchies between slave and master, boy and man, female and male, between the loved object and amorous subject.

Baudrillard thinks of seduction as a dynamic relation between the real and representation analogous to a *trompe l'oeil,* in which an image or impression appears *as if* it were real, passing for real just long enough for us to recognise that we have been seduced by signs. Such a tricky play between a production of the imagination, the simulation, and the real or material form cannot be reduced or resolved by reference to the real or substantial. However, while the potency of seduction is its capacity to draw us in and accept, there is a limit to its depth; it resists being mined, interpreted or worked on: 'Seduction cannot possibly be represented, because in seduction the distance between the real and its double, and the distortion between the Same and the Other, is abolished' (Baudrillard 1990a: 67). The mirror shows the limits of seduction: it presents the self to the self as if it were another person but the distortion of the mirror image (its two-dimensionality, its reversal of relations between components) goes unnoticed. Once the image is broken – as when Narcissus breaks the surface of the pool – the relationship between reality and image disappears. The strategy of seduction plays to the mirror, trying to enter the image, to obliquely conquer the object without its being aware, as if in a dream. At its extreme, this can become a form of self-seduction that threatens to destroy the diadic form of sex, which, as we have seen, is characteristic of the hierarchical distinctions that are the foundation of discourses of sexuality.

Modernity has reached a stage when the strategy of seduction has escaped into discourses other than that of sexuality ('Everything is sexualized ... ' – Baudrillard 1990a: 177). Consumption may be the other side of production, but it is seduction that replaces both as forms of social engagement. The ambiguity and reversibility of seduction do not themselves shape the age but are instead incorporated into it. Baudrillard treats seduction as a form equivalent to aesthetics that becomes the 'informal form of politics', a mode of sociality that at least appears to undermine the rigidity and interest basis of democratic politics. Just as the politics of spin and public relations appears to cut through the institutional rigmarole of democratic politics, but merely obscures the operation of the law and of interests, so seduction will not be a sufficient way to overcome the bureaucratic principles of modernity.

The concept of seduction, as Baudrillard uses it, sounds as if it might lead to freeing at least the discourse of sexuality from some of its more ponderous and repressive moves. But the prospect of 'transsexuality' is treated as evidence of a world in which distinctions have been flattened into meaninglessness in his *Transparency of Evil* (1993b), originally published in 1990, more than ten years after *Seduction* (1990a [1979]) introduced the term. The interminable play of signs that comes with the possibility of transvestism – the possibility of cloaking oneself in signs of sexuality – leads to artifice rather than pleasure.

This changing of the signs of sexuality extends to operations to change the organs of sex as well as the more easily modifiable signifiers of clothes and make-up: 'The myth of sexual liberation is still alive and well under many forms in the real world, but at the level of the imaginary it is the transsexual myth, with its androgynous and hermaphroditic variants, that holds sway. After the orgy, then, the masked ball' (Baudrillard 1993b: 22). It is 'the look' that is paramount, not the search for pleasure, and it is a signal of the disingenuous, of indifference to sexual difference. The game has no end, no function other than the pleasure of the play of signs.

It is in the light of the ambivalence of transsexuality (and transaesthetics and transeconomics) that Baudrillard explores the impact of extreme phenomena that appear to manifest 'evil': AIDS, catastrophe, terrorism. These extreme phenomena that we all fear and would like to build defences against are, says Baudrillard, themselves defences against the self-destruction of modernity. In the face of AIDS, the discourse of sexuality has to address itself once again to sex, to the practices that have bodily effects as well as pleasures (AIDS is the species 'generating an antidote to its principle of sexual liberation' – Baudrillard 1993b: 66). The discourse of sexuality, along with those of money and information, was one based on the free circulation of signs through the latter half of the twentieth century. This free circulation of signs went into reverse as a public educational discourse emerged employing celebrities to speak on behalf of the state about condoms and homosexual practices. The discourse of sexuality shifted from one about freedom of expression and possibility to one of restraint and control. The effect was to dispel much of the pleasure in the discourse of sexuality, introducing a deadly serious note to the seductive play of innuendo and *double entendre*, dragging into the mainstream the pleasures of a demi-monde of sexual perversities (anal sex, non-penetrative sex, oral sex) so that their degree of risk could be judged.

Cloning (Baudrillard calls it a 'bionic mirror' – 1990a: 167) removes sexual reproduction and along with it both father and mother, and so transcends sexuality in a way that transvestism and transsexualism cannot achieve. Transvestism is a playing with signs that undermines any link with the real, but the real remains, fixed and decodable beneath the surface of the signs. Transsexuality brings the play of signs to the real, ensuring that there is no unmasking; reversibility is not so playful any more but the real is no longer biologically fixed. Cloning, however, suspends reversibility, play and the possibility of seduction. It is a fatal strategy that shuts down the dialectic of sexuality for good – it is the end of sex. The result is not that a self engenders a self but that there is a branching or budding, in which the genetic code produces the new self. The process of reproduction is transformed so that 'it is the matrix of the genetic code that will "give birth" without end in an operative manner purged of all contingent sexuality' (Baudrillard 1990a: 169). Cloning is the result of the death drive reasserting itself through a return to a pre-sexual form of reproduction that destroys the 'other' in favour of an endless reproduction of the same (Baudrillard 1993b: 114).

Cloning becomes a recurrent trope for Baudrillard because, along with a series of other bio-technical advances (the Pill, *in vitro* fertilisation, surrogacy, artifical insemination by donor), it signals the end of sex as reproduction. As he says, 'We've been sexually liberated, and now we will find ourselves liberated from sex – that is, virtually relieved of the sexual function' (Baudrillard 2000: 10). There are also technological advances which signal the end of death (cryonic suspension, spare part surgery), and together the end of sex and death signal the end of the modern idea of the individual subject with distinctive, genetic characteristics and internal drives for sex and freedom. Just as it appears that the role of critique is redundant as there is no longer any individual to be free, Baudrillard restates the plot of critical theory, that it is first of all culture that clones us, long before biological cloning has fully arrived:

> It is the matrix of acquired traits that, today, clones us culturally under the sign of monothought – and it is all the innate differences that are annulled, inexorably, by ideas, by ways of life, by the cultural context. Through school systems, media, culture, and mass information, singular beings become identical copies of one another. (2000: 25)

For Baudrillard, seduction is not simply about the discourse of sexuality; as a mode of energy that exerts influence over beings and things it also has a political dimension. In opposition to the natural law of sex (the biological imperative, the pleasure principle), seduction takes on the form of an arbitrary rule in a game. As such it cannot establish a system of prohibitions or interdictions that operate beyond the play of signs; seduction cannot be implicated in a repressive discourse, any more than it can in a liberatory one. The effect is that seduction is neither a fatal nor a banal strategy (see Chapter 7), it is one that can be played endlessly with little more impact than to undermine the strategies that claim they are based on a 'truth' – it is one way to resist 'monothought'. Because it has no history, or memory or any accumulation, seduction leaves no residue, no mark on the world. Seduction is not about changing, transgressing or opposing the laws of either the physical or the social worlds, but about living within it. It is a ritual of rule following and game playing that enables the world to carry on without fixed beliefs or points of reference.

Conclusions

In Freud's theory, the sexual libido not only draws on bodily desires but also looks outwards to society and culture for 'objects' that will excite and stimulate it. In the mature individual, the search for sexual pleasure is modified by the reality of societal and cultural constraints; sexuality can no longer be thought of as merely biological. The critical theorists pick up this idea to explore both how society channels and moulds sexuality and how sexuality might provide a route towards 'free', unalienated individuality. The cultural explosion of eroticism in modernity may appear to promise freedom of sexual action for the individual, but the logic of such freedom, as can be seen from Sade's writing, is a form of pleasureless repression. This is because sexuality becomes managed according to a discourse which articulates the needs of the society to produce and to reproduce, to work and to sustain the workforce. That same discourse specifies what shall be pleasures and which desires shall be met under what conditions.

The apparent freedom of sexuality in modern societies is illusory: a 'repressive desublimation' brings 'ravishment' by the image and seduction by the signs of sexuality that are disconnected from the experience of bodily desire and pleasure. The critique of sex and sexuality warns us that the appearance of freedom is likely to be illusory if it is offered by the culture – but does this mean that all that our libido draws us to will lead to unfulfilled desire and hollow pleasure? For Baudrillard, the end of sex with the technical possibility of cloning threatens the end of the individual mortal 'self' and presages a return to the pre-modern unity of the immortal self, that is, 'species' or genetic inheritance. But this has not yet made it impossible to experience the feelings of freedom and pleasure that come with fulfilment of sexual desire.

Summary

- *Freud*: Human sexuality is seen as originally polymorphous and perverse but develops as a drive to sexual excitation (libido) that is shaped both from within and without the body. Sexual drive is modified by the pleasure principle, which includes the avoidance of unpleasure, and further modified by the reality principle. Freud later speculates that a death instinct, expressed as a compulsion to repetition, works in tension with the libido.
- *Lefebvre*: In modern society sexuality emerges from the private sphere into the public domain as a shocking and brutal eroticism in the media and advertising.
- *Adorno and Horkheimer*: The media exploit titillation – unresolved desire – while the rationality of the 'libertine' (Sade's *Juliette*) destroys pleasure and desexualises sex.
- *Marcuse*: The reality principle becomes the 'performance principle' in modern societies as individual action is shaped by organised domination. The culture seems to increase sexual freedom but repression is sustained through the management of certain channels for sexual expression. 'Repressive desublimation' leads to increased individual sexual freedom but is accompanied by the commodification of sex and its direction

towards a specific form: heterosexual, genital, reproductive rather than aestheticised, bodily and playful.

- *Barthes*: Sade's 'libertinage' is viewed as a regime of the rational discourse that exerts power over pleasure to pervert desire while the *Lover's Discourse* (1979b) of modernity is one of 'ravishment' by the idea and the image that fails to be realised in pleasure or satisfaction.
- *Baudrillard*: Sexuality is disconnected from bodily desire in modernity as it becomes a play of signs inscribed on the body's surface that circulate the values of fashion and eventually becomes 'transsexuality'. 'Seduction' emerges as a symbolic strategy notable for its reversibility and ambivalence that has little to do with sex but displaces production in the sphere of culture. Scientific sex – cloning – threatens the end of sex and sexuality altogether.

Further reading

Sex and sexuality have become central topics of scholarly work and debate in the humanities and social sciences, and in recent years some very good discussions have become available. Amongst these, Jeff Weeks's *Sexuality and its Discontents* (1985) is particularly relevant to the discussion here, and Gail Hawkes's *A Sociology of Sex and Sexuality* (1996) puts some of the issues into a distinctively sociological context. Feminist writing on sexuality has produced some stimulating and provocative contributions such as those to be found in collections such as Janet Holland and Lisa Adkins's *Sex, Sensibility and the Gendered Body* (1996) and Sue Wilkinson and Celia Kitzinger's *Heterosexuality* (1993).

Notes

1 Interestingly he derives his concept of repression as much from Malinowski as from Freud (Lefebvre 1971: 148 fn) and suggests that the limitations of Marcuse's analysis of repression are due to his lack of a concept of the quotidian. However, Malinowski had himself been impressed by Freud's *Totem and Taboo* and had attempted to utilise his theoretical ideas.

2 Of course the French term *ravissement* does not translate easily into the archaic English form 'ravishment'; Barthes's term connotes the delight, rapture and ecstasy of the subject imagining the love object.

SIX

Art and Entertainment

The enjoyment of both art and entertainment is usually passive, so that unlike the activity of work, and the non-work of leisure activities such as sports or gardening, all one has to do is take in the sights, sounds, movements, impressions and emotions, and respond to them. With virtually no expenditure of energy or investment of physical effort, there is no product or 'work' that we can point to – other than paying attention. As Adorno puts it, 'culture originates in the radical separation of mental and physical work' (1983: 26); culture utilises our mental capacities but does not demand the output or the same level of responsibility as mental work. Art and entertainment are, however, both dimensions of culture in which the members of a society are communicating with each other through shared meanings and understandings. When I watch a film and laugh along with everyone else, including those watching the same film at other times and places, it shows that I am responding to more or less the same quality evoked by a particular sequence of words and actions as everyone else. In a similar way the queues filing past a painting by a long-dead master respond with something of the same awe and attention as those who saw the painting the previous day or a hundred years ago.

The cultural products of art and entertainment are reflective communications that are in themselves purposeless: they do not impart information or bring about any change in the world. But responses such as laughter and awe indicate that values are being exchanged between the audience and the cultural product; this exchange both reaffirms values and provides the opportunity for their development and variation. Getting the joke is not only dependent on understanding the language but also on being in tune with the current culture of humour. The same sort of circularity is found with art: the quality of an old master is determined by the state of art criticism within a cultural milieu, and the state of classic art criticism is to be found in what is presented as an old master. The values exchanged may, however, extend beyond those of the form so that comic films may establish what is funny but they may also undermine ethical values and ideas about political propriety. The painting may establish what is mastery in fine art but also provide a perspective on the ostentation of wealth or the human integrity that survives in poverty.

The products of culture enable a society to review and replay its values, opening them to question at the same time as distributing them through the society. They can introduce new ideas and challenge existing values, passing on to their audience new ways of thinking about the world they live in. Art and entertainment are not 'useful' in our everyday lives through fulfilling bodily and practical needs, but they may bring *pleasure*, making the indivi-dual feel better through the moment of laughter or awe. The shared experience of pleasure and exchanged values can cohere society, giving its members a sense of collective identity, of belonging to a larger group with whom they may have no direct contact. There is a conservative tendency for culture to sustain already established values and reinforce the existing social order, but the fluidity of the connection between the individual and the society through the cultural sphere – as compared with, say, the law – also gives it the poten-tial for critique. Critique is itself a reflective form, an attempt to both under-stand the organisation of society and at the same time intervene in the taken-for-grantedness of that social form. Cultural products which offer a critique do not have to adopt a rational form, presenting reasons for their con-tent, so they can circumvent the dominant mode of knowledge and achieve a subversive effect more directly and subtly. To provoke laughter or awe in the audience may be far more effective in shifting their perspective on social life than to present a rational argument.

Given this capacity of art and entertainment to both confirm existing values and critique them, it is easy to see why for critical theorists the stuff of culture has attracted considerable attention. The Frankfurt critical theorists attempt to rescue 'autonomous art' and the tradition of aesthetics from their conformist and conservative tradition and to subject the 'culture industry' of entertainment to critique because of its role in supporting the instrumental rationality of industrialised capitalism. Adorno has some doubts about whether art can be enjoyable in the same way as entertainment – but then he is doubtful that entertainment is enjoyable either: 'The words "enjoyment of art" sound funny. If in nothing else, Schoenberg's music resembles popular songs in refusing to be enjoyed' (Adorno 1991: 30). But later critical theorists tend to blur the distinction between art and entertainment because of course art can be entertaining and there is the possibility that entertainment can be art and that, for many, both can be enjoyable. However, common in the approach of critical theorists to art and entertainment is the idea that they are worthy of attention for three reasons. Firstly, the *content* of art and of enter-tainment provides a potentially revealing account of the way that the human, social, world works in much the same way as myth can. Cultural forms poten-tially offer a mimetic representation of the world of lived experience. Secondly, the *means* by which art and entertainment are produced reflect something of the way that the society operates. The means of representation and its relationship to the real are significant in themselves. Thirdly, art, if not entertainment, can show how life could be *other* than it is. The products of imagination can explore the realms of possibility beyond the alienated experience of modern life.

Adorno and Horkheimer: The culture industry

Theodor Adorno and Max Horkheimer (1979) argue that in advanced capitalist societies, the culture industry produces material that deadens the masses, while the potential of art to provoke critical thought is drowned by the peddling of endlessly bland and repetitive cultural commodities. Just as manufacturing industry generates *things* as products, so the culture industry generates and circulates *ideas* as products. As with commodity production in general, the social form fetishises cultural products, creating specific cultural and economic value in intangible commodities such as the entertainment value of a film or the artistic value of a painting (Adorno 1991: 33–5). The culture industry results from the penetration of the organisation and business practices of industrial capitalism into the sphere of culture early in the twentieth century. Cultural commodities are directed not to the material needs of human beings, such as food and clothing, but to people's minds: their conscious and subconscious selves. Capitalism has an interest in the state of those minds: it needs workers who are happy enough to accept uncritically their position within the system.

Horkheimer described the aims of the Frankfurt Institute as being to explore 'the interconnection between the economic life of society, the psychic development of the individual and transformations in the realm of culture' (quoted in Held 1980: 33). At the centre of their project was the way that culture mediated between individuals and the wider society in which they lived. Working first in Europe and later in the United States they noted the emergence of new forms of culture – in particular, radio and film – that were enthusiastically used by the Nazis for propaganda purposes but which also contributed to the development of capitalism. The mass rally involved communication of one to many who had gathered in a stadium or public space, but radio brought a speech to each listener, usually in their own homes, who had to do nothing more than turn on. The technology of new forms of mass culture meant that a relatively small production process, concentrated in place and personnel, could reach many people with identical cultural goods, even when dispersed in time or place.

The mass-produced new media of movies and radio delivered a product that, once consumed, leaves nothing but memories. Like dreams beamed in from outside, their partial residue remains mixed in with the memory of experiences of direct human action and interaction. Unlike dreams, however, the mass media products are uniform: everyone receives precisely the same thing and any sense of a personal experience is illusory. This is mass production and the producers have left no work for the consumer to do but absorb it: the 'industry robs the individual of his function' (Adorno and Horkheimer 1979: 124). Technological rationality standardises the form of the new media but it also excludes the possibility of response: '... the technique is that used for any type of propaganda' (Adorno and Horkheimer 1979: 123). Production is within a commercial system tied to the banks and the electricity suppliers, oriented to the consuming public rather than to any aesthetic principles. The expensive business of setting up a radio station or making a film requires gathering together entrepreneurial capital to invest and take the risk of a sufficient return, yet the cost to its mass of consumers is small. Managing the investment for society-wide culture involves the state in funding, licensing or censoring the products. The culture industry creates 'conspicuous production' in which companies compete to advertise themselves, their investment, their brand names, their size and technical capacity, their star properties and the size of the audience they are reaching (Adorno and Horkheimer 1979: 124).

Classic works of literature or music that had previously been produced as art are adapted for mass entertainment, but consumers get the bonus of advertisements. The careful packaging of mass cultural commodities leads to a 'style' that contradicts the individuality of art with a tried and tested way of presenting the content. There is, say Adorno and Horkheimer, an illusory difference between products: the stuff of 'hit songs, stars, soap operas' consists of 'cyclically recurrent and rigidly invariable types' (1979: 125). The rigidity of style helps backers to predict whether the audience will buy the product, but the effect is to manipulate the audience, forcing them to follow the plot and giving them no space in which to reflect or use their own imagination. Adorno and Horkheimer quote Nietzsche on style as 'a system of non-culture, to which one might even concede a certain "unity of style" if it really made any sense to speak of stylized barbarity' (quoted in 1979: 128). The simplification of cultural products follows a tested pattern, which, because it is repeated so often, becomes 'natural' – so, for example, the idiom of romantic movie talk becomes the nature of romantic talk. Including sex, violence, fun and laughter in the content creates the illusion of enjoyment. But the repeated exposure of sexuality devalues it to titillation that is in the end just frustrating, offered to 'stimulate the unsublimated forepleasure which habitual deprivation has long since reduced to a masochistic semblance' (Adorno and Horkheimer 1979: 140). Love is 'downgraded to romance', and violence directed against characters is in fact a form of violence against the spectator: we are assaulted by what we see (Adorno and Horkheimer 1979: 140). All is washed down with hollow laughter: 'Fun is a medicinal bath. The pleasure industry never fails to prescribe it. It makes laughter the instrument of the fraud practised on happiness. Moments of happiness are without laughter; only operettas and films portray sex to the accompaniment of resounding laughter' (Adorno and Horkheimer 1979: 140–1). The entertainment produced by the culture industry gives the illusion of happiness through laughter, dulling the sensibilities of the masses and preparing them for work in the 'rational organization' (Adorno and Horkheimer 1979: 147).

It would be easy to read the culture industry thesis as an argument against 'low art' or modern cultural forms like film, although Hohendahl (1995) argues persuasively that to dismiss Adorno and Horkheimer as elitist cultural snobs would be to miss the point. Adorno (1991) is specific about the effects of industrial forms on the contents of culture in a number of media – radio evangelists, television, film, astrology in magazines – but his discussion of music is the most specific and detailed.

Classical music produced and consumed in accordance with the rules of the market becomes industrialised entertainment; Adorno lists the compositions of Irving Berlin, Gershwin, Sibelius, Tchaikovsky and Schubert as 'fetishes' in the world of musical life (1991: 31). The performances of Toscanini, who presented classical music as a series of 'hits' in concerts around the world, were just as much part of the star system promoted by the culture industry as any pop music. But Adorno's most famous critique is reserved for popular music and what Adorno refers to as 'jazz', including the music of Tin Pan Alley, swing bands and dance bands that play 'standards' and 'hits'. His accounts of jazz and popular music are intemperate and dismissive, rather like everyone's father, complaining about the bland 'noise' of the younger generations' taste in music. Here he is on jazz:

> The ban on changing the basic beat during the course of the music is itself sufficient to constrict composition to the point where what it demands is not aesthetic awareness of style but rather psychological regression. The limitations placed on metre, harmony and form are no less stifling. Considered as a whole, the perennial sameness of jazz consists not in the basic organization of the material within which the imagination can roam freely and without inhibition, as within an articulate language, but rather in the utilization of certain well-defined tricks, formulas and clichés to the exclusion of everything else. (Adorno 1983: 123)

The problem with this criticism is that it is directed at 'jazz' as if it was a unitary 'style' – there are of course many types of music played as jazz and Adorno is not specific about what music he is referring to. Much jazz does retain a regular and continuous beat throughout a 'song' or 'tune' and many lesser players do little else but play clichés, tricks or 'slick-licks'. But what Adorno does not seem to have heard are the harmonic variations introduced through altering chords and improvising in different versions of the same song, or the ways that rhythms vary the feel of a syncopated beat, pushing or pulling it to create atmosphere. The musical heritage of a jazzer is often discernible but players are able to create music that is recognisably unique in articulation and improvisation. They may play a 'standard' hundreds of times without repeating the same performance twice although each is marked with their own distinctive tone. Jazz persists as a cultural form very much on the margins of the culture industry without attracting significant investment and with few players earning a good living. In other words, some jazz seems to fit precisely what counts for Adorno and Horkheimer as 'art', that is, cultural production that is autonomous and free, unshaped by the market forces of capitalism, created under the impetus of the artist; 'purposefulness without a purpose' (Adorno and Horkheimer 1979: 158). But Adorno's argument about the content of popular music is to do with its standardised form. He accepts that it is can often be melodically, harmonically or rhythmically more complex than serious music, but says: 'In hit music, however, the structure underlying the piece is abstract, existing independent of the specific course of the music. ... For the complicated in popular music never functions as 'itself' but only as a disguise or embellishment behind which the scheme can always be perceived' (Adorno 1990: 305). It is the standardised form of popular music which means that it is 'pre-digested' for the listener, who always feels on 'safe ground' even when faced with apparent complexity and the 'pseudo-individualization' of the improvised solo. It is the predictable and rigid form of the jazz 'standard' that makes it a standardised product and means it is seriously limited as a work of art.

Traditionally art has been protected from the market by patronage, but selling in a market does not require that it becomes standardised. So what is art that is autonomous and free? Adorno was himself a composer who wrote extensively on music and was also a critic of the contemporary 'serious' music of his day. He particularly respects the music of Arnold Schoenberg because it 'requires the listener spontaneously to compose its inner movement and demands of him not mere contemplation but praxis' (Adorno 1983: 150). The passivity that I have ascribed to both art and entertainment here gives way to an active listener who must bring something to the music. But this is not merely a game in which the composer sets up difficulties for the listener, or adds ornamentation that must be penetrated. Adorno tells us that Schoenberg's music follows the basic principle of 'the "developing variation"; everything that appears strives to be developed logically, to be intensified and then resolved in an equilibrium' (1983: 154). In contrast to the constant repetition of the entertainment products of the culture industry, art develops by moving systematically from variation to variation, creating a near dream state in which an 'other' world can be imagined. Adorno describes the last movement of Schoenberg's Second *Kammersymphonie* which 'sounds as though it came from another world, from the realm of freedom' and the instrumental introduction which contains 'the sound of truth, as though the music had been freed of all chains and was soaring above and beyond enormous abysses towards that other planet evoked in the poem' (1983: 159). Purposeless art can inspire its audience to transcend the earthly limits of their experience, to imagine the freedom of an alternative and to engage in a critical praxis with the world about them. Through having imagined something different, the audience resist the taken-for-granted, the status quo, the sameness. This is art as liberation, culture that has not been suborned to the dictates of the market and not packaged as a commodity.

In Adorno's later *Aesthetic Theory* (1997), an unfinished work published after his death, he discusses how autonomous art, even when affirming the cultural values from which it emerges, establishes itself as other to the society in which it is produced. As Adorno explores the aesthetic philosophy of Kant and Hegel, he develops a concept of art as truth in which it stands apart from the empirical world of lived experience and offers a reflection on human circumstances – as he puts it, art 'opts for a praxis beyond the spell of labour' (1997: 12). Art, he argues, is historical but its aesthetic is not determined by history so much as by the dialectical tension that is established between its content and lived experience:

> All artworks, even the affirmative, are a priori polemical. The idea of a conservative artwork is inherently absurd. By emphatically separating themselves from the empirical world, their other, they bear witness that that world itself should be other than it is; they are the unconscious schemata of that world's transformation. (Adorno 1997: 177)

For Adorno, then, art does not merely represent the empirical, social world but is itself a form of critique of that world. It demands a critical engagement to grasp the polemic, but mere entertainment can have no such effect. Reading his work, one wonders whether or not he would have been entertained by the cultural satire of cartoons like *The Simpsons*, and if he did find himself smiling, whether he could also see it having effect as polemic. The show is very much a product of the culture industry, produced as entertainment, yet the characters and the situations critique advanced industrial society, as if drawing on the perspective of critical theory. Perhaps what is lacking in Adorno's dialectical approach is the recognition of irony in cultural products – the idea that a cultural artefact could be doing at least two things at once, such as being art and being entertainment.

Benjamin: The mechanical reproduction of culture[1]

A key dimension of the 'culture industry' thesis is the impact of new forms of cultural production that use technological developments to reproduce sounds and images – the mechanical and later electronic devices of the camera, radio, cinema and television. Adorno and Horkheimer offer a critique of these new media that focuses on their cultural impact, but Walter Benjamin, a colleague but never a member of the Frankfurt Institute, offered a rather more detailed and sympathetic critique of these media in the 1930s. Despite the divergences between Benjamin and Adorno (see Buck-Morss 1977: 136–84; Jay 1996: 197–212; Wiggershaus 1994: 214–18), both were interested in how the cultural product would be changed by new means of mass reproduction. But while Adorno saw only commodification, Benjamin saw new possibilities for authenticity and critique.

Benjamin's essay 'A Small History of Photography' (1985a), written in 1931, reflects on the philosophical implications of photography becoming available to a mass audience – for example, on visiting cards, the mobile phones of their day. Photography threatened painting and drawing because it brought the fullness and particularity of past reality alive in the present, a quality Benjamin calls the 'spark of contingency' (1985a: 243). Photography can capture detail that the human consciousness cannot grasp even if the eye sees it: how a horse's legs move at speed, or the detail of plants' form. This capacity of photography – Benjamin calls it the 'optical unconscious' – captures what was there in the past and alters how we might see the same thing in the future. Early photography required long exposure times so that the human subject almost 'grew into the picture', producing an effect of 'aura', a mysterious quality of the light which seared the real presence of people into the image (Benjamin 1985: 245). The notion of 'aura' is for Adorno associated with the authenticity of an artwork, the spiritual enchantment such works absorb through religious ritual or the work of their creation that enables them to stand for their culture (Adorno and Horkheimer 1979: 19). But Benjamin was delighted by a new form of photography, particularly Eugène Atget's documentary photographs of shopfronts, doorways, fireplaces and workers in the streets, that 'pump[ed] the aura of reality out of the photograph like water out of a sinking ship' (Benjamin 1985: 250). The documentary photograph such as Atget's does not just represent reality, but becomes a comment on the world – and so begins to achieve something of that distance that Adorno identifies in the work of art.

Painting has a market value based on the picture's uniqueness, distinctiveness and desirability but photography could reproduce, endlessly, what had once been unique. The theme of Benjamin's most well-known essay, 'The Work of Art in the Age of Mechanical Reproduction' (1973b), originally published in 1936, was the cultural impact of the image as a commodity that has to compete with an infinite number of identical photographic images, each costing a few pence to produce. The extension of industrial and mechanical means of reproduction (lithography, photography, film) to cultural products had a potentially transformatory impact on the traditional form of art. Benjamin suggests that the 'aura', the authenticity, specialness, uniqueness of the artwork, 'withers in the age of mechanical reproduction' (1973b: 215). From magical and religious rituals to the exhibition that situated individual works within the *oeuvre* of an artist or school of painting, cultural practices gave the value and meaning of aura to artworks by establishing their distance from the profane and mundane everyday world. For Benjamin, the destruction of aura in modernity was driven by the desire of the contemporary masses to bring their lived world closer: '... the adjustment of reality to the masses and of the masses to reality is a process of unlimited scope, as much for thinking as for perception' (1973b: 217).

With moving film it is the technical choice of angles, intercut shots, close-ups, and so on, that reduces reality to just two dimensions; acting too becomes technical as performance is fragmented over a long period without an audience for inspiration. The whole process depends on the machinery of camera, lights and sound, which disappears from the finished product (Benjamin 1973b: 227). The film's audience takes the position of the camera, from which they can be critical without any obligation to the actor, who lacks the aura of the stage actor's human presence. To make up for this failing aura, Benjamin notes that beyond the film the actor becomes a personality, a celebrity, a star, whose presence is enhanced by promotional pictures and personal stories. But '[t]he cult of the movie star, fostered by the money of the film industry, preserves not the unique aura of the person but the "spell of the personality", the phoney spell of a commodity' (Benjamin 1973b: 224).

Benjamin does not treat the loss of aura as a sign that art has become mere entertainment; Charlie Chaplin's movies can be enjoyed as entertainment but understood as critique. In fact, mechanical reproduction produces new critical possibilities as film precisely represents the details of behaviour, can be replayed endlessly and viewed in segments (Benjamin 1973b: 229). But mechanical reproduction creates a mass audience whose response determines the individual's; each is distracted rather than engaged in contemplation and reacts with the crowd. The narrative flow of the running film demands that the spectator's eye follow the action, not giving her or him time to contemplate or reflect. The effect is rather like the Dadaist attempt to destroy the aura of their work by using ready-made objects that do not appear worthy of contemplation (see below p. 127). The lack of contemplation provoked by film is what for Adorno stultifies imagination because action is precisely represented, taking up the same time period as if it were real (1991: 55). But for Benjamin, contemplation is not the only way to absorb the work of art: we engage with architecture through the habit of sight and touch rather than through standing, looking and thinking. Spectators receive film, as they do architecture, in a 'state of distraction', but this does not prevent either form contributing to the culture and the spectators having a critical attitude (the 'public is an examiner, but an absent-minded one' – Benjamin 1973b: 233–4).

For Benjamin, the past can be seized only as a 'dialectical image' that is recognised in the moment it 'flashes up' (1973a: 247). The photograph offers an image of the past that has been arrested so that it *can* be seen again and again – Benjamin calls this 'dialectics at a standstill' (1983: 13). The metaphor of the 'dialectical image' as a point at which the present and the past meet is characteristic of Benjamin's method of understanding culture as history:

> ... image is that wherein what has been comes together in a flash with the now to form a constellation. In other words, image is dialectics at a standstill. For while the relation of the present to the past is a purely temporal, continuous one, the relation of what-has-been to the now is dialectical: is not progression but image, suddenly emergent. – Only dialectical images are genuine images. (Benjamin 1999: 462)

The dialectical image does not speak for itself; it must be read by the critic, who brings the image into the present to unravel its purely temporal link to the past. History for Benjamin serves a more important purpose than simply gathering evidence to establish order, sequence and cause, because it is through reflection on the past that we can engage with a process of redemption that may lead to happiness. Through sharing these reflections with others – and this is the point of critical writing – the critic can contribute towards the collective redemption of humanity. The work of history is to gather and connect the fullness of human experience, to recognise details that at the time seemed minor or trivial. This is not a disinterested activity, and Benjamin refers to the edge that historical materialism gives to engaging critically with the past; each generation that reflects must resist the tendency of the ruling class towards conformism (see Chapter 7, p. 142).

Benjamin takes quite a different view of the impact of the culture industry from Adorno and Horkheimer because he recognises that the new, mass forms of 'mechanical reproduction' make culture available to the proletariat. The mass art form of film lent itself to the reproduction of the mass itself in news reels, parades, rallies and sports events which could then be used in propaganda to bring the mass to confront itself. The loss of aura does transform art but does not suspend the critical possibilities of art or the possibilities of criticising art. But there are risks. In the epilogue to the 'Work of Art' essay, Benjamin says that '[t]he logical result of Fascism is the introduction of aesthetics into political life' and the logical result of pushing aesthetics into politics is war, exemplified by the Futurists' claim that 'war is beautiful' (Benjamin 1973b: 234). For Benjamin, the culture industry may provide the means for a potent propaganda machine for the Nazis, but it also promises a means by which the masses might become a class in and for itself.

Marcuse: Art as liberation

Benjamin's analysis of the changing role of art provided one of the sources for Adorno and Horkheimer's account of the impact of the culture industry. Marcuse provided a much less problematic support, in an essay published in 1937, with his concept of 'affirmative culture'. This universal, bourgeois form of culture, Marcuse argues, posits a better, purer world, a good life

> that must be unconditionally affirmed: a world essentially different from the factual world of the daily struggle for existence, yet realizable for every individual for himself 'from within', without any transformation of the state of fact. It is only in this culture that cultural activities and objects gain that value which elevates them above the everyday sphere. (Marcuse 1968c: 95)

Affirmative culture is at once critical, in that it identifies a better life, and yet bourgeois, in ignoring the material conditions of society and relocating the better life within the individual as 'beauty of the soul', 'internal freedom' and 'the realm of virtue' (Marcuse 1968c: 98). Bourgeois culture had separated art from its ties to religion and tradition and could inspire the individual with the promise of freedom and happiness – but only for the rich few and only internally, through imagination. For Marcuse, this aspiration of art to critical and reflective distance must be transformed through a negation of its affirmative aspect so that it can turn outwards and inspire all to live their lives differently – to produce a 'nonaffirmative culture' (1968c: 132).

For Marcuse, the sphere of art offers the possibility of articulating a negation that in *One-Dimensional Man* (1972b) he calls the 'Great Refusal' (see above, Chapter 3, pp. 50–1). Art as a critical sphere of life has been dissolved in advanced capitalism as it has been commodified, advertised, packaged and offered for exchange value – as entertainment. The two-dimensional, critical, alienating effect of art becomes incorporated into the exchange values of one-dimensional technological society. The 'romantic' heroes of seventeenth- to nineteenth-century bourgeois art – artists, criminals, outcasts – whose activities provided a critique of the form of society, had by the twentieth century lost their subversive or destructive force as they became commodities, produced *en masse* and bought as entertainment. Bach became background music for the kitchen and classical literature was sold as paperbacks in the drugstore, but in the process became 'deprived of their antagonistic force' and had their 'contradiction to the status quo … flattened out' (Marcuse 1972b: 63). The availability of the arts to a wide audience through the broadcast media and cheap publishing Marcuse accepts as a good thing, but he bemoans the neutralisation of the 'estrangement effect' of art that dissociates its audience from their everyday world. Even avant-garde art forms, including modern poetry, surrealism, Dada and Brechtian drama, which appear to capture the negation of the Great Refusal, in fact 'share in the function of entertaining' (Marcuse 1972b: 67). Affirmative, bourgeois art sublimates the angst or troubles of life as they take on an imaginary rather than real form in the artwork. Industrial society *desublimates* these works by fitting them back into the flow of ordinary life, but because they are used as entertainment or accompaniments to other activities their critical force is negated. The snippet of Vivaldi, Beethoven or Bach used as part of an advertisement stops it being music that arrests us – it becomes just part of the advertisement. The effect is to reduce and absorb opposition in the sphere of politics, culture and even instinctual behaviour. It produces a society of people whose critical faculties have atrophied into a 'Happy Consciousness' that 'reflects the belief that the real is rational, and that the established system, in spite of everything, delivers the goods' (Marcuse 1972b: 74).

Benjamin warned that the aestheticisation of politics could lead to fascism and war, but Marcuse's later work is optimistic that a politicisation of art can break its separation from the world of lived experience and individual insularity. In *An Essay on Liberation* (1969) he describes how the appropriation of language by the hippie movement and black power subverted and negated affirmative culture. For example, he points out how the word 'soul', which traditionally represented everything tender, deep, immortal and human, has become embarrassing, corny, false in the established universe of discourse, has been desublimated and in this transsubstantiation, migrated to the Negro culture: they are soul brothers; the soul is black, violent, orgiastic; it is no longer in Beethoven, Schubert but in the blues, in jazz, in rock 'n' roll, in 'soul food'. (Marcuse 1969: 36)

The 'new sensibility' that emerges within modern culture depends on an aesthetic sense that is radical, subversive and questions established forms. Marcuse lists the new forms ('non-objective, abstract painting and sculpture, stream-of-consciousness and formalist literature, twelve-tone composition, blues and jazz' – 1969: 38) which break from what he calls 'illusionist' art to confront a new reality. But the transformation of culture is not just an aesthetic process; it must involve a praxis that relates the content of art to lived experience if it is to be liberatory. Marcuse warns that the revolt in art must be urgent and transitory because it is quickly absorbed within the traditional institutions of culture: the art gallery, the concert hall and the market. In place of beauty and the sublime of traditional culture – Marcuse mentions Beethoven's 'Ode to Joy' – it must put in its place music that is sensuous, electrifying, and of 'frightening immediacy' (1969: 47).

Subversive art in these entertaining forms can only be a transitional move in liberation that must go hand in hand with a transformation of the material conditions of existence: an attack on the very mechanisms of advanced capitalism. For Marcuse, it is through the development of solidarity in the face of exploitation rather than through the march to revolution that change will come about; art, even if it is entertaining, can contribute to the subversive build-up of that solidarity. Art can provide the possibility of transhistorical truth and an imperative towards change without being utopian or representing the perspective of a class. Instead, Marcuse sees the political potency of art in Benjamin's view of Poe, Baudelaire, Proust and Valéry, who express a '"consciousness in crisis": a pleasure in decay, in destruction, in the beauty of evil; a celebration of the asocial, of the anomic – the secret rebellion of the bourgeois against his own class' (Marcuse 1979: 19–20). Art alone will not liberate humanity but it offers the possibility of catharsis as individuals question their conditions of existence and feel solidarity with those in similar circumstances. There is a dialectical potential in art that is in one moment socially negative, going against the status quo while demonstrating competence with artistic form and affirming the tradition that constitutes art, and in the second moment undermining that form as anti-art and beginning to establish a new form. When art is successful in representing the extremes of human experience (such as death, madness, incarceration) it cannot help but be beautiful. Marcuse embraces this dialectic between aesthetics and real existence as providing a dynamic for change that can be steered in the direction of human emancipation: '...art represents the ultimate goal of all revolutions: the freedom and happiness of the individual' (Marcuse 1979: 69).

Lefebvre: Representing the quotidian

Henri Lefebvre does not share the Frankfurt theorists' celebration of bourgeois culture. He inverts the significance that Adorno and Horkheimer see in 'style' by arguing that as an aesthetic of everyday life it has been superseded by 'culture' (see Chapter 4, p. 73). He is scathing of the 'classics' of nineteenth-century French literature: Baudelaire is a 'half-starved bohemian clown', Flaubert 'the petty bourgeois who hated the petty bourgeoisie', and Rimbaud 'practiced simple hallucination' (Lefebvre 1991a: 108–9). Nineteenth-century art, he argues, celebrated the 'marvellous' or fantastic and promoted an intellectual excess, all of which amounted to 'a sustained attack on everyday life' (Lefebvre 1991a: 105). This attack continued in the twentieth century with magic realism and surrealism, which, while it aspired to be revolutionary, merely merged real life into the dream life of the individual while avoiding analysis or reflection.

What makes Lefebvre angry and suspicious is the distance between art and everyday experience – precisely the attraction of art within the Frankfurt School of critical theory. For Lefebvre, surrealism was motivated by a desire to overthrow the tradition and institutions of art, but unlike Dada's anarchism, which was a reaction to the events of the First World War, surrealism aspired to penetrate the everyday world with what he calls 'spiritual charlatanism' (1991a: 116). Like the Frankfurt School, Lefebvre blames instrumental rationality for disenchanting modernity. But his complaint is that rationality removed the mysterious, sacred, diabolical, magical, ritual and mystical elements from the everyday world. The 'weird and the bizarre' movements of modern art contribute to this process by producing a state of 'mental confusion':

> This state of deliberate semi-neurosis, partly play-acting, often little more than an ambivalent infantilism, allows the 'modern' intellectual to push far from his lips the bitter chalice of an everyday life which *really is* unbearable – and will always be so until it has been transformed, and until new foundations for consciousness are established. (Lefebvre 1991a: 120)

The authentic which Adorno finds in the autonomous work of art exists for Lefebvre in everyday life from which the mystery has not been abstracted. The negation of ordinary experience in art that Marcuse sees as stimulating a critical consciousness is seen by Lefebvre merely as the avoidance of the brute reality of ordinary experience; modern art is devoid of authenticity because it represents the mysterious and abstracted. Despite these differences Lefebvre cannot resist commenting critically on the contents of culture; it does at least hold the possibility of representing experience.

Writing in 1958, Lefebvre modifies his 1947 attack on surrealism as at least partially unjust when he says that its 'scorn for the prosaic bourgeois world, its radical rebellion, did mean something' (1991a: 29 fn49). However, in modern society the public has become fascinated by a 'technical aestheticism' (distinguishing new categories and techniques) that the critics mediate through the press, instead of engaging with art itself. The result is that art is treated as part of 'culture', distinct from everyday life, a trend that Lefebvre attributes to the way romanticism developed into a mass culture in which everything is transformed into 'a *spectacle*, that is, essentially *non-participatory*. Pure spectacle, television, cinema. I participate by looking: by operations which give me the illusion of participation, but which at the best offer only mystifying identifications and deceptive projections' (1995: 337).

Lefebvre, however, is enthusiastic about some modern artists, such as James Joyce, whose novel *Ulysses* (1922) tells an epic story that inserts dreams and mysticism into the triviality of one particular day in the life of ordinary people that is at the same time indicative of the cyclical, repetitive time of everyday life in general: '... the I merges with Man and Man is engulfed in mediocrity' (1971: 3). The symbolism is not fantastic but both cosmic and quotidian; the history of a single day is also the history of civilisation in a way that is 'essentially dialectical' (Lefebvre 1971: 5). Another literary character who catches the quotidian without mystical abstraction is Alfred Jarry's *Ubu Roi* (1896), who 'stands for the Father, the Head, the Boss, the Master, in fact for the father-figure of everyday life. Ubu links everyday life and modernity' (Lefebvre 1971: 133). But Lefebvre dismisses those writers concerned with the abstract, with the unreal and with technical virtuosity, and bourgeois art that indulges in 'metalanguage', by which he means that it merely reflects on itself without restoring the social context (1971: 132).

Strangely, the films of Charlie Chaplin seem to be a meeting point for critical theory. Benjamin (1973b: 227) and Adorno (1991: 155) both mention them without dismissing their obviously entertaining quality. For Horkheimer, Chaplin provided a model for Hitler's 'abrupt and exaggerated gestures' (1947b: 118). But for Lefebvre, Chaplin's films are as effective in rendering the modern world as Joyce because as the little man fights with mundane objects (an umbrella, a deckchair, a motorbike, a banana skin), the difficulties of the everyday are rendered visible to us:

> Always surprised, always delighted by the strangeness and richness of things, always awkward when faced with ritualized practices (essential behaviour, necessary conditioning), Chaplin captures our own attitude towards these trivial things, and before our very eyes. ... Via this deviation through disorientation and strangeness, Chaplin reconciles us on a higher level, with ourselves, with things and with the humanized world of things. (1971: 11)

Lefebvre calls this effect of Chaplin's early films a 'reverse image': the character on the screen reflects our lives back to us through a mirror showing not the smoothness and familiarity with which we live everyday life but the reverse – the clumsiness, chaos, accident and strangeness that's also there. For Lefebvre, the reverse image means that Chaplin's films are not simply entertaining. They do more than make us laugh; they offer a critique of everyday life that is optimistic and human. For example, Chaplin's character of 'the Tramp' is the product of the bourgeois world just as much as the machines and the proletariat that works at them. But the tramp figure is a deviant, a negative character, a reverse image that Lefebvre argues has characteristics of the proletariat as described by Marx and expresses the pure alienation of humanity. This figure is not going to raise political consciousness or start a revolution but for Lefebvre he is going to 'stir up the masses profoundly' (1991a: 12).

While for most critical theorists the model of art is classical literature, painting and music, for Levebvre it is the festival, the gathering of ordinary people as they break from the routine of everyday life: 'Festival differed from everyday life only in the explosion of forces which had been slowly accumulated in and via everyday life itself' (1991a: 202). In a nostalgic mode he describes the enjoyment of collective eating, drinking, dancing and sports as a community consumes its surplus production. This merry-making, although characterised by excess, was not simply indulgence, he argues, but involved a ritualistic and spiritual reflection on the relation between the human community and the natural world, celebrating the gifts of nature and the joy of life. These celebrations provided a calendar of events that punctuated the routine, marking the seasons and the variation in human activities that went with them. The ritual of gathering contributions from each household and family towards the communal celebration emphasised the relationship between household and community – Lefebvre reminds us that the word 'symbol' has a Greek origin that 'means initially "to pay one's share", hence: to participate in the magic action, in the effectiveness of the ritual' (1991a: 204). Contributions to the collective event, a form of family sacrifice, also reflected wealth, so that the rich were involved in expressing their obligation to the community through their contributions. But this ritual expression of the order of society began to be separated from everyday life by organised religion with its set rituals and abstract beliefs controlled by a church rather than a sense of magic. The Dionysic joy in the human community of the festival has given way to ritual observance as a precaution against bad times: 'Drearily, plunged in an immense boredom which is like an ultimate sacrifice: people "give up" the time, put up with the inconvenience' (1992: 211). Lefebvre is, however, optimistic that art can be a part of a revolution in culture as he sloganises, 'Let everyday life become a work of art!' (1971: 204) and calls for play to be seen as a work of art and the life of the city as play. And it is towards the rediscovery of the festival that part of his critique is directed, aiming to recover a balance between the conditions of happiness and unhappiness in urban society with a harmonisation of festivity and everyday life (Lefebvre 1971: 206).

Barthes: Reading culture

Barthes's *oeuvre* is that of the cultural critic. Although most famous for his commentaries on modern 'mythologies' (Barthes 1979a, 1993a – see Chapter 2, p. 31), most of his work does not address the content of mass culture. It is the writing of Michelet, Racine, Balzac, Flaubert, Sollers, the music of Schubert and Schumann, the art of Cy Twombly, Erté and Arcimboldo, and the films of Eisenstein that attract him (see, e.g., Barthes 1991). Barthes's critical aim is to analyse the works of these artists to find out how they impact on culture, how they become available for reading, how they are uttered – how their writing gives them a particular cultural presence. He established a distinctive critical perspective in his first published book, *Writing Degree Zero* (1968), where he argues that writing is a form of representation that cannot escape from the circumstances in which it is produced. Writing is always at least tied to the 'idiolect' or style of the author – her or his way of putting something – which derives from the language that the author has learnt. A particular literary or political form may shape an idiolect; Barthes describes how Marxist writing is derived from 'a lexicon as specialized and as functional as a technical vocabulary' but is also shaped by its value judgements and orientation to action (1968: 22). What fascinates him is the possibility that poetry and novel writing could achieve a transparency through which the world could be seen unshaped by learnt form – a writing degree zero. Flaubert's attempt to establish a craftsmanship of writing seems a possible candidate, but this very visible form of neutrality still manages to weave a 'spell' over the reader (Barthes 1968: 68). Barthes argues that in modernity a self-consciousness about the ideological effect of language has led to serious attempts to make writing represent the world as it really is, without interpreting it or embedding values in the description. But all these attempts at colourless or neutral writing ultimately fail because the process of writing always situates itself in relation to the present or the past. A writing degree zero would be ambivalent and yet representative: 'Proportionately speaking, writing at the zero degree is basically in the indicative mood, or if you like, amodal; it would be accurate to say that it is a journalist's writing, if it were not precisely the case that journalism develops, in general, optative or imperative (that is, emotive) forms' (Barthes 1968: 76–7). Writing which attempts to rid itself of any modality – Camus's *The Outsider* (1942) is Barthes's example – seems to achieve neutrality. But as it is read, referred to, taken as an example, even such amodal writing takes on habits and a regularity of form. Because writing cannot stand outside society or above history it can never achieve 'degree zero' and must always take on a form – this for Barthes is the reason why the analysis of cultural representation can be a way of approaching the distinctive form of societies (1968: 87).

The problematic of how representation relates to the society to which it refers and from which it emerges guided Barthes throughout his working life. Writing and reading interested him most, but he also explored how photographic images might represent culture. He says of the news photograph, for example, that it appears to have the status of a *'message without a code'* and appears to be the 'perfect *analogon'*, an exact representation of a scene – a potential image degree zero (Barthes 1977a: 17). But techniques (trick effects, the pose of the subject, use of objects, lighting, references to other artwork/art forms, juxtaposition to text) enable the photograph to conceal its cultural meanings and associations behind an apparently direct representation of reality. Just as writing can never escape its historical and social situatedness, the same happens with photography:

> The type of consciousness the photograph involves is indeed truly unprecedented, since it establishes not a consciousness of the *being-there* of the thing (which any copy could provoke) but an awareness of its *having-been-there*. What we have is a new space-time category: spatial immediacy and temporal anteriority, the photograph being an illogical conjunction between the *here-now* and the *there-then*. (Barthes 1977b: 44)

Unlike writing, the photograph reveals little of its form of production but always carries something of the form of the world that was in front of the camera. This moment of the past is brought into the moment of the present, impressing on the viewer the phenomenological effect of something or someone 'having-been-there' (this is not unlike Benjamin's 'spark of contingency' – see p. 115 above and Dant and Gilloch 2002).

In *Camera Lucida* Barthes reconsiders the way that photographs animate and move the viewer: '... as a wound: I see, I feel, hence I notice, I observe, and I think' (1993b: 21). He presents a personal reading of particular photographic images through which he pioneers a new language to express the disinctive and enduring power of photographic representation. In a move reminiscent of Benjamin's 'dialectical image' (see p. 116 above), Barthes finds the model of the potency of photography in the static, masked and white-faced performances of the tableau vivant (1993b: 31–2, 91, 118). The adventure of visually reading a photograph depends on 'the co-presence of two discontinuous elements' (1993b: 23): the *'studium'* and the *'punctum'*. The *studium* is the typical or ordinary meaning of the image as a cultural object that results from the reader's education. For the individual, though, the photograph only comes alive, becomes a matter of love and passion, when a detail or a fragment interrupts, disturbs or stands out from the image. This is the *punctum* – the accidental, the coincidental feature of the image which 'pricks' the reader. The *punctum* 'is what I add to the photograph and *what is nonetheless already there'* (Barthes 1993b: 55).

The second part of *Camera Lucida* finds Barthes caught up in an emotional reviewing of old photographs. One, of his mother as a child aged five with her seven-year-old brother in a Winter Garden, catches his attention in a way that goes beyond the *studium* and the *punctum*. The photograph shows a unique, unrepeatable, historical moment – the undeniable presence of his mother as a child – that confirms the historicity of our being and for Barthes becomes its essential characteristic. From the present, of course, the viewer knows what happens later, and Barthes is painfully aware that whatever youth and optimism is displayed in the image, these people are now dead: 'In front of the photograph of my mother as a child, I tell myself: she is going to die: I shudder … over a catastrophe which has already occurred. Whether or not the subject is already dead, every photograph is this catastrophe' (1993b: 96).

The capacity of the photograph to be a 'certificate of presence' is always backwards-looking, a 'prophecy in reverse' (1993b: 87). The past is brought forcefully into conjunction with the present so that hindsight can interplay with prophecy; we know the future of the past. Barthes bemoans the limits of the photograph as an object that is flat and impenetrable (1993b: 106). The 'camera lucida' is an optical device with a prism through which an artist looks at both the scene being drawn and the page on which she or he is drawing. One eye takes in the depth of reality as the other constructs its two-dimensional image on the flatness of the sketchpad. For Barthes, the photograph is the camera lucida in reverse: we read from the two-dimensional image the three-dimensional reality that lies in the past, a reality 'that-has-been' (*Ça-a-été* – 1993b: 80). Like the camera lucida, the photographic camera provides an 'emanation of the referent' but this time one from the past, fixed by the transformation of chemicals on a plate or paper.

Photography emerged as a form of 'writing' through which the truth of the past could emerge as content almost without form, almost at degree zero, but Barthes was also interested in art that is at the same time writing. He was delighted by the work of Erté, who created a fantastic alphabet formed from human figures; his 'Z', for example, is a woman kneeling who leans backwards and holds out her arms, the 'O' is drawn from the figures of two acrobats linking hands to feet (Barthes 1991: 127). The letter which normally is only a sign when it becomes part of a word is given a depth of connotative meaning; this is writing at its furthest from degree zero. In a similar way Cy Twombly's artworks highlight the lack of neutrality of writing, the emotionality and meaning that is carried in its form. Twombly's works on paper use charcoal, pen, pencil and sometimes paint or crayon to scrawl and scribble; sometimes there are clear words or phrases, sometimes it just looks like the looping scrawl of a child who is learning to write. Things are scratched out, erased, overwritten, but however careless and unskilled the artwork appears at first glance, a little reflection shows that the image has been carefully worked on. What appeals to Barthes is the ambiguity of something that is both writing and image, moving hesitantly between the two – discourse and figure. As Barthes says, Twombly's line is 'inimitable'; this is not a text that could be transcribed and retain any meaning, nor an image that could be copied (1991: 170).

loes not share the Frankfurt critical theorists' account of the
t of the culture industry or the domination of instrumental reason.
inalysis shows that cultural forms, modes of 'writing', are never
reducible to the mechanics of their production or to the rational control of
meaning. His approach argues that the capacity of cultural products to entertain is tied to the way that they communicate, not to their autonomy, or lack
of it, as art. For Barthes, art is entertaining when it shares meanings; it draws
the 'reader', 'spectator' or 'viewer' into a process of making sense that is not
predetermined or ultimately controlled by the social system, though it may
be inflected towards the status quo. Art may liberate consciousness – but so
can a family photograph.

Baudrillard: Culture as simulation

Jean Baudrillard's work mounts a critique of the form of modern societies that
lays great emphasis on the sphere of culture and consumption (see Chapters 3
and 4) as the principal means through which the individual is connected to
society. Baudrillard picks up the threads of Benjamin's interest in reproduction
and Barthes's interest in signs and writing to explore how the culture of consumption escapes from the auratic, the classical and the bourgeois tradition to
become a play of simulations in which the affirmative may also be a negation.

Baudrillard sets out three orders of simulacra: the 'counterfeit' as the dominant form in the classical period from the Renaissance to the industrial revolution; 'production' as the strategy in the industrial era; and 'simulation' as
the dominant mode in the 'code-governed phase' of late modernity (1993a:
50). Each is a mode of culture in which the real is represented – 'writing' in
Barthes's terms – and each accords to a social structure. The 'counterfeit' is
exemplified by the use of stucco as a building material to imitate the nature
of all manner of things: velvet curtains, wooden cornices and fleshy curves of
the body. The capacity of this one substance to stand for most things provided a unifying form of representation appropriate to a centralised location
of cultural power. Industrial 'production' utilised the technology of mechanical reproduction to produce a series of like objects – Baudrillard recognises
that Benjamin grasped the cultural significance of this period of industrial
power and of technological rationality (1993a: 55). These earlier modes of
representation have not disappeared but have conceded dominance in late
modernity to the digital 'code' of the computer and DNA, which in themselves are 'illegible, and for which no possible interpretation can be provided'
(Baudrillard 1993a: 57). It is at the level of simulation via the code that the
distinction between the real and its representation disappears into hyperreal-
ity: the 'generation by models of a real without origin or reality: a hyperreal'
(Baudrillard 1994a: 1). Once encoded digitally, a representation can no longer
be traced back to an original, a model in reality against which a 'counterfeit'

or serial copy could be judged. The endless series of reproductions are simulacra, simply permutations of the code, none of which can claim authenticity, aura or authority. Baudrillard has spun Barthes's degree zero into a system of signification without a signified.

The world of art provides Baudrillard with illustrations of these forms of simulacra, such as the signature on a painting that guarantees its authenticity as not a counterfeit or copy of another artwork. The signature is evidence of the originator of the work and necessary for the painting to have cultural value and to be received as readable as a cultural object. As with Barthes, for Baudrillard the written sign is a key part of painting as a cultural product: 'The painting is a signed object as much as it is a painted surface' (Baudrillard 1981: 102). Once mechanical reproduction has become established, modern art no longer needs to represent 'the literality of the world' and instead focuses on the 'gestural elaboration of creation – spots, lines, dribbles' (Baudrillard 1981: 106). Rather as Twombly's works demonstrate their gestural specificity to Barthes as being 'inimitable', modern art suggests that it cannot be counterfeited: the content has become the signature. Baudrillard refers to Robert Rauschenberg's painting *Factum I* (1957), which looks as if it is a quick daub – but a second painting, *Factum II* (1957), is a precise copy of the first. Rauschenberg is playing with the idea of the copy and of the individuality of the painting – he can forge the painting that seems to be as idiosyncratic as a signature.

Modern art also sends up the process of mechanical reproduction with the ready-made, such as Marcel Duchamp's *Bottle Rack* (1914), which was an industrially produced, everyday artefact found in many French homes (Baudrillard 1990b: 10; 1993b: 16; 1996b: 28–9, 76–7; 1997: 10). The artist did no more than *sign* something that had been manufactured along with hundreds and thousands of exactly similar pieces. In 1917 Duchamp went even further by submitting for exhibition a urinal which he entitled *Fountain* and signed as 'R. Mutt' – retaining the significance of a signature to identify the work but destroying the capacity of the signature to allow the work to be placed in an *oeuvre*. Copies of this work are to be found in a number of museums around the world; no one is sure whether the 'original' exists. Some of these copies have been 'authorised' by Duchamp – by his signing them on the bottom. Both the bottle rack and the urinal were mass-produced objects and neither their design nor their production could be claimed as autonomous art. But signed by an artist and removed from use to display in a gallery, they can take on the authority of art that can play with representation as 'counterfeit', as 'mechanical reproduction' and with the real as representing itself.

The consequence of the third stage, of simulacra, is that the contents of culture can be produced and copied more quickly and circulated endlessly ('culture degree Xerox' – Baudrillard 1993b: 9). Art and entertainment become merged as information once they are reproduced and mediated – the digital image of a classic artwork, the MP3 encoding of a pop song. There is an implosion of meaning in the increasing volume of media output and an implosion of society into the mass (Baudrillard 1980 – see Chapter 7). The media situate information of various sorts in relation to each other, setting them in a circuit of exchange that gives them value. Baudrillard gives the example of how the events of May 1968 were 'mediatized' as reports and images of the general strike were broadcast throughout France. The effect was that the broadcasts 'neutralized the local, transversal, spontaneous forms of action' because political action had been generalised and taken out of the realms of particular and lived action (Baudrillard 1981: 176). Sounding very like the Frankfurt critical theorists' account of how the culture industry drowns out critique and fascinates rather than enlightens or provokes an audience, Baudrillard argues that mediatisation overwhelms meaning and critical thought:

> Critical thought judges, discriminates, and produces differences. It is by this selection process that it acts as the guardian of meaning. The masses, on the other hand, do not choose, do not produce differences but indifference; they preserve the fascination of the medium, which they prefer to the critical demands of the message. For fascination does not stem from meaning, it is rather exactly proportionate to the alienation of meaning. (Baudrillard 1980: 146)

In *The Evil Demon of Images* (1987) Baudrillard spells out the diabolical quality of entertainment images that are so seductive in their form that any message they may contain is neutralised. The images presented in the modern cinema appear more truthful, more faithful in their representation of 'reality', of life as it presents itself to our senses, than previous forms of art. The perfection of special effects, the painstaking and extravagant way that feature films re-create the real, gives viewers an illusion of verisimilitude. This destroys any dialectical relation between image and reality for the captivated viewers, who don't notice how they are diverted or what distortions there are in the representation. How we understand the world we live in is mediated by these carefully produced simulacra that can precede rather than follow real history. One of Baudrillard's examples is *The China Syndrome* (1979) a film about an accident at a nuclear plant that preceded, so diminishing its horrifying implications, a real nuclear accident at Harrisburg: '... is the real (Harrisburg) only the symptom of the imaginary (... *The China Syndrome*) or vice versa?' (1987: 20). We become caught in the 'fatal process' of investing our trust in the imaginary because it seems so realistic; but it is a process with no end in which images lead to endless images but never back to the real.

Baudrillard's elusive category of the 'fatal strategy' (see Chapter 7, pp. 148–9) seems to be well illustrated in the brief introduction he wrote for the French edition of J.G. Ballard's novel *Crash*, where he explores how its characters confront fate (1994a: 111–19). The anti-hero, Vaughan, collects images of the effects of injuries from car crashes and, by reconstructing the crashes, tries to recapture the moment that body and commodity/object meet and merge. A car crash epitomises the spontaneity of a real, bodily, unintended event, and Vaughan and other characters find the idea of giving themselves up to such

violent and uncompromising bodily sensations erotic – an escape fr
simulated sexuality of contemporary culture. For Baudrillard, thi
fronting of fate transforms the highway accident into the 'Accident', an
that symbolically and ritually reconnects the body to the object. There is an
enduring nostalgia in Baudrillard for a time of symbolic exchange when
things meant something and when the subject was confronted by an object
that resisted; when sex and fear rather than the simulation of sex and fear
moved the body. What he despairs of is the realm of simulation in which so
much pretence at reality keeps us from the simplicity of existence – but that
is all we have, and there is no going back.

Conclusions

Both art and entertainment represent the world we live in, allowing us an
opportunity to stand back from the everyday and reflect on how things are
and how they might be. Critical theory argues that in modernity the process
of representation enters a new phase – of the culture industry, mechanical
reproduction, of direct representation, of representation that precedes reality –
that sustains the social order of advanced capitalism and threatens to slide
towards even greater repression. But at the same time the possibility for a
politicised reflection – of historical possibility, of the mass, of everyday experience, of the form of art itself – lies in a liberatory art that can be joyful and
playful as well as being part of a praxis through which the world might be
critiqued and even changed.

Summary

- *Adorno and Horkheimer:* (1) Culture becomes an industry shaped by capital investment, business organisation and industrial processes to produce
  entertainment commodities to be sold in a market.
- (2) The authenticity of the individual and distinctive autonomous artwork,
  shaped within a tradition of the creative imagination of the artist that
  allows form to develop, is displaced by cultural products that have the
  same pre-formed structure, albeit embellished by features that give the
  appearance of variation and complexity.
- (3) The critical and polemical quality of art that stimulates its audience to
  imagine a world different from the one they experience gives way to a
  stultifying, repetitive and predictable form appealing to 'fun' and entertainment that encourages mass acceptance of the instrumental rationality
  of modernity without provoking the individual imagination.
- *Benjamin:* Mechanical reproduction (e.g. photography, film) destroys the
  traditional 'aura' of the artwork but produces new possibilities for critical
  awareness through, for example, the 'dialectical image', which allows the

mass to confront itself and the conditions of its historical emergence. The aestheticisation of politics mean that mechanical reproduction is used to create propaganda that supports Fascism and provokes war.

- *Marcuse*: Affirmative culture aspires to a better life for the individual but within the constraints of bourgeois society; critical art, however, offers the possibility of a negation of the existing form of society and liberation for all. Advanced industrial society repackages art as entertainment to limit its critical effect and promote a 'Happy Consciousness', but a politicisation of aesthetics can subvert and negate affirmative culture, prompting individuals towards a solidarity in aspiring to freedom.
- *Lefebvre*: Modernity brought a 'culture' that celebrated the romantic, bourgeois concern with the fantastic at the expense of the 'styles' of everyday life that reflected ordinary existence. The non-participatory 'spectacle' of modern mass culture can be contrasted with some art (James Joyce, Charlie Chaplin) that links quotidian experience with that of humanity as a whole. The 'reverse image' can provide a critique showing the chaos and accidental in the everyday, while the playful form of the festival can offer a joyful break that celebrates and reflects on mundane experience.
- *Barthes*: Modern culture aspires to the 'zero degree' in which experience is untainted by individual style or the form of representation (neutral writing, the photograph as analagon). But cultural products are always caught in the contextual history of their utterance, which is precisely what can move the reader/viewer as she or he recognises a reality 'that-has-been'.
- *Baudrillard*: In late modernity culture is dominated by 'simulacra' that have no origin in a reality other than the 'code' and that can be endlessly copied. The creation of the illusion of similitude produces copies that precede reality and give it meaning – 'culture degree Xerox'.

Further reading

There are a wide range of sources that discuss various theoretical approaches to the study of culture including critical theories. Amongst the most useful are Dominic Strinati's *An Introduction to Theories of Popular Culture* (1995), Mark J. Smith's *Culture: Reinventing the Social Sciences* (2000) and Alan Swingewood's *Cultural Theory and the Problem of Modernity* (1998).

Note

1 My thanks to Graeme Gilloch for discussions and collaborative work (Dant and Gilloch 2002) on which this section draws heavily.

SEVEN

Knowledge, Action and Politics

Part of Marx's legacy from Hegel, Henri Lefebvre tells us, was the notion that the process of history and of becoming was central to knowledge about the life of mankind (1968: 28). However, while, for Hegel, knowledge reached its height in the synthesis achieved by the overcoming of previous forms of knowledge, for Marx this was too abstract, remaining as it did at the level of consciousness – he famously declared that philosophers had interpreted the world but the point was to change it (1975: 423). Hegel was a philosopher through and through, as Lefebvre puts it, whereas Marx *'thought* as a man of *action'* (1968: 27) – and it is this link between knowledge and action that makes his philosophy distinctive. For Lefebvre, the dynamic orientation of Marx's philosophy can be summed up in the concept of *'praxis'*: thought must be realised, tested and judged in the context of action. Thought or reflection cannot be judged by internal standards of truth in order to establish knowledge; it has to be applied to the world of experience that is cumulatively grasped as history.

It is the relation between knowledge and action that is the theme of this chapter. Critical theorists engage in the production of thought, ideas, theory and knowledge, but they are concerned about how such abstractions are applied in the world of lived experience. As the Frankfurt theorists mount their critique of pragmatism, traditional theory, positivism and one-dimensional thought, they are concerned with how these types of knowledge are applied to the world of action to dominate nature and people. This form of rationality can be summed up in the phrase 'instrumental reason': knowledge that is generated to achieve specific purposes but which is careless of other consequences. Rather than replace it with a 'pure' form of knowledge, one that is separate from the world of experience and action, critical theory proposes an engaged form of knowledge that is reflective and addresses the consequences for ordinary lives, for individuals and for their freedom. Critical thought always questions the basis of any form of knowledge and is unwilling to accept a system, or method, as sufficient to legitimate knowledge.

For the French tradition, a slightly different approach to the Hegel–Marx line of dialectical thinking produces a different orientation but with very similar concerns. The concept of praxis, for example, enables Lefebvre to explore the link between history and experience with the political aim of liberation without revolution – an aim broadly shared with the Frankfurt critical theorists. Praxis rehabilitates the realm of the senses into knowledge by linking human material and emotional needs with the cultural processes that recognise needs and collaborate to meet them. In Lefebvre's formulation, praxis is distinctively the realm of human action oriented to other human beings, to relationships, to the production of ideas about human relationships – in other words to philosophy, politics, art, culture and the state. These are precisely the same fields that interest the Frankfurt theorists and later theorists who will be discussed in this chapter. And in so far as thought addresses itself to the world of human action, it is entailed in praxis: 'Through praxis thought is re-united with being, consciousness with sensuous or physical nature, the mind with spontaneity' (Lefebvre 1968: 58).

Lefebvre's use of the concept of praxis to link theory and action is consistent with the way that critical theory grounds its theorising in the world around it. Many of the critical theorists are philosophers by inclination and training and all demonstrate an informed understanding of what philosophers have to say. But critical theory is a distinctive form of theoretical reflection that always orients itself to what is wrong or limited in the world and hints, though usually in the most elliptical and negative terms, at what would make it better.

Horkheimer: The origins of critical theory

In a series of essays Max Horkheimer (1947a, 1947b and 1947c) mounts a critique of philosophical forms – especially pragmatism and positivism – to identify the constraints thought has acquired in modernity. He is keen to free thought from a programmed, centralised and systematised invocation to act in certain ways and to reintroduce spontaneity and imagination to enable action to be the result of the wishes and desires of people. At root, the problem is about reason. It is as reason that thought and consciousness can be brought to bear on the world of practical action, and it is through reason that reflective imagination can be redirected from fantasy and myth to engage with lived experience. One of Horkheimer's early moves is to distinguish *subjective* from *objective* reason. Subjective reason is the form of thought that deals with classification, inference and deduction; it is the type of thinking that is concerned with means and ends (Horkheimer 1947a: 3–57). As a utilitarian moment in the orientation of the individual mind to its practical and immediate interests, subjective reason, Horkheimer argues, is symptomatic of the development of modern western thought. He contrasts it with the much longer tradition – which he identifies with the Greek philosophers – of objective reason, a force not only within the individual mind but also in the objective world of human social relationships seen as a totality. It is objective reason that focuses on concepts that extend beyond the interests of the individual: '... on the idea of the greatest good, on the problem of human destiny, and on the way of realization of ultimate goals' (Horkheimer 1947a: 5).

It is the dominance of subjective reason as a mode of thought that has led to the instrumental and pragmatic approach to knowledge in which truth is demonstrated by success in practical action: 'Concepts have become "streamlined", rationalized, labor-saving devices. It is as if thinking itself had been reduced to the level of industrial processes, subjected to a close schedule – in short, made part and parcel of production' (Horkheimer 1947a: 21). This type of praxis formalises and limits how reason is related to action. When empirical science, potent as a technological force in industrial production, is applied to all forms of intellectual life, reasoned thought ceases to be autonomous and becomes an instrument. Instrumental reason is used 'as a mere tool by man' to dominate nature, and once the 'natural' form of lower species and races has been distinguished, this includes human nature (Horkheimer 1947b: 108). Reason is paradoxically both 'a part of nature, [and] at the same time set against nature' (Horkheimer 1947b: 125).

The 'reality' of empirical reason has displaced earlier forms of religious and mythological thought that entertained the realm of the possible and sustained the reflective judgement of objective reason. In a number of essays Horkheimer defends the realm of mind, spirit, soul and metaphysics against the attacks it receives from pragmatism, positivism and instrumental reason. For Horkheimer, a younger generation who reject spiritual concepts on the grounds that they have provided a smokescreen for torture, murder and oppression do not recognise that such spiritual reason was precisely concerned with morality: '"Soul" is becoming, in retrospect as it were, a pregnant concept, expressing all that is opposed to the indifference of the subject who is ruled by technology and destined to be a mere client. Reason divorced from feeling is now becoming the opposite of *Anima* or soul' (Horkheimer 1974c: 60).

Scientific reason, when applied to the inner life of human beings as psychology and psychoanalysis, reduces the mind to a system that can be explained as merely animal action. The capacity to replicate some of its functionality in an 'automated apparatus' (Horkheimer seems to anticipate the debate about artificial intelligence – 1974c: 58) further demonstrates the irrelevance of the immortal soul. But what is lost as 'purposive systematic procedures' replace imagination and emotion is the centrality of moral principles to civilisation and its continuity, including '[r]espect for neighbor, sense of responsibility, and capacity for friendship and love' (Horkheimer 1974c: 60).

As instrumental reason displaces the mysteries of nature and spirit, Horkheimer points out that the very way that human beings are taught to think has changed. Young people are encouraged to adopt rational attitudes and to orient their thinking towards specific goals instead of learning through their instinctual and mimetic impulses (Horkheimer 1974b: 114). Mimesis is the process by which human beings learn through imitating others' patterns of behaviour and, by acting within them, learn about different possibilities for action. The mimetic impulse produces a form of knowledge not based in thought or reason but characteristic of that embodied in myth and art: an imitation of life that stimulates reflection on its form. But science and the notion of progress replace mimesis as a mode of learning with a willingness to adapt and to be shaped by external reason (Horkheimer 1947b: 115). The mimetic impulse does not disappear completely: as Horkheimer reminds us, a technique of the Nazis was to imitate the Jew as a way of identifying the otherness of the outsider, while sustaining a position of power and apparent rational superiority.

The most important impact of abstract reason, however, is its application to producing commodities in a way that separates thought from action and experience. The capitalist mode of production uses instrumental reason to dominate nature through the creation of machine tools that control and manipulate raw materials. During the first half of the twentieth century a developing industrial system of production built a wealthy and prosperous economy: a world created by human beings that appeared to be their world. But Horkheimer points out that, paradoxically, it is also not their world – it is the world of capital. The domination of nature extends beyond industrial processes to produce a social world characterised by a material culture that is manifestly man-made and displays the successful domination of nature. As Horkheimer says:

> The objects we perceive in our surroundings – cities, villages, fields and woods – bear the mark of having been worked on by man. It is not only in clothing and appearance, in outward form and emotional make-up that men are the product of history. Even the way they see and hear is inseparable from the social life-process as it has evolved over the millennia. ... The sensible world which a member of industrial society sees about him every day bears the marks of deliberate work: tenement houses, factories, cotton, cattle for slaughter, men and, in addition, not only objects such as subway trains, delivery trucks, autos, and airplanes but the movements in the course of which they are perceived. The distinction within this complex totality between what belongs to unconscious nature and what to the action of man in society cannot be drawn in concrete detail. Even where there is a question of experiencing natural objects as such, their very naturalness is determined by contrast with the social world and, to that extent, depends on the latter. (1972: 200–2)

The material world reveals the impact of industrial action that is the result of systematic forethought and planning which has applied reason and theory to its production. The knowledge that is used is embedded within the products so that the world is presented to the senses 'preformed'. Instrumental reason pre-forms not only the material stuff of the world through machine technology but also pre-forms the ideas and even the senses of the people who live in that world. The historical process of an emerging technological rationality has not only dominated nature but feeds back to dominate human beings, capturing them in the process, making them part of it. As Horkheimer says, tools are not only the prolongation of human organs, human organs are also the prolongation of the tools (1972: 201).

It is 'traditional' theory that generates the 'useful' knowledge that has brought about this historical transformation, most obviously through leading to technical knowledge – engineering, mechanics, materials science, and so on. But pure science that does not have immediate applicability is also part of traditional theory when it accepts the economic conditions that create a demand for it and also the resources to pay for it. Theoretical knowledge oriented to the process of production does not stop with science and techno-logy; economics, management science and psychology all contribute to the understanding of industrial organisations. The institutionally valid forms of these disciplines that attempt to articulate objective facts are underpinned by the separation of theory from action and of value from research – this is what characterises 'traditional theoretical thinking' (Horkheimer 1972: 208). It is, for example, the spread of instrumental reason that produces the 'scientific', calculative, analysis of the opinion poll, which, Horkheimer argues, appears as a 'substitute for reason' (1947a: 31). Instead of using their own judgement, ordinary people are influenced by modern techniques of communication that emphasise the majority (e.g. the opinion poll) as the arbiter of cultural life. Public opinion has been hijacked by instrumental reason that feeds it with pre-packaged contents of thought, which are then re-cycled through the feed-back loop of opinion polls to tell people what they should think.

Critical theory is a form of knowledge that resists not only usefulness and applicability but also the institutional demarcation of theory and application. Horkheimer is, however, keen to distance critical theory from the internal speculation of idealist philosophy and wants to emphasise its direct engage-ment with the human condition and overarching interest in identifying 'the reasonable conditions of life' (1972: 199). Critical theory intercedes in the flow of history not to instigate a diversion into metaphysical thought (although Horkheimer does accept that it may at times appear as subjective, speculative, one-sided or useless) but to apply rational thought to the totality of human existence. Its aim is nothing less than the transformation of society, and it is committed to a future society, as a community of free men and women. This means that critical theory must articulate the social contradic-tions inherent in all social locations, including that of the theorist, and so cannot be tied to the situation of a single class. But if this is the case, what is the basis for its value orientation? How can critical theory underpin its basis in judgement?

In a number of places Horkheimer (e.g. 1972: 222) toys with the idea of the critical theorist as a member of what Karl Mannheim, after Alfred Weber, called the 'free-floating intelligentsia', referring to those whose perspective was not tied to any particular location within the social and economic struc-ture. But critical theory is more committed than this phrase suggests and does not attempt to stand apart from the flow of social life or 'hang suspended over it' (Horkheimer 1972: 223). It accepts a commitment to Marx's analysis of political economy, taking as axiomatic that in the modern era, the capitalist mode of production drives the social system towards a new barbarism, riven with tensions and contradictions. There is also a commitment to an historicism, also derived from Marx, that refers to the totality of western social formations and which serves critical theory as 'the unfolding of a single existential judgement' (Horkheimer 1972: 227). However, critical theory confronts the cultural rather than the economic impact of the mode of production, and it is the individual not a class that is its subject: 'Its subject is rather a definite individual in his real relation to other individuals and groups, in his conflict with a particular class, and, finally, in the resultant web of relationships with the social totality and with nature' (Horkheimer 1972: 211).

Critical theory does not seek objective distance but aims to be adopted as a mode of knowledge and action by all human beings so that their decisions shape their history, rather than their actions following mechanically those of a system. Struggle and change are components of the critical attitude as much as a critique of the existing order. As Horkheimer puts it, it is not simply a matter of generating 'the theory of emancipation; it is the practice of it as well' (1972: 233), and practice involves a continuous review and modification of theory. The dynamic relation between theory and practice means that contradictions continually emerge, preventing critical theory from settling as a system of classification that might provide a basis for sociology. It does not offer a detailed description of society or of interaction or suggest the possibility of a suprahistorical subject, nor are there general criteria on which it can be judged, 'for it is always based on the recurrence of events and thus on a self-reproducing totality' (Horkheimer 1972: 242). Horkheimer's account of critical theory underlies the perspectives that have been gathered together under the label of 'critical theory' in this book. It has much in common with philosophy and yet is distinctive in adopting a position on political economy and taking as a goal the freedom and happiness of all individuals. Critical theory also takes up an argumentative stance that has 'the dialectical function of measuring every historical stage in the light ... of its primary and total content' (Horkheimer 1972: 251). It is through dialectics that thought is related to action and reason is confronted with the changing nature of history.

Marcuse: From dialectics to aesthetics

Horkheimer does not attempt to specify a dialectical method for critical theory, while Adorno (1973) engaged in a debate with a series of key contributions to western philosophy, particularly that of Hegel, aiming to establish a distinctive philosophical method. Adorno's *Negative Dialectics* (1973) attempted to remove the affirmative traces left by Hegelian dialectics to produce a method in which, as Held helpfully summarises it, '[t]hinking is a form of praxis, always historically conditioned; as physical labour transforms and negates the material world under changing historical circumstances, so mental labour, under changing historical conditions, alters its object world through criticism' (1980: 204).'

Adorno's evolving position on the relationship between knowledge and action is too complex and distinctive to be summarised here (though see especially Buck-Morss 1977). Marcuse (1941) also engaged with Hegelian philosophy in detail to reveal a radical and critical strand – again a substantial work that stands alone and is too complex to deal with here. However, in a series of earlier essays that, like Horkheimer's, were concerned with establishing the ground of critical theory, Marcuse (1968a, 1968b, 1968c) developed a dialectical approach, derived from Hegel, that identified contradictions between life as it is experienced and life as it could be. This, he argued, can lead to a society 'that disposes of the goods available to it in such a way that they are distributed in accordance with the true needs of the community', one in which 'instead of life being placed in the service of labor, labor would become a means of life' and 'men would themselves take on the planning and shaping of the social process of life and not leave it to the arbitrariness of competition and the blind necessity of reified economic relations' (Marcuse 1968a: 73). Marcuse argued that reason presupposes a free mind and that a free mind seeks only freedom (1968c). Individual freedom is, however, dependent on self-sufficiency and property, which require a critical theory to produce a society where 'individuals can collectively regulate their lives in accordance with their needs' (Marcuse 1968c). Marcuse's account of critical theory was not utopian because it did not describe an ideal end, merely a set of aims that should motivate critique: freedom, happiness and transformation of the economic order. He describes a theoretical imagination that employs fantasy to address possibilities other than those prescribed by the current social order, but must also apply a rigorous analysis of the economic and political relations of society.

These early themes of dialectics, freedom, happiness and imagination that Marcuse derives from Hegelian philosophy are set against a critique of modern society in One-Dimensional Man (1972b). The single dimension that dominates ordinary life in late modernity is that of the 'performance principle' (see Chapter 5), by which knowledge is linked to action according to direct, practical and rational criteria. One-dimensional thought blanks out opposition, so that all thought follows the lines of the technological rationality of advanced capitalism. Marcuse's Hegelian Marxism promotes two-dimensional, dialectical thought that allows for the possibility of disagreement, negation and therefore critique; two-dimensional thought frees the imagination to entertain possible forms of existence and compare them to current experience. Marcuse argues that the social sciences, which we might expect to be critical, have succumbed to one-dimensional thought as questions of value have been abandoned in favour of empiricist and operationalist knowledge, often based on counting (money, people, tasks and outputs).

By the end of the 1960s, however, Marcuse was optimistic that the 'Great Refusal' was beginning to emerge as a response to advanced capitalism amongst students, in the urban ghettos and through a remobilisation of anarchist and socialist political groups (1969: vii). The very capacity of technologically advanced systems of production meant that there was no longer a problem in meeting the real needs of people and there were sufficient resources to abolish poverty and misery and create solidarity. However, the exploitative apparatus had continued to stimulate drives and aspirations in the individual that could be met through the provision of consumer goods. By following a lifestyle oriented to a form of subjective 'happiness', individuals have lost touch with their own vital needs within advanced capitalism. Needs and the means of their satisfaction are socially engineered through institutions and media: 'The entire realm of competitive performances and standardized fun, all the symbols of status, prestige, power, of advertized virility and charm, of commercialized beauty – this entire realm kills in its citizens the very disposition, the organs, for the alternative: freedom without exploitation' (Marcuse 1969: 17).

Critical theory offers a reappraisal of the values that had become endemic to advanced societies, and in the *Essay on Liberation* (1969) Marcuse shows how bodily shame, sexual mores and consumer values are constructs of the ideology of capitalism. An aesthetic aspect of the political response to the culture of advanced capitalism is concerned with the environment and the form of the world in which people live. Marcuse anticipates the green movement as he suggests that such an aesthetic would 'insist on cleaning the earth of the very material garbage produced by the spirit of capitalism' (1969: 28). Such a political practice would, he recognised, be based on stimulating the imagination to move beyond the concepts and logic of instrumental reason and would be against the will of the great majority. And here is the catch in the relationship between knowledge and action in Marcuse's version of critical theory: the theorist knows what true needs are, what a more humane form of life would be, what would count as liberation, what freedom is – but the mass and even the majority do not know. Because the system of advanced capitalism has been so successful in co-opting the mass of individuals into accepting the system's needs as their own, the values they hold are those that need to be changed. As Marcuse puts it, 'the general will is always wrong' (1969: 65), echoing Horkheimer's suspicion of the opinion polls' account of the values of the majority. The solution for Marcuse is persuasion, but as mass media techniques are not available to the 'leftist minority', strategies of resistance and subversion, 'uncivil disobedience' and direct action must be used to challenge and alter the status quo. Such radical strategies face almost inevitable defeat in the short term but are necessary for the move from a 'representative democracy' towards a 'direct democracy'. Marcuse sees the potential for action to become knowledge: 'law and order becomes something to be established *against* the established law and order: the existing society has become illegitimate, unlawful: it has invalidated its own law' (1969: 78). Here the language of law and order is doing double-duty to refer to that which *is* established and that which is *to be* established, but there are no criteria to distinguish one from the other.

Marcuse aspires to a state of civilisation 'where man has learned to ask for the sake of whom or of what he organizes his society' (1969: 90). Many individuals do no doubt continually ask this question of their own actions and those of others, including institutional actors such as governments and commercial corporations. But as a practical political criterion it does not count as knowledge that can lead to action – individuals will come up with different answers and it is difficult to imagine ever achieving a consensus in which we could safely refer to the action of a generic subject such as 'humankind'. The Great Refusal is opposed to the existing consensus and aspires to reclaim the autonomy of individuals to express their own needs. This means that critical theory cannot anticipate what values will guide those individuals or it will cease to be dialectical; but without a clearly articulated set of values, knowledge that can guide action is impossible. Marcuse's skill in remoulding philosophy to the purposes of critical theory is impressive but ultimately raises more questions than it answers.

The early essays by Horkheimer and Marcuse, published in the Frankfurt School's house journal, the *Zeitschrift für Sozialforschung,* in the late 1930s and early 1940s, are programmatic rather than substantive or methodological. They exemplify the essayistic style of the Frankfurt critical theorists and mobilise a series of concepts – totality, history, theory, practice, instrumental reason, technological rationality, dialectics – and establish a series of orientations – Marx's critique of political economy, the liberation of the individual, the comprehensive cultural form of industrialised society – that are developed later, especially in Adorno and Horkheimer's *Dialectic of Enlightenment* (1979), and Marcuse's *One-Dimensional Man* (1972b). And in these general ways we can see a continuity between their understanding of the relationship between knowledge and action, particularly political action, that is characteristic of later 'critical theories'. But these early position papers lack clarity about the concepts of freedom and liberation and the methods by which 'facts' can be adduced. The studies of the Frankfurt School deal in generalities, and while the work of its members in the United States became much more specific and empirical (see, for example, Adorno 1991), it is not always easy to see how the link between their summary remarks on knowledge and historical totality can realistically lead to action that might change society.

Lefebvre: The primacy of everyday life

Many of the stimulations and resources that Henri Lefebvre calls upon are very similar to those of Marcuse and yet neither refers substantially to the other's work. Both looked to the social changes brought about by the Second

World War as potentially creating a new social order. Both were inspired by the philosophical debate between Hegel and Marx to want to understand the alienation of individuals in modernity, and both explored how critique could have an impact on practice. Both moved away from Marx's concern with economics and production to address consumption and culture. But then there are differences: whereas Marcuse used Freud to understand the psyche of the modern individual (the transformation of the reality principle into the performance principle, sublimation into repressive desublimation), Lefebvre focused attention on everyday life as the sphere in which individuals expressed their needs and desires and responded to the social pressures on them to live or act in certain ways. Both Marcuse and Lefebvre are interested in the history of capitalism since Marx: for Marcuse, 'advanced capitalism' is characterised by 'technological rationality'; and for Lefebvre, 'modernity' has a culture that is scientific and operational.

For Lefebvre, philosophy is too self-reflective, too abstract and divorced from the everyday life of material existence, 'of possessions and needs' (1971: 17). Nonetheless a philosophical approach is invaluable for 'assessing disconnected material' and projecting an image of 'a "complete human being", free, accomplished, fully realized, rational yet real' (Lefebvre 1971: 12). Philosophy in itself is self-destructive and self-contradictory unless it is applied to the non-philosophical, and so Lefebvre proposes 'a philosophical inventory and analysis of everyday life that will expose its ambiguities' (1971: 13). This is a direction that Marx has already moved in, taking a lead from Hegel, and he achieved a shift from addressing the role of the state to addressing the role of the working class as the realisation of philosophical thought in the realm of the non-philosophical. But Lefebvre wants to go further than Hegel, further than Marx's account of rationality as the outcome of labour and production, to use philosophy to address the most non-philosophical dimension of existence: the quotidian. To do so he turned not to the form of critique favoured by the Frankfurt theorists, as he followed this path from philosophy to modern life, but to the Socratic form of question and answer, the 'maieutic'.

As he redirects philosophical inquiry to the mundane and ordinary he identifies a form that recurs frequently in critical theory as the mimetic, but for Lefebvre is articulated slightly differently as the theme of 'recurrence':

> Everyday life is made of recurrences: gestures of labour and leisure, mechanical movements both human and properly mechanic, hours, days weeks, months, years, linear and cyclical repetitions, natural and rational time, etc.; the study of creative activity (of *production* in its widest sense) leads to the study of re-production or the conditions in which actions producing objects and labour are re-produced, re-commenced, and re-assume their component proportions or, on the contrary, undergo gradual or sudden modifications. (1971: 18)

The regularities of everyday life are constituted in the form of such recurrences; it is through these that individual action takes on meaning and can be recognised as social action rather than individual behaviour. The currency of images, language and music suggests the modes in which such meaning is grasped in the non-philosophical realm of the everyday; what philosophy can do is to explicate the relationship between the imaginary and the real, the 'inner' and 'outer' life. Through addressing the cyclical time of recurrence, the linear form of becoming, so attractive to abstract philosophy, is confronted by ordinary corporeal existence.

Lefebvre identifies the key features of Marx's method of applying philosophy to the substance of existence: analysing the whole in terms of expansion and development; using dialectical reason and a conceptual language; seeking causes; identifying contradictions; distinguishing form from content, base from superstructure (1971: 69–70). But both the method and Marx's analysis have proved inadequate to keep up with the hundred years of history since it was set out. The social world of modernity has become fragmented and the underlying system has become obscured by the complexity of modern sub-systems – the institutions and public offices of the modern state. Not only are Marx's categories inadequate for the analysis of modern society, so are the categories of modern society itself: the forms, functions and structures that are identified in its own strategies and political discourses. Lefebvre's solution is to take up a critical perspective, inspired by Marx, and to apply it to the space-time complex of everyday life that lies behind all the sub-systems and that is a product of the organised society of controlled consumption (1971: 72).

Lefebvre recognises that the human, especially the social, sciences have already addressed the relationship between practical activities and ideologies, but, like the Frankfurt theorists, he points out that it is their 'operativeness', their concern with means and ends, that fails to confront the conflict between the rational and the irrational. What the operative sciences accept – and here he cites Durkheim – is the compulsion entailed in the reality of existence. Lefebvre wants to generate knowledge by studying not simply production, but how the social existence of human beings is produced: 'Such a critical analysis corresponds to a study of compulsions and partial determinisms; it aims at a reversal of the upside-down world where determinism and compulsion are considered rational even though reason has always attempted to control determinism' (1971: 23).

Through confronting rationalism and science, knowledge can move beyond accepting the status quo and actively contribute to releasing human creativity and freedom. Lefebvre proposes opening up the unquestioned, regular, insignificant, humble, solid nature of everyday life through an analysis of the ethics of routine action and the aesthetics of familiar settings. His critique focuses on the character of the quotidian that emerged in modernity as the industrial revolution began to relieve the ubiquity of want and of vulnerability to nature. As wants were met, unequally and unevenly, through the application of reason, the irrational and the realm of the imagination were undermined. What Lefebvre proposed for his three-volume *Critique of Everyday Life* was a critical comprehensive study of society that would explore the relation between knowledge and action, rather than a collation of endless facts (1971: 28).

Instead of proletarian revolution, Lefebvre proposes a revolution in the way we lead our everyday lives. In place of the technological rationality that is characteristic of modern society, he argues for a dialectical reason linking thought and action into praxis. Whereas philosophy tends to reflect in abstractions and ideas independent from the flow of life, Lefebvre wants thought that engages with triviality and the minutiae of everyday life. Whereas leisure seeks a break from the everyday, a dialectical reason can engage with it: 'The true critique of everyday life will have as its prime objective the separation between the human (real and possible) and bourgeois decadence, and will imply a *rehabilitation of everyday life'* (Lefebvre 1991a: 127). Philosophy and history have traditionally sought a pure metaphysical form of reason and dealt only with the lives of kings, generals and bishops. Lefebvre argues for a praxis of 'thought-action' based on everyday life to replace the mythic, ideal form of understanding that stands apart from the flow of history (1991a: 135).

Benjamin and Barthes: History as the past in the present

Neither Benjamin nor Barthes attempts to establish a systematic account of knowledge and how it relates to social action, but both review the role of history in understanding modernity. Both were influenced by Marx and to some extent Hegel but neither routinely draws on either to make his arguments or to reference his methods. There is common ground between their work (see, for example, Dant and Gilloch 2002) that can best perhaps be summed up as a concern with writing and with history.

For Benjamin, history was a process of becoming that was beyond human control, even through political action; in a strange fragment he argues that there are countervailing dynamics of history, one of which is the 'profane', 'the quest of free humanity for happiness', the other of which is the Messianic, the end of history, where 'the Messiah himself consummates all history, in the sense that he redeems' (1985b: 155). The coming of the Messiah is not a goal to which politics can be directed, but despite its promise of happiness, politics must fight against the very possibility of such an end of history. For Benjamin, history is a struggle, but not simply between human, rational, political forces, but also with the process of history itself that is embedded within the beliefs of human culture. In his 'Theses on the Philosophy of History' (1973a) Benjamin warns that historical materialism cannot simply shake off previous history, because whatever changes are made now will affect not only the future but also how we understand the past. As human action responds to wishes and desires that have been felt in the past, it must recognise the impact of other past traditions on the present and the future. In a famous trope, Benjamin describes history as an angel facing the past, being blown backwards towards the future by the storm of progress from Paradise: 'Where we perceive a chain of events, he sees one single catastrophe which keeps piling wreckage upon wreckage and hurls it in front of his feet' (1973a: 249). Benjamin is warning that knowledge directed to changing the world, to bring about freedom and happiness, has more to contend with than the apparent political or economic interests of others. He also warns of too eagerly embracing the idea of progress, especially technological and social progress – both of which were a feature, albeit in different forms, of fascist and socialist ideologies which were dominant at the turn of the 1940s. In criticising 'historicism', which sees history as cumulative and sequential, a series of causes and facts, Benjamin commends a more active approach to history, 'historical materialism', that is 'based on a constructive principle' (1973a: 254). Historical materialism treats history not as something that can be settled but as something that is continually worked on both at the level of conscious knowledge and at the level of human action.

There is nothing of Benjamin's Messianism in Roland Barthes's view of history, but he also critiques its traditional form as a matter of getting the facts straight and identifying the causal structure of progress: '... historical discourse does not follow reality, it only signifies it; it asserts at every moment: *this happened*, but the meaning conveyed is only that someone is making that assertion' (Barthes 1970: 154). In Barthes's history of the famous nineteenth-century French historian Jules Michelet, he shows that the past has always to be read into contemporary social context and that it cannot be reduced to a systematic causal process. Barthes identifies in Michelet's writing an understanding of the 'vegetal character of historic growth', in which the objects of history do not cause each other but are connected because they are 'merely different moments of the same stem' (1987: 35). Like Benjamin, Barthes refuses linear, causal history and embraces a history in which themes are associated by juxtaposition, the past being read in terms of the present. An historian like Michelet is reinterpreting the lives and deeds of people who are dead ('administering the estate of the dead' – Barthes 1987: 82), putting their actions in order so that they make sense and fit together. He makes sense of what was unclear to people when they were alive; but this is not, Barthes emphasises, a grand task at the 'level of ideas, of forces, of causes or systems' (1987: 82).

In a rather later essay, Barthes (1989) develops an approach to the problem of the consumer faced with the homogeneity of mass culture that explores the multiple levels of meaning. He argues that there is a division of languages, so that as readers or interpreters, we 'lock ourselves into our own social, professional cell' in order to 'adapt ourselves as best we can to the fragmentation of our society' (Barthes 1989: 116). Power varies according to the 'sociolect', the way of speaking or writing linked to one's social location within discourse. Speech from within the circuits of power he calls 'encratic discourses' and those outside, 'acratic discourses' (Barthes 1989: 120). While encratic discourse conforms to the 'doxa' – public opinion, the general – acratic discourse speaks out against the doxa and so is 'paradoxical'. Here we can map Barthes's theoretical account onto the tension between critical theory and the dominant mode of discourse within instrumental reason. Encratic discourse does not present itself as an ideological form, a system of values, but appears to be unmarked, natural, universal – just good sense. What is more, there is no simple parallel between the doxa and class power because other classes will borrow the doxa for their own purposes to subvert or challenge power. This theory of discourse extends the idea that in modernity there can be no 'degree zero' (see Chapter 6) for speech and writing which is always oriented to power and constitutes language as including or excluding. Barthes recognises the sociolects of Marxism, Freudianism, structuralism and of the human sciences as acratic discourses that reassure those within and offend those outside. They achieve their purpose, he argues, not by invading or intimidating, not by means of a rhetoric or technical attack, but by 'obligatory rubrics', or a stereotyped form outside which members cannot speak or think and that 'aims at keeping the Other from speaking' (Barthes 1989: 123).

At first glance this seems an extreme view of the way that language constricts utterance, but at second glance we can see that the meaning of any utterance is dependent on the way meanings and inflections are shaped within the sociolect. Like history in general, linguistic meaning and effect are not stable either over time or across the use of language within any linguistic community. Meaning is a product of usage, and usage occurs within discursive contexts that develop a specificity of meaning. Barthes's critique of writing produces a critique of culture that challenges all claims to simply speak the truth. Of course, he offers no ground on which to establish critique – Marxism and Freudianism are no more than sociolects that challenge the doxa – and does not open the question of reflexivity; in what sociolect is *his* utterance formed? The Frankfurt critical theorists would no doubt regard his approach as too agnostic about value orientations to be acceptable, and they would reject it as they did Mannheim's sociology of knowledge (see, for example, Adorno 1979: 115 1983: 35–49; – see also Dant 1991). Like the Frankfurt critical theorists, Barthes sees the engagement with culture as a mode of critique that questions knowledge and opens up the possibility for change. Like Benjamin, his view of history is of a dynamic process of understanding. But unlike the Frankfurt theorists, Barthes does not clearly articulate an aim of liberation from alienation and oppression, and he is willing to spell out the limits of acratic discourses such as critical theory.

Baudrillard: The critique of repressive simulation

While Lefebvre (1991a) engaged in a lengthy debate with Marx and explored the limitations of Marxism in understanding everyday life, Jean Baudrillard cuts to the quick and turns the tools of Marxism back on itself. He mounts a critique in *The Mirror of Production* (1975) that argues that as Marx develops conceptual tools to critique the apparent universality of bourgeois thought (mode of production, dialectics, labour power), these concepts themselves begin to appear as universals. Such concepts take on a mythical importance as they cease to be devices for interpretation and are canonised into an inflexible scientific form of Marxism that Baudrillard calls 'repressive simulation' (1975: 48). It is the failure of the conceptual tools of Marx and Freud to explain social life both in primitive societies and in advanced capitalist societies that undermines their claims to universal applicability. Despite its dialectical method, the critique of capitalism begun by Marx has become trapped in a rationalism in which his theory has become descriptive rather than analytical, a product of the time that produced it, unable to describe other historical periods.

Baudrillard argues that Marx was engaged in an exchange of conceptual signs between political economy and historical materialism. Just as Marx argued that the materialist critique of religion was played out and unable to deal with different historical forms, Baudrillard argues that modern societies have undergone a cultural revolution with new commodities and new techniques of production that leave Marx's critique of political economy outmoded. A new mode of material *reproduction* has emerged that involves social relations of domination based on criteria of difference, that is, on a process of signification, on a code. These relations of domination to do with sex, race, age, language, species and culture are far more complex than private property (Baudrillard 1975: 142). Politics is as much to do with the exchange of signs in a code as of commodities, and the media are, for Baudrillard, a productive force (in his early work he criticises Marx for overlooking the impact of the railways and language on the mode of production – Baudrillard 1981: 164). Critique must shift to the political economy of the sign, to forms that are symbolic as well as material, and include the conceptual tools of political economy. There is a clear development of what is to count as 'knowledge' as Baudrillard displaces terms like 'production', 'commodity', 'value', and replaces them with terms that include 'seduction', 'sign', 'meaning' and 'fashion'. Sign exchange, which becomes the characteristic form of consumer societies, is always 'nothing but a gigantic *simulation model of meaning*' that is haunted by the symbolic (Baudrillard 1981: 161). But the relation is not open to systematic analysis of the link between signs and their referents in the real world because 'what is outside the sign, of what is other than the sign, *we can say nothing*, really, except that it is ambivalent, that is that it is impossible to distinguish respective separated terms and to positivize them as such' (Baudrillard 1981: 162). As Baudrillard puts meaning at the centre of the social relations of consumer societies he tells us that we have to approach it through strategies that at best 'allude' to the real – there is no system of meaning waiting behind signs to be decoded.

What frustrates and irritates many of Baudrillard's critics is the attention that he gives to the cultural content of consumer societies: its advertisements, films, material culture, shopping malls, and so on. He does not criticise their ideological role in sustaining capitalism or attack their hollowness and banality as the Frankfurt theorists do. These media exemplify the form of modern culture as sign exchange and have the effect of 'burying the social beneath a simulation of the social' (Baudrillard 1983: 67). The media – Hollywood films, magazine features, television soap operas – endlessly produce and reproduce human social relations so there appears to be an explosion of the social, but it is one which fails to represent real experience: 'Media, *all* media, information, *all* information, act in two directions: outwardly they produce more of the social, inwardly they neutralize social relations and the social itself' (Baudrillard 1983: 66). The explosion is only at the level of sign exchange, while the social, with all its divisions of interest, classes, political energy and conflict, 'implodes' into the mass. Baudrillard argues that there are no polarities within the mass, so there is no possibility of alienation of one from the other; all read the same news and watch the same programmes whatever their class or interests. The real lived relations may be complex and various but the mass who sit down to watch a football match on television are addressed as a unitary being that shares the same interest in their side winning: '... they react in their own way by reducing all articulate discourse to a single irrational and baseless dimension, where signs lose their meaning and peter out in fascination: the spectacular' (Baudrillard 1983: 10–11).

The effect of the massive increase in the circulation of information strengthens those institutions which we treat as characteristic of modern society (Baudrillard mentions social security, the city, work, medicine and insurance). For Baudrillard, it is the mass media – television and films, pop music and magazines – which are the model for the passive absorption of information flow. The media supplant traditional forms of entertainment that involved two-way communication (the laughs, cheers, heckles and applause of the audience in the theatre and concert hall) and prepare us to accept the one-way information flow in institutions. In place of human dialogic interaction, communication becomes one-way through, for example, a self-completed form which puts information into a system that responds without negotiation, judgement or discretion. The individual is left without the resources that would enable her or him to be 'socialised', to take a place as a member of society who interacts directly with other individuals.

Baudrillard argues that '[i]nformation devours its own contents; it devours communication and the social' (1983: 97), and gives two reasons. Firstly, the circulation of information in late modernity wears itself out in the 'staging of communication' as opportunities for exchanging meaning are reformed in order to be inserted within the mass media. So, for example, the 'phone-in' radio 'stages' a dialogic exchange that is illusory because the process is controlled by the media (the caller is screened and can always be cut off), and for those just listening it remains a one-way flow of information. Baudrillard's second reason for the implosion of meaning in the media is that the very volume of information produces a deadening effect. In early modernity, information energised people, gave them the power to act and to express their will. But people bombarded with information in late modernity become a fluid, mute mass, a lifeless object, a 'silent majority' with no voice. One way in which the mass can express its view is through the spread of the democratic process of polling votes to polling opinions. But opinion polls are published in the media and influence the very political processes they are meant to study (see p. 135). Politics has shifted from its traditional arena in the public space – the town square, the meeting hall, the conference room – and lost its responsive and negotiated quality as it has adapted to the media context. The soundbite of the modern politician, the speech tailored by a team of writers to resonate with the widest media audience, the concern with smiles and suits, party symbols and colours, all reduce communication to its capacity to elicit and manage a response.

Baudrillard does not see the silent majority as passive. The mass is a potent historical force that keeps consuming and wants to consume more of whatever is on offer: news, movies, science, technology, gadgets, fashion, medicine, social security. The action of the mass confounds any attempt to distinguish use values or needs by consuming the useless and finding a need for everything. It may not be reacting in the rational or political way that critical theory would normally recognise as 'praxis', but paradoxically there is action in inertia. Baudrillard identifies a strategic response in the mass's refusal to accept the terms of reason and rationality and its willingness to absorb the endless play of signs: 'Thus the strategic resistance is that of a refusal of meaning and a refusal of the word – or a hyperconformist simulation of the very mechanisms of the system, which is a form of refusal and of non-reception' (1983: 108). This is not quite the Great Refusal that Marcuse wrote of (see pp. 50–1); Baudrillard writes of the refusal of millions of people to show interest in current political events by watching a football match on television instead (1983: 12). But for Baudrillard those movements that work towards liberation, emancipation and the resurrection of the subject of history 'do not seem to see that they are acting in accordance with the system, whose imperative today is the overproduction and regeneration of meaning and speech' (1983: 109). An alternative to refusing the circulation of information is the strategy of terrorism. The meaninglessness of terrorist action matches that of the mass, which also represents nothing, but is very different from the inertia of the masses. As Baudrillard points out, the terrorist act of violence plays the media game by seeking to fascinate rather than persuade, to panic rather than reason; it is a form of black magic that is aimed at the white magic of the media and the masses (Baudrillard 1983: 50–1). We, the mass, are fascinated by the televised spectacle of human disasters, whether they are real (the events of 11 September 2001) or whether they are imaginary (the Hollywood films of terrorism, hijackings, burning buildings, alien invasions, aircraft in trouble, and so on). However fatal it is, terrorism is not a strategy that Baudrillard recommends, but he points out that we are vulnerable to the way it cuts through the stasis of consumer culture.

Baudrillard's critique of the flow of knowledge in consumer culture is persuasive about the tendency to disengage with the social and the growth in mediatisation (fewer people go to church or turn out to vote; more people go shopping, hire videos and go on holiday). But this does not mean that as individuals we feel powerless to exchange meaning. The terrorist attacks of 11 September 2001 stimulated a whole range of political responses, each attributing different meanings to the act. The people who made up the mass began to have stories to tell – novelists and writers rushed to express in print their responses; people usually without a voice in the media (survivors, rescuers, victims' families) all began to act as a conduit for feelings and meanings that were surfacing from the silent majority. Baudrillard assumes that the mass media are consumed passively and that each watching of the screen is equivalent. But while some may remain silent, others will shout, switch channels, turn off or talk with someone in the room. Conversations within families and between friends relate mediated events to direct experience, and it is in these contexts that meaning is exchanged and the imaginary is connected to the real. The development of technological rationality and information systems may have led to a profound shift towards quantitative data rather than complex knowledge, but it is in the context of human lives that information is given meaning and turned back into knowledge. Facts, the contents of databases and information, have to be reinserted into discourse, where they take on value and meaning.

Rather than the distinction between strategy and tactics that Michel de Certeau develops (see Chapter 4), Baudrillard plays with the tension between the silent majority's strategy of simply absorbing the flow of mediated sign exchange and the terrorist's strategy of violent and meaningless intervention. Baudrillard's writing does not refer to freedom, to the possibility of objective reason, or even to the possibility that the individual can escape from the mass and domination by the system, and in this sense he is not a critical theorist. And yet he keeps writing, developing a language of concepts and metaphors that return and are remodelled and reused. The only effect that the writing can have is critical – his readers' understanding of the world around them shifts in response to his remarks, which push against the existing social order as he persuades us to re-evaluate all that we take for granted.

In the end Baudrillard tells us that there is perhaps only one 'fatal strategy': theory (1990b: 181). Exactly what a fatal strategy is never becomes transparent, but it is to do with the relationship between knowledge and the world, between subject and object. To claim objective knowledge – what Horkheimer would call subjective or instrumental reason – is a banal strategy in the sense that it presumes that history is amenable to human interventions. What Baudrillard argues consistently throughout his work is that 'the object' has a strategy of its own and will not bend easily to the will of human action. The object is at once both the individual physical object but it is also all that which is beyond the human subject – 'the object is *what escapes the subject*' (Baudrillard 2000: 80). The fatal strategy is one, then, that accepts that history is determined at least in part by fate and tries to work with that fate. The banal strategy is banal because it lacks irony; it does not allow for something to be exactly the opposite of what it appears to be (see Baudrillard 2000: 74–80). The fatal strategy is one that dissembles, makes moves that are indirect, duplicitous:

> And when I speak of the object and its profound duplicity, I speak of all of us and our political and social order. The whole problem of voluntary servitude should be re-examined in this light, not to resolve it but to sound out the enigma: obedience, in effect, is a banal strategy, which doesn't need to be explained, for it secretly contains – all obedience secretly contains – a fatal disobedience to the symbolic order. (Baudrillard 1990b: 182)

The apparently banal strategy of simply succumbing to the mediated knowledge of consumer societies contains hidden within it the fatal strategy of refusal. The silence of the masses drains the volume of meaning that is exuded by the media in its frantic exchange of signs, and rather than confront it with a recovery of symbolic exchange, of a subjective and lived relation between representation and the real, it stays quiet. Baudrillard's critical theory seems to argue that we should make knowledge claims most sparingly and resist acting in ways that will sustain the system – even if this means not acting much at all.

Gorz and Touraine: Return of the subject of politics

Both André Gorz (1989) and Alain Touraine (1995) review a series of accounts of modernity and reject the pessimism of earlier critical theories that see individual freedom as subject to domination by a social 'apparatus'. And in contrast to Baudrillard, both offer a theory of how individuals can, and do, recognise their situation in the world and act in various strategic and collaborative ways to claim their freedom; informed action by individuals can have a political effect. Gorz argues that the 'economic reason' of advanced capitalism that sought economic efficiency through automation has left the worker as a mere minder of machines, no longer bodily at the centre of the process of production. Rejecting the traditional socialist position that links political power to occupational work, Gorz argues that it lies in those areas of non-work life in which the individual has some level of autonomy. The critical theorists, writing in the middle of the twentieth century, saw free time as vulnerable to domination through the cultural system, but Gorz sees it as a sphere of life in which individual interests, perhaps shared with other members of the family or community, can be pursued outside the sphere of economic rationality. The self-rewarding activities of 'making bread ... playing an instrument, gardening, campaigning, exchanging knowledge and so on' are those that will shape unalienated individual identity (Gorz 1989: 168).

In a more complex sociological analysis of what he calls 'hyper-modern society', Alain Touraine recovers themes from his earlier work (the 'programmed society' – see Chapter 3; the social actor; new social movements) and argues that the individual can once again take centre-stage in the arena of political action, or praxis (1995: 271–2). Against the Frankfurt theorists' account of a society dominated by instrumental reason as a mode of thought (he cites and disputes with Marcuse and Horkheimer), Touraine argues that there is merely a coherence in the way late modern society is administered. The programmed society, which includes the 'culture industries', is one in which 'managerial power consists in predicting and modifying opinions, attitudes and modes of behaviour, and in moulding personalities and cultures' (Touraine 1995: 244). Unlike the Frankfurt theorists, Touraine recognises that the refusal to accept this administration begins to constitute individuals as Subjects. The debates around an endless sequence of practical issues (health services, education, building new roads, care for elderly people, euthanasia, use of illegal drugs, and so on) demonstrate a resistance that affects a significant proportion of the population. Individuals express their disagreement with government and institutions more or less regardless of any identification with political parties. As pressure groups form around what are often, to begin with at least, local issues, a voice of dissent is articulated; spokespeople come forward, similar problems in different localities are linked, the media become involved and a new form of political debate takes off. While the aim may ultimately be to bring about a change of public policy, the social movement directs itself to public opinion rather than to simply lobbying representatives.

For Touraine, these are expressions of the 'new social movements' that he identified in the aftermath of the events of 1968. It was not, he argues, the workers' strike that captured the political imagination but the students who conjoined a series of cultural issues in a general resistance to oppression. The women's movement, for example, grew out of this process and became a political force independent of any politico-economic dispute. Social movements around ecology, anti-globalisation and industrial co-operatives all follow this model of resistance and dispute. They do not necessarily use the political means of representative democracy (the ballot box, the elected representative, the parliament and council chamber) but do use the public sphere (marches, rallies, sit-ins, demonstrations). Touraine argues that the political repertoire of social movements has shifted from the violent slogans and the aim of seizing power of the industrial era, to actions that are often accompanied by attention-grabbing 'performances' of music and costume. This is at least partly a result of the centrality of women, who focus on issues around the rights of individuals – rights to contraception and abortion, for example – but who also bring a different style of making political representation in the public arena. The media have become a public sphere that social movements address, and Touraine points to the centrality of television, which 'turns everything into entertainment'; but '[t]he appeal of the least demanding programmes, which reduce viewers to being consumers, is, fortunately, not great enough to overshadow the ability of the best to ask questions to force us to look at and become part of issues that are both close to home and far away' (1995: 246).

The media are not simply propaganda machines for a single point of view, and the audience is not an inert 'silent majority'. Touraine is optimistic that the public space is becoming more open as the power of traditional party politics is being replaced by social movements battling for public opinion. It is often seen as a weakness that new social movements are directed to a single issue, but Touraine sees as one of their strengths that they are not attempting to seize power and bring about structural change throughout society. The very fact that the movements are 'flexible and fragile' means that they respond to changes with speed and subtlety and are not trying to produce their own form of domination (Touraine 1995: 248). A further strength is the willingness of those people involved to identify with others who are far away but affected by restrictions on human rights, hunger or poverty. At the heart of these movements is an ethical consciousness that is concerned with the identity and dignity of people rather than with socio-political strategy.

In the discussion of lordship and bondsman in the *Phenomenology of Spirit*, Hegel says: 'The individual who has not risked his life may well be recognized as a *person*, but he has not attained to the truth of this recognition as an independent self-consciousness' (1977: 114). The idea that personhood is one thing but that taking an active and aware part in the political process is something else lies behind Touraine's notion of the 'Subject'. Against the historicism of Hegel and Marx, in which social forces always overwhelm the knowledge and action of the individual, he argues that individuals, in certain circumstances, can have historical agency. At a certain stage of late modernity people turn away from traditional politics but do not abandon all political interests that extend beyond their personal economic interests. It is consciousness of the importance of some issues beyond the person that leads to the emergence of the 'Subject', whom Touraine defines as 'a dissident, a resistance fighter' (1995: 264). This is a social subject who self-consciously acts and who takes a hand in the shaping of history, acting for her or his freedom and that of others. Even in the alliance of subjects in social movements, the

Subject does not give up her or his own rationality to accept a creed or dogma from a political party or a leader. As Tourraine puts it: *'The Subject is an individual's will to act and be recognized as an actor'* (1995: 207).

The Subject is, then, directed by reason but fuelled by human passion, a locus of energy directed towards freedom that engages in struggle with the established order of determination of life by institutions. Political action does not respond to abstract ideals but to the quality of ordinary individuals 'who respect, understand and love others, and who sacrifice their social success or intellectual prowess to those demands' (Touraine 1995: 212). It is when these values are threatened that the subject rebels against the use of what are seen as unjust powers, usually of the state, to control minds and bodies. The subject is a social movement founded on the ethics of human rights. It is the system of values that recognises the rights of individuals to be Subjects free of domination and control, which provides the foundation for the subject as a social movement. It is through love of, and solidarity with, the 'other-as-subject' that ethics emerges to replace the trade of interests that is politics; the affirmation of the freedom of the subject is a non-social principle with multiple social effects.

> Nothing must distract us from our central assertion: *the subject is a social movement.* It is constituted, not in self-consciousness, but in *the struggle against the anti-subject,* against the logics of apparatuses, especially when they become culture industries and *a fortiori,* when they have totalitarian goals. This is why the consciousness of the subject is so constantly associated with a critique of society. (Touraine 1995: 274)

What is rather disquieting about Touraine's concept of the Subject or the subject (the capital distinguishes a distinct being from a category) is that it is not difficult to see how it could serve many ends. The terrorist acting in the name of a subject people becomes a Subject who acts as a conscious individual in the name of freedom. Within the context of his life, his actions are rational; they are actions based on knowledge of the constraints on human rights. Terrorism is a form of praxis in this sense: a political action that is informed by knowledge. In contrast, the action of a state in defending its citizens against the violence of terrorism invokes a series of actors – security guards of various sorts – who are not subjects in Tourraine's sense because they are simply following orders rather than being motivated by a desire for freedom. Of course, the terrorist may also be simply 'following orders' from an ideologue or superior authority, as may the 'marshal' for a social movement's demonstration. All could be claimed to be 'subjects' or not according to how we interpret their conscious commitment to their actions – the notion of the Subject hangs on the link between an individual's consciousness and her or his actions. All exercise rationality either directly or via the collaborative work of a group to further the freedom of themselves and those around them.

The turn to the individual is a feature of the resistance in 'postmodern' theories of late modernity, and both Gorz and Touraine see in the individual the possibility for knowledge to be formed in consciousness and applied to action that can affect the society. Early critical theory also saw the reflective individual as the agent of history, where knowledge meets action: 'The fully developed individual is the consummation of a fully developed society. The emancipation of the individual is not an emancipation from society, but the deliverance of society from atomization, an atomization that may reach its peak in periods of collectivization and mass culture' (Horkheimer 1947c: 135). Like Touraine, Horkheimer identified the emergence of the free, conscious individual in the development of modernity in Greek civilisation. Both identified liberalism and free enterprise as producing an individual oriented to self-interest who became part of the mass disinterested in the wants of everyone else. Yet while Horkheimer blames the media and the system of production for submerging individuality in obedience despite its rhetoric of individualism (1947c: 158), Touraine sees the media as a public sphere in which the individual can participate and emerge as a Subject.

Conclusions

Without exploring the epistemological positions of the various critical theorists, we have found in this chapter a number of different perspectives on how knowledge about society is constituted in the culture and how it is connected to action. Marx argued that '[t]he question whether objective truth can be attributed to human thinking is not a question of theory but is a *practical* question' (1975: 422). This dilemma of how knowledge might engage with lived experience as praxis is a recurring theme in critical theory, which always argues that knowledge cannot be produced by a set, systematic method but must always be reflectively concerned with its basis. Knowledge cannot stand apart from action, and the problem is to reconnect it with lived experience. However, as Martin Jay suggests, for the Frankfurt School this led to a position in which '[t]heory ... was the only form of *praxis* still open to honest men' (1973: 280). While critical theorists like Lefebvre and Touraine hint at going further than this, the political impact of their writings is no more than a theoretical praxis that may stimulate others to action but does not incite or even promote it.

Summary

- *Horkheimer.* (1) Subjective reason is deductive, calculative and oriented to the individual and to means and ends. Objective reason is concerned with the social totality, values and interests beyond the individual: human destiny.

- (2) The application of the logic and methods of industrial production to social organisation as instrumental (subjective) reason has led to the domination of nature (including human nature) in modernity so that 'our world' is in fact the world of capital.
- (3) Critical theory adopts objective reason to question the consequences of 'useful' and 'applied' knowledge for the freedom of the totality of individual human beings. Critical theory promotes free, imaginative thought by individuals that shapes their actions to their own interests but with respect for humanity as a whole – a 'self-reproducing totality'.
- *Marcuse*: (1) One-dimensional society is characterized as a product of the 'performance principle', which ignores opposition, disagreement, negation and critique and follows the logic of technological rationality. The awareness of 'true' needs is distorted by mass adoption of the needs of the (capitalist) society as equivalent to individual needs.
- (2) Resistance to the apparatus requires critique and negation of the standardised, instrumental forms of reason – the Great Refusal.
- *Lefebvre*: A philosophical approach to the routine, regular 'recurrences' of everyday life through a 'maieutic' of question and answer can lead to a critique of the reproduction of human existence and the relation between the imaginary and the real. Such a critique can link thought and action into a praxis that will rehabilitate everyday life.
- *Benjamin*: A redemptive form of historicism that is not causal or cumulative can come to terms with the present through a continual reinterpretation of the past.
- *Barthes*: (1) History is viewed as the past being continually re-read in terms of the present.
- (2) 'Acratic' discourse speaks within the status quo with the constraint of a 'sociolect', while 'encratic' discourse mounts a critique by speaking against received wisdom from outside the 'doxa'.
- *Baudrillard*: In late modernity critique must shift from the mode of material production to the mode of cultural reproduction, the process of circulating signs that expands with the development of the media. The social 'implodes' into the mass as lived social relations give way to mediated relations to produce a 'silent majority' that in its hyperconformism refuses to negotiate or confirm the 'simulational model of meaning'.
- *Touraine*: Within the 'programmed', 'hyper-modern society' there are opportunities for resistance through pressure groups and 'new social movements' (e.g. the women's movement) which shift the ground of politics to the public space of communication and the media. This new politics depends on the emergence of a Subject who grasps her or his political situation and acts in accordance with it.

Further reading

The sociology of knowledge has fallen out of fashion – for the moment – though some of the themes discussed here are set within its context in my *Knowledge, Ideology and Discourse* (1991). More recently, many of the writers who have tried to grasp critically the impact of postmodernism have reviewed the impact of critical theories of knowledge. For example, Steven Seidman's *Contested Knowledge: Social Theory in the Postmodern Era* (1998) puts critical theory in a context from traditional to postmodern social theory, while Gerard Delanty's *Modernity and Postmodernity* (2000) situates critical theory in a more philosophical tradition from Kant through to Lyotard, Foucault and Derrida. Larry Ray's *Rethinking Critical Theory: Emancipation in the Age of Global Social Movements* (1993) explores the development of critical theory through Habermas's writing, while Craig Calhoun takes a much broader view of what is involved in *Critical Social Theory* (1995).

EIGHT

The Idea of a Critical Theory

The various versions of critical theory that have been discussed in this book describe the features of late modern society that restrict or constrain individuals from living in freedom. The aim of critical theory, however, is not cool description but a radical transformation of the social world of advanced capitalism that will bring freedom for all from such constraints. Critical theory does not aim to bring about social change through revolutionary means, through confronting the practical and economic arrangements with political opposition. In a major development from Marx's analysis of capitalism, critical theory recognises that culture is as much a determinant of the form of society as political economy. Any change in the form of society will ultimately have economic and political effect but it cannot be achieved without transformation of the culture of modernity. The form of society has a material dimension: the economic and practical arrangements for meeting needs, the laws governing social actions and the specific institutions that make practical arrangements. But the material form of society is given meaning, communicated and understood through the society's culture: the ideas, understanding, reasons, images, writing and other modes of expression that accompany the material dimension. Critical theory mounts its critique of society as culture, rather than as political system or economy.

Each version of critical theory challenges how history and society are currently understood within the entrenched patterns of power which shape modern society. The challenge amounts to critique because it argues that how the social world has been previously understood is part of the reason why it is the way it is. Rather than seeing history as transparent to knowledge, critical theories argue that a particular history produces a particular knowledge that obscures the constraints on lived experience that it engenders. The critique of the culture of modern society is intended to initiate change; it is not disinterested description or mere criticism of mistakes.

The phrase 'critical theory' is of course very loose. As Susan Buck-Morss explains in her tracing of the origins of Adorno's method in relation to the work of the 'Institute for Social Research' (the Frankfurt School), 'Critical Theory was never a fully articulated philosophy which members of the Institute applied in an identical fashion. It was far more a set of assumptions which they shared, and which distinguished their approach from bourgeois, or "traditional", theory' (1977: 65).

If Buck-Morss's detailed work on the connections between the work of the members of the Frankfurt School fails to identify 'critical theory' with 'substantive precision', my attempts to link the work of a diverse group of European theorists certainly does not claim that they are all operating with a shared and 'fully articulated philosophy'. What I have been trying to show throughout this book is that the disparate set of cultural critics I have referred to as 'critical theorists' take up similar themes, make use of similar theoretical resources, and, above all, set themselves against the established order that assumes the trajectory of modernity is towards progress. The theorists I have discussed are all dissenters, not about details or facts but about how the modern world is organised. They do not share a systematic method, an analytical device or a technical procedure for mounting their critique. But then one of the things that they have in common is a fundamental distrust of such methods – which are to be found in considerable number in the humanities and social sciences. I have chosen to refer to writers whose work exemplifies a continuity in the approach of critical theorists from two theoretical traditions – the Germanic and the Gallic – that spans the latter half of the twentieth century. Though there are divergences on matters of detail, these authors offer a largely consistent perspective, whereas others whose work I decided not to refer to, and who might also be considered critical theorists, would have taken me too far into other areas (see Chapter 1 for a discussion of those writers who might have been included in this project).

The writing that I have claimed as 'critical theory' has argued that the form of modern society is repressive and constricting in ways that it need not be. Rather than mounting a critique of the political structures, or the economic arrangements of modern societies, this strand of critical theory has directed its attention to their culture. Culture is treated not simply as the artistic and communicative stuff of society but as the way that ordinary lives are lived: at work, at leisure, through sexuality, as consumers, as minds that are curious and seek to be entertained, as social subjects that are knowing and have an interest in the way society is organised. It is these themes that I have attempted to draw out in the previous chapters by looking at the work of a necessarily restricted group of writers. My hope is that the impetus of this critical approach to society will not be lost for a new generation, for whom there are many new problems and new theories to consider. For the current generation, critical theory may seem rather parochial with its focus on 'modernity' in a way that overlooks the complexity of global social, economic and cultural relations; famine, ecology, war, disease, slavery and physical repression seem far more urgent. But in the western nation states, characterised as they are by democratic political systems, rising standards of living, improved working conditions and increasing longevity, the form of modern society still constrains the freedom of individuals to realise their full potential. The concerns and criticisms of the critical theorists, although in some cases voiced half a century ago, are still pertinent today. Indeed it is a quality of the generality of their critical theorising that it dates very slowly and will only disappear as irrelevant when the relationship between the organisation of society and the lived experience of culture has changed radically.

Social change

Marx transformed how society might be understood by treating its material form, the economic relationships that sustain its members, as historical, as a product of the lives of people and not determined by a force outside of history such as 'nature' or 'God'. Critical theory responds to the resistance of those economic relationships to be transformed through the exertion of political will, recognising that the ideas and beliefs of societies are inextricably entwined with the material means of existence and that history cannot be steered by any single mechanism. Revolutions, whether economic, political or both, have failed to redirect the course of history to free the people of a society from the social consequences of its economic strategy. The Frankfurt critical theorists were responding to the failure of socialist revolution in Russia to lead to such a solution and to the dire consequences of a direct political transformation initiated by the Nazis. The French critical theorists responded to the continuing failure of socialist movements in post-war Europe to achieve transformation by more gradual political means through a series of political moves that culminated in the events of 1968.

The idea of freedom that motivates critical theory is not freedom from physical bondage or violent repression but freedom for individuals to live their lives to the full: freedom from alienation. Freud provides a critical account the inner life of the individual being that recognises mind and body as indivisible components of subjective experience. His theory of the inner life of human beings in modernity is not accepted with the same degree of confidence as Marx's analysis of the mode of production, but his thinking dispels the notion of a mystical soul that lives beyond bodily experience. Like Marx, Freud shows how human lives can be understood without reference to the mystery of nature or religion. Freedom cannot be left to an afterlife, and the psychic experience of all must be free if freedom is to be complete. Freud's own account of how modern civilisation constrains the individual's inner life pre-figures, if it does not inspire, much that critical theory argues.

The critical theorists reject social transformation that depends on the use of military force and an hierarchical, authoritarian structure, but they also reject social democratic responses that appease the forces of capitalism and so maintain the form of an unequal society. Revolution spills blood for little long-term gain, while working within the channels of social democracy achieves some gains but leaves intact basic structures of domination. So the strategy of critical theory is to identify culture as both the sphere in which modern society takes on its form and the means by which it can be changed. In political terms, critical theory is a failure because it leaves no agenda for action, no blueprint to work towards, no manifesto around which to organise struggle. To bring about social change requires liberating people from within; it may be the structures of social relations that oppress, but liberation is a felt transformation not a structural change. Social transformation will come about only by changing the way that our understanding of how societies work contributes to the working of those societies.

So how does critical theory propose to bring about change? Its aim is the freedom of all people in modernity: rather than the interests of some dominating the rest, the interests of all should be identified and accepted. Contemporary politics in the western democracies has made some progress in recognising the interests of all individuals within a nation state as in principle equivalent regardless of class, sex, ethnicity, adult age and ability. As these social divisions are challenged, attention is turned to the human rights of those in other countries, to the rights of children and even animals, so that what counts as 'society' and 'culture' is extended. Perhaps most importantly, the impracticality of drawing boundaries around the nation state as 'society' has brought about the recognition of 'global' cultural and social forms. The critical theory discussed in this book appears rather outdated in its narrow view of what counts as society and culture, and it offers no clear account of what a society would be like that is 'liberated', in which individuals are 'free'. But it does outline the structures of domination and how they have developed in modernity, especially during the twentieth century. Without articulating what 'freedom' would look like, critical theory nonetheless describes what 'unfreedom' is in advanced capitalist societies.

From the writings of Karl Marx, especially through his debate with Hegel on the nature of philosophy, it is clear that domination is not achieved by means of repressive force alone. Domination under advanced capitalism is more than ever brought about by ideological means; it is through a culture that presents the interests of the few as the interests of all that freedom is curtailed. Unfreedom is more than lack of food, shelter and the minimal material requirements of human existence – though the lack of such basics is a continual reminder of the extent of inequality and unfreedom. Unfreedom is more than the absence of the recognition of basic rights of humans as equal – though the failure to recognise human rights is also a sharp reminder of the extent of unfreedom. Critical theory identifies unfreedom as also to do with the capacity to think and act freely. Unfreedom is the way that instrumental reason has taken on the potency of myth, that sexuality is defined and specified, that work is distinguished from non-work, that art is transformed into entertainment, that everyday life is shaped and knowledge is separated from action.

The idea of a critical theory

Critical theory addresses the particular relations between the individual and society, and between thought and action, that are characteristic of modern societies. In these societies unfreedom is the consequence of the domination of culture by a mode of thinking – 'instrumental reason', 'technological rationality' – that provides the ideational means by which society is organised and administered. Different critical theories identify the distinctive form of these societies using different terms: the 'industrial apparatus', the social 'system', the 'programmed society', the 'dual society', the 'post-industrial society', the 'society of bureaucratically controlled consumption', the 'consumer society'. What is common in these various versions of critique is the challenge to the received ideas that underlie the structural and institutional components of modernity. But rather than confronting directly the material means of oppression with direct material resistance, critical theory identifies a mode of resistance that is itself cultural. Its critique is not only aimed at culture, it is also itself a contribution to culture.

Critical theory adopts a mode of engagement that can be described as praxis – knowledge as action. It calls for active thought that continually challenges the existing state of affairs in society. The praxis of critical theory is in its provocation to thought – thinking differently about the social world will lead to change in the way society is lived. To be sure, sexuality, work, art, entertainment, consumption, and so on, have material dimensions in which bodies act on things, including other bodies. But these forms of social action are entwined with the consciousness that accompanies them such that the material experience can never be divorced from the understanding of that experience. Critical theory does not offer a programme of change in material experience – and in this sense is not utopian – but it does offer a mode of understanding that can transform how material experience in modernity is understood.

Now, it must be admitted that the way I have presented critical theory in this book is not itself critical; I have attempted merely to describe critical theory and the way that it presents various aspects of society and culture. This has been a discussion *about* critical theory and neither an exemplification of nor a critique of it.[1] But other writers have subjected the very idea of critical theory to rather more critical attention, and Raymond Geuss, in his *The Idea of a Critical Theory* (1981), has used the approach of analytical philosophy to explore just what it might entail. Geuss has very little to say *about* critical theory but focuses on what its constituents must be if it can claim to be a critical theory rather than a scientific social theory. His debate is principally with critical theory as exemplified in the work of Jürgen Habermas, but much of what he has to say is of direct relevance to the form of critical theory as I have discussed it. His focus is on critical theory as a critique of ideology; it makes claims to knowledge about the real interests of members of modern societies that they are unable to recognise because they accept the prevailing ideology which obscures what their interests are: 'Critical theories aim at emancipation and enlightenment, at making agents aware of hidden coercion, thereby freeing them from that coercion and putting them in a position to determine where their true interests lie' (Geuss 1981: 55). In contrast to scientific theories, which rely on empirical verification to establish objective knowledge with which to manipulate the external world, critical theories claim to be reflective and recognise their own context of origin within society as a form of knowledge. Critical theory is not then objective in the sense of making knowledge claims independently from the culture in which they arise, but recognises its role within that culture – this is what I have referred to as praxis which has the goals of emancipation and enlightenment. As Geuss presents it, critical theory recognises that the members of modern societies are deluded, they suffer from a 'false consciousness', they live within an ideology that is false and which constrains them from living freely according to their own interests. Critical theory's emancipatory role is to enlighten the members of a society to their true interests and the falseness of the ideological world-picture that they routinely accept ('The agents in a society impose coercive institutions on themselves by participating in them, accepting them without protest, etc.' – Geuss 1981: 60). And it is through stimulating 'self-reflection' that critical theory can assist society's members towards realising their own emancipation by showing them that their world-picture is false and that they have only accepted it under conditions of coercion.

Geuss's analytical philosophical method challenges the logical steps that must be made if a theory is able to claim to be critical, and he questions the implications of each step. He argues, for example, that if critical theory is to be successful in stimulating self-reflection, it must appeal to the 'epistemic principles' of the members of the society – that is, it must accord with already accepted standards of reason within that society. In other words, critical theory does not need to establish new epistemic principles, a new set of rules as to what will count as true knowledge. And we have seen that what the critical theorists do is precisely to recover a traditional form of rationality ('objective reason') that has been displaced by the ideological domination of a particular form of rationality ('subjective reason') that in modern societies appears to address everyone's needs as 'instrumental rationality'. By arguing that reason must take into account value orientations of the whole society, of the 'totality', and not take as its model the individual's sense of her or his own immediate interests, critical theory challenges the appropriateness of a certain form of reason (that which is characterised in scientific thought) for addressing cultural and political matters for a society as a whole. Its aim is to provoke and stimulate a form of reason that is not alien but which is so often presented as inadequate ('unscientific') in modern societies. Systematicity and precision have to be sacrificed in order that cultural and political knowledge addresses the variable and historically emergent values of the society as a whole but which ultimately affect each individual.[2]

Geuss points out the difficulties and limitations in a critical theory: it depends on claiming that members of society are deluded by modern capitalist society's ideology about their true interests and yet, using only the cognitive tools available within that ideology, argues that they can be persuaded to think differently. I have chosen in this book not to discuss ideology directly (though see Dant 1991), but what I have treated as 'culture' is very much the same as what Geuss means by 'ideology'. Critical theory somehow has to identify the delusions and unpack the reasons used to support them but cannot transcend the ideological environment in which all members of the society have to think. The crucial motivation for members of a society to accept that critical theory has something to say to them is a recognition that they are unhappy, frustrated, dissatisfied and alienated. And yet as advanced capitalism develops and is able to meet increasing needs for increasing numbers of people it becomes even more difficult to get society's members to recognise the unconscious desires the critical theory attributes to them and to freely recognise that they are unhappy and frustrated. Geuss recognises that traditional critical theory attempts to expose unconscious desires by describing the 'good life' that can be 'found expressed in certain works of art, and in religious and metaphysical doctrines, or can be derived from particular aesthetic or religious experiences' (1981: 82). This is why critical theory is not concerned simply with the material arrangements in modern societies but addresses the culture of those societies as being the sphere in which the majority of aspirations to a good life are unfulfilled.

It could be argued that critical theory has failed in that it has not brought about a general enlightenment and the emancipation of all the members of advanced industrial societies. Instrumental reason continues to dominate those societies and its effects continue to restrict the lives of individuals. Nonetheless, we can see critical theory as providing a reasoned and historically based support for thinking and acting differently than would appear to be normative for the members of modern societies. Acting differently does not necessarily mean overt political action but can simply mean resisting or refusing to accept, and providing reasons and arguments for such a resistance based on a sense of the needs of the social totality – it is precisely this style of resistance that has emerged in the ecology and anti-globalisation movements. As political action, these new social movements often become polarised on particular situations and the particular ways in which modern society acts within the logic of instrumental reason and against the values of the social totality. Activists who attempt to stop the trade in nuclear fuels for reprocessing or prevent the introduction of genetically modified crops are often focused on the specific activities of multi-national corporations. But behind their practical political action we can see a form of reason that has been informed by critical theory and which can be shared by many more people who are less confident about the nature of direct action. Their refusal to take for granted a system of thinking and a set of values that are characteristic of the culture of capitalism shows the effect of a critique that challenges the basis of established norms of thinking.

Critical theory offers a series of judgements that can be summarised as follows:

- The lives of individual human beings in modern societies are unnecessarily dominated, constrained and restricted, in terms of both what they can do and what they can think, by the cultural forms through which they must live their lives together as a society.
- These restrictions are not the result of natural or supernatural forces but the product of human history.
- These restrictions may have their origins in the patterns of economic arrangements for collectively meeting material needs that Marx describes as 'capitalism', but they are sustained, refined and experienced at the level of culture – that is, as ideas, signs, images, beliefs, knowledge, language, attitudes, protocols, systems, programmes, rules, injunctions, and so on.
- These restrictions, which constitute a degree of 'unfreedom', could be undone to liberate individual lives without creating chaos or increasing the restrictions on the lives of other people.
- The way in which these restrictions can best be undone is through their collective recognition and rejection through cultural means; through refusal to accept what is taken for granted, resisting that which is not desired, criticising and negating received ideas and values that are presented as universal.
- The theoretical strategy of 'critique' exposes the cultural form of constraints and restrictions in such a way as can contribute to their recognition and rejection.

Critical theory suggests a series of moves – to refuse, to resist, to reject, to disagree, to criticise, to imagine and to think otherwise – by which the critique of culture may bring about change in society. Critical theory invites its readers to share its judgements and aspire to a 'good life' – a different way of living in and experiencing the modern world that challenges those who treat the form of life in modernity as fundamentally given and unchangeable in its trajectory. Through questioning the foundations of knowledge we can recognise that rather than accepting the domination of a single form of calculative rationality that produces reliable knowledge about purely material processes (science), a different mode of rationality must be applied when thinking about the problems of human society. Through self-reflection we can interrogate how our needs and desires are related to those of the rest of the society of the modern world. Through imagination we can entertain values other than those presented as universal regardless of their undesired consequences. Through a critical praxis we can resist the domination of instrumental reason and explore other possible ways of living. We can think differently and do different critical theory can help us achieve both. We still need critical theory.

Further reading

I have focused my attention on the work of a particular group of critical theorists that is readily available in English translation; the references and bibliography indicate the sources I have used. Here I will indicate their key texts that might provide a good starting point and mention a few of the secondary sources that help make accessible what is often elliptical and unsystematic writing.

Theodor Adorno and Max Horkheimer's *Dialectic of Enlightenment* (1979) remains a central text that exemplifies critical theory. The collection of Adorno's essays on *The Culture Industry* (1991) provides a more accessible and substantive introduction to his work. Herbert Marcuse's *One-Dimensional Man* (1972b) is still a provocative and persuasive indictment of the cultural system that has spread out from post-war America to encircle the globe. Amongst the many secondary sources on the Frankfurt theorists, David Held's *Introduction to Critical Theory* (1980) and Martin Jay's *The Dialectical Imagination* (1973) continue to provide excellent accounts of the links between the various writers and their thinking. Rolf Wiggershaus's *The Frankfurt School* (1994) also provides a clear historical, biographical and intellectual background. Walter Benjamin's work has, since the 1970s, attracted increasing interest with translations and secondary texts. An early collection of translated essays, *Illuminations* (1973c), provides a good introduction and Graeme Gilloch's *Walter Benjamin: Critical Constellations* (2002) gives the much broader context of his work as a whole.

Henri Lefebvre too seems to be enjoying a revival of interest but one of the earliest of his works to be translated, *Everyday Life in the Modern World* (1971), is still one of the most accessible and imaginative. The first volume of Michel de Certeau's *Practice of Everyday Life* (1984) is well known and read, but the second volume, with its empirically grounded close study of ordinary life in France, is less well known (Certeau et al., 1998). Together they make a powerful case for a critique of culture that engages directly with lived experience. An unusual book that brings together a series of critical perspectives on everyday life is Michael E. Gardiner's *Critiques of Everyday Life* (2000).

Like many of the critical theorists, Barthes wrote in fragments, essays and short books; his *Mythologies* (1993a), although almost half a century old, continues to be a fascinating account of modern culture. Michael Moriarty's *Roland Barthes* (1992) provides a helpful overview and critical discussion. Jean Baudrillard's *The Consumer Society* (1998) is a stimulating and uncharacteristically direct critique of modern society. His later work often borders on the literary, but a recent collection of lectures, *The Vital Illusion* (2000), powerfully sums up his views on where 'progress' might be leading us. Amongst a large and growing secondary literature on Baudrillard, Mike Gane's *Baudrillard's Bestiary* (1991) is still helpful, readable and yet provocative.

Alain Touraine's *Critique of Modernity* (1995) is quite hard-going as it summarises history and ideas but in the polemical final sections inspires new ways of thinking politically. In a different vein but with even more optimism, Michael Hardt and Antonio Negri's *Empire* (2000) is punchy in bringing a critical approach in line with other modern theories.

Notes

1 Although I have hinted in a number of places where critical theory seems to depend on claims that are rather weak, such as in the discussion of needs in consumer societies in Chapter 4.

2 Geuss goes on to point out that Habermas develops a 'transcendental argument' for universal standards of distinguishing true and false knowledge that are embedded in the very form of language in our speech community (1981: 65–8). For Habermas, the traditional form of critical theory was inadequate because it depended on standards of knowledge and reason that are historically emergent and therefore could not be applied to all societies under all conditions. As Geuss spells out, the transcendental argument shifts the ground for a critical theory, and this is the reason why I have not tried to represent Habermas's work as within the critical theory tradition I have described in this book.

Bibliography

Adorno, Theodor W. (1973 [1966]) *Negative Dialectics*, London: Routledge.

Adorno, Theodor W. (1974 [1951]) *Minima Moralia*, London: Verso.

Adorno, Theodor W. (1979 [1969]) 'On the Logic of the Social Sciences', in T. Adorno, H. Albert, R. Dahrendorf, J. Habermas, H. Pilot and K. Popper, *The Positivist Dispute in German Sociology*, London: Heinemann.

Adorno, Theodor W. (1983 [1955]) *Prisms*, Cambridge, MA: MIT Press.

Adorno, Theodor W. (with Simpson, George) (1990[1941]) 'On Popular Music', in S. Frith and A. Goodwin (eds) *On Record: Rock, Pop and the Written Word*, London: Routledge.

Adorno, Theodor W. (1991) *The Culture Industry: Selected Essays on Mass Culture*, London: Routledge.

Adorno, Theodor W. (1997 [1970]) *Aesthetic Theory*, London: Athlone Press.

Adorno, Theodor W. (1998 [1963, 1969]) *Critical Models: Interventions and Catchwords*, New York: Columbia University Press.

Adorno, Theodor W. (2000 [1993]) *Introduction to Sociology*, Cambridge: Polity.

Adorno, Theodor W. and Horkheimer, Max (1979 [1944]) *Dialectic of Enlightenment*, London: Routledge.

Arendt, Hannah (1958) *The Human Condition*, Chicago: University of Chicago Press.

Barrett, Michèle (1988) *Women's Oppression Today: The Marxist/Feminist Encounter*, London: Verso.

Barthes, Roland (1968 [1953]) *Writing Degree Zero*, New York: Hill and Wang.

Barthes, Roland (1970) 'Historical Discourse', in M. Lane (ed.) *Structuralism: A Reader*, London: Jonathan Cape.

Barthes, Roland (1973 [1964]) *Elements of Semiology*, New York: Hill and Wang.

Barthes, Roland (1976 [1971]) *Sade, Fourier and Loyola*, New York: Hill and Wang.

Barthes, Roland (1977a [1961]) 'The Photographic Message', in *Image–Music–Text*, ed. Stephen Heath, Glasgow: Fontana.

Barthes, Roland (1977b [1964]) 'Rhetoric of the Image', in *Image–Music–Text*, ed. Stephen Heath, Glasgow: Fontana.

Barthes, Roland (1979a) *The Eiffel Tower and Other Mythologies*, New York: Hill and Wang.

Barthes, Roland (1979b [1977]) *A Lover's Discourse*, London: Cape.

Barthes, Roland (1982 [1970]) *Empire of Signs*, New York: Hill and Wang.

Barthes, Roland (1987 [1954]) *Michelet*, Berkeley: University of California Press.

Barthes, Roland (1988 [1967]) 'Semiology and Urbanism', in *The Semiotic Challenge*, Oxford: Blackwell.

Barthes, Roland (1989 [1973]) 'The Divison of Languages', in *The Rustle of Language*, Berkeley: University of California Press.

Barthes, Roland (1990 [1967]) *The Fashion System*, Berkeley: University of California Press.

Barthes, Roland (1991 [1982]) *The Responsibility of Forms*, Berkeley: University of California Press.

Barthes, Roland (1992 [1987]) *Incidents*, Berkeley: University of California Press.

Barthes Roland (1993a [1957]) *Mythologies*, London: Vintage Books.

Barthes, Roland (1993b [1980]) *Camera Lucida*, London: Vintage Books.

Barthes, Roland (1993c [1963]) 'Mythologies de l'automobile', *Oeuvres Complètes Vol. 1: 1942–1965*, Paris: Éditions du Seuil.

Baudrillard, J. (1975 [1973]) *The Mirror of Production*, St Louis, MO: Telos.

Baudrillard, J. (1980) 'The Implosion of Meaning in the Media and the Implosion of the Social in the Masses', in K. Woodward (ed.) *The Myths of Information: Technology and the Postindustrial Culture*, London: Routledge and Kegan Paul.

Baudrillard, Jean (1981 [1972]) *For a Critique of the Political Economy of the Sign*, St. Louis: Telos.

Baudrillard, Jean (1983 [1978]) *In the Shadow of the Silent Majorities*, New York: Semiotext(e).

Baudrillard, Jean (1987) *The Evil Demon of Images*, Sydney: Power Institute of Fine Arts.

Baudrillard, Jean (1990a [1979]) *Seduction*, Houndmills, Basingstoke: Macmillan.

Baudrillard, Jean (1990b [1983]) *Fatal Strategies*, London: Pluto Press/New York: Semiotext(e).

Baudrillard, Jean (1993a [1976]) *Symbolic Exchange and Death*, London: Sage.

Baudrillard, Jean (1993b [1990]) *Transparency of Evil*, London: Verso.

Baudrillard, Jean (1994a [1981]) *Simulacra and Simulation*, Ann Arbor, MI: University of Michigan Press.

Baudrillard, Jean (1994b [1992]) *The Illusion of the End*, Stanford, CA: Stanford University Press.

Baudrillard, Jean (1996a [1968]) *The System of Objects*, London: Verso.

Baudrillard, Jean (1996b [1995]) *The Perfect Crime*, London: Verso.

Baudrillard, Jean (1997) *Art and Artefact*, London: Sage.

Baudrillard, Jean (1998 [1970]) *The Consumer Society*, London: Sage.

Baudrillard, Jean (2000) *The Vital Illusion*, New York: Columbia University Press.

Benhabib, Seyla and Cornell, Drucilla (eds) (1987) *Feminism as Critique: Essays on the Politics of Gender in Late Capitalist Societies*, Cambridge: Polity.

Benjamin, W. (1983) *Understanding Brecht*, London: Verso.

Benjamin, W. (1985a [1931]) 'A Small History of Photography', in *One-Way Street and Other Writings*, London: Verso.

Benjamin, W. (1985b [1931]) 'Theological-Political Fragment', in *One-Way Street and Other Writings*, London: Verso.

Benjamin, W. (1973c [1939]) 'On Some Motifs in Baudelaire', in *Illuminations*, London: Fontana.

Benjamin, W. (1999 [1982]) *The Arcades Project*, Cambridge, MA: Harvard University Press.

Benjamin, Walter (1973a [1940]) 'Theses on the Philosophy of History', in *Illuminations*, London: Fontana.

Benjamin, Walter (1973b [1936]) 'The Work of Art in the Age of Mechanical Reproduction' in *Illuminations*, London: Fontana.

Benjamin, Walter (1973c) *Illuminations*, London: Fontana.

Berger, Peter & Luckmann, Thomas (1966) *The Social Construction of Reality*, Harmondsworth: Penguin Books.

Braudel, F. (1992 [1979]) *The Structures of Everyday Life: The Limits of the Possible*, Berkeley and Los Angeles: University of California Press.

Braverman, Harry (1974) *Labor and Monopoly Capital: The Degradation of Work in the Twentieth Century*, New York and London: Monthly Review Press.

Buck-Morss, Susan (1977) *The Origin of Negative Dialectics: Theodor Adorno, Walter Benjamin and the Frankfurt Institute*, Hassocks: Harvester.

Bulfinch, Thomas (1981) *Myths of Greece and Rome*, London: Penguin.

Calhoun, Craig (1995) *Critical Social Theory*, Oxford: Blackwell.

Certeau, Michel de (1984 [1980]) *The Practice of Everyday Life*, Berkeley: University of California Press.

Certeau, Michel de, Giard, Luce and Mayol, Pierre (1998 [1980]) *The Practice of Everday Life, Volume 2: Living and Cooking*, Minneapolis: University of Minnesota Press.

Chaney, David (2002) *Cultural Change and Everyday Life*, London: Palgrave.

Dant, Tim (1991) *Knowledge, Ideology and Discourse: A Sociological Perspective*, London: Routledge.

Dant, Tim (2000) 'Driving Identities', paper presented to 'Mobilizing Forces: Social and Cultural Aspects of Automobility', Gothenburg, Sweden.

Dant, Tim and Gilloch, Graeme (2002) 'Pictures of the Past: Benjamin and Barthes on Photography', *European Journal of Cultural Studies*, Vol. 5 (1): 5–23.

de Sade, Marquis (1991 [1797]) *Juliette*, London: Arrow.

Delanty, Gerard (2000) *Modernity and Postmodernity*, London: Sage.

Delphy, Christine (1984) *Close to Home: A Materialist Analysis of Women's Oppression*, London: Hutchinson.

Dews, Peter (1989) 'Adorno, Poststructuralism and the Critique of Identity', in A. Benjamin (ed.) *The Problems of Modernity*, London: Routledge.

Douglas, Jack (1971) 'Understanding Everyday Life', in J. Douglas (ed.) *Understanding Everyday Life: Toward the Reconstruction of Everyday Knowledge*, London: Routledge and Kegan Paul.

Ferguson, Harvey (1996) *The Lure of Dreams: Sigmund Freud and the Construction of Modernity*, London: Routledge.

Foucault, Michel (1978 [1976]) *The History of Sexuality, Volume 1: An Introduction*, London: Allen Lane.

Foucault, Michel (1980) *Power/Knowledge: Selected Interviews and Other Writings 1972–1977*, ed. Colin Gordon, Brighton: Harvester.

Freud, Sigmund (1928) *The Future of an Illusion*, London: Hogarth Press.

Freud, Sigmund (1962 [1930]) *Civilization and its Discontents*, New York: Norton & Co.

Freud, Sigmund (1976 [1900]) *The Interpretation of Dreams*, Harmondsworth: Pelican.

Freud, Sigmund (1977) 'Three Essays on Sexuality', in *On Sexuality*, Harmondsworth: Pelican.

Freud, Sigmund (1991 [1920]) 'Beyond the Pleasure Principle', in *Metapsychology*, Harmondsworth: Penguin.

Frisby, David and Featherstone, Mike (eds) (1997) *Simmel on Culture*, London: Sage.

Fromm, Erich (1963 [1956]) *The Sane Society*, London: Routledge and Kegan Paul.

Galbraith, J.K. (1962 [1958]) *The Affluent Society*, Harmondsworth: Penguin.

Gane, Mike (1991) *Baudrillard's Bestiary: Baudrillard and Culture*, London: Routledge.

Gardiner, M.E. (2000) *Critiques of Everyday Life*, London: Routledge.

Geuss, Raymond (1981) *The Idea of a Critical Theory: Habermas and the Frankfurt School*, Cambridge: Cambridge University Press.

Giddens, Anthony (1976) *New Rules of Sociological Method: A Positive Critique of Interpretive Sociologies*, London: Hutchinson.

Gilloch, Graeme (1996) *Myth and Metropolis*, Cambridge: Polity.

Gilloch, Graeme (2002) *Walter Benjamin: Critical Constellations*, Cambridge: Polity.

Goffman, Erving (1971 [1959]) *Presentation of Self in Everyday Life*, Harmondsworth: Pelican.

Gorz, André (1989 [1988]) *Critique of Economic Reason*, London: Verso.

Gorz, André (1997 [1980]) *Farewell to the Working Class*, London: Pluto Press.

Gouldner, Alvin (1976) *The Dialectic of Ideology and Technology: The Origins, Grammar and Future of Ideology*, London: Macmillan.

Gouldner, Alvin (1980) *Two Marxisms: Contradictions and Anomalies in the Development of Theory*, London: Macmillan.

Graves, Robert (1996 [1955]) *The Greek Myths*, London: Folio Society.

Grint, Keith (1998) *The Sociology of Work: An Introduction*, Cambridge: Polity.

Habermas, Jürgen (1984 [1981]) *The Theory of Communicative Action, Volume 1: Reason and the Rationalization of Society*, Boston: Beacon Press.

Habermas, Jürgen (1987 [1981]) *The Theory of Communicative Action, Volume 2: Lifeworld and System: A Critique of Functionalist Reason*, Cambridge: Polity.

Hardt, Michael and Negri, Antonio (2000) *Empire*, Cambridge, MA: Harvard University Press.

Hawkes, Gail (1996) *A Sociology of Sex and Sexualities*, Buckingham: Open University Press.

Hegel, Georg W.F. (1977 [1807]) *Phenomenology of Spirit*, Oxford: Oxford University Press.

Held, David (1980) *Introduction to Critical Theory*, London: Hutchinson.

Heller, A. (1984 [1970]) *Everyday Life*, London: Routledge and Kegan Paul.

Hohendahl, Peter Uwe (1995) *Prismatic Thought: Theodor W. Adorno*, Lincoln and London: University of Nebraska Press.

Holland, Janet and Adkins, Lisa (eds) (1996) *Sex, Sensibility and the Gendered Body*, London: Macmillan.

Horkheimer, Max (1947a) 'Means and Ends', in *Eclipse of Reason*, New York: Oxford University Press.

Horkheimer, Max (1947b) 'The Revolt of Nature', in *Eclipse of Reason*, New York: Oxford University Press.

Horkheimer, Max (1947c) 'Rise and Decline of the Individual', in *Eclipse of Reason*, New York: Oxford University Press.

Horkheimer, Max (1972 [1937]) 'Traditional and Critical Theory', in *Critical Theory: Selected Essays*, New York: Herder and Herder.

Horkheimer, Max (1974a [1957]) 'The Concept of Man', in *Critique of Instrumental Reason*, New York: The Seabury Press.

Horkheimer, Max (1974b [1966]) 'The Future of Marriage', in *Critique of Instrumental Reason*, New York: The Seabury Press.

Horkheimer, Max (1974c [1967]) 'The Soul', in *Critique of Instrumental Reason*, New York: The Seabury Press.

Jameson, Fredric (1990) *Late Marxism: Adorno, or, The Persistence of the Dialectic*, London: Verso.

Jameson, Fredric (1991) *Postmodernism, or, The Cultural Logic of Late Capitalism*, London: Verso.

Jameson, Fredric (1998) *The Cultural Turn: Selected Writings on the Postmodern, 1983–1998*, London: Verso.

Jay, Martin (1973) *The Dialectical Imagination: A History of the Frankfurt School and the Institute of Social Research, 1923–1950*, Berkeley: University of California Press.

Jay, Martin (1996) 'Preface to the 1996 Edition' of *The Dialectical Imagination*, Berkeley: University of California Press.

Kierkegaard, Soren (1999 [1843]) *Diary of a Seducer*, London: Pushkin Press.

Landry, Donna and MacLean, Gerald (1993) *Materialist Feminisms*, Oxford: Blackwell.

Latour, Bruno (1993) *We Have Never Been Modern*, London: Prentice Hall.

Lazzarato, Maurizio (1996) 'Immaterial Labor', in P. Virno and M. Hardt (eds) *Radical Throught in Italy: A Potential Politics*, Minneapolis: University of Minnesota Press.

Lefebvre, Henri (1968 [1966]) *The Sociology of Marx*, Harmondsworth: Penguin Books.

Lefebvre, Henri (1971 [1968]) *Everyday Life in the Modern World*, London: Allen Lane, The Penguin Press.

Lefebvre, Henri (1991a [1947/58]) *Critique of Everyday Life: Volume 1*, London: Verso.

Lefebvre, Henri (1991b [1974]) *The Production of Space*, Oxford: Blackwell.

Lefebvre, Henri (1995 [1962]) *Introduction to Modernity*, London: Verso.

Lévi-Strauss, Claude (1968 [1958]) *Structural Anthropology*, Harmondsworth: Penguin.

Marcuse, Herbert (1941) *Reason and Revolution: Hegel and the Rise of Social Theory*, New York: Oxford University Press.

Marcuse, Herbert (1968a [1936]) 'Concept of Essence', in *Negations: Essays in Critical Theory*, London: Allen Lane, The Penguin Press.

Marcuse, Herbert (1968b [1937]) 'Philosophy and Critical Theory', in *Negations: Essays in Critical Theory*, London: Allen Lane, The Penguin Press.

Marcuse, Herbert (1968c [1937]) 'Affirmative Culture', in *Negations: Essays in Critical Theory*, London: Allen Lane, The Penguin Press.

Marcuse, Herbert (1969) *An Essay on Liberation*, London: Allen Lane, The Penguin Press.

Marcuse, Herbert (1972a [1955]) *Eros and Civilization*, London: Abacus/Sphere Books.

Marcuse, Herbert (1972b [1964]) *One-Dimensional Man*, London: Abacus/Sphere Books.

Marcuse, Herbert (1979 [1977]) *The Aesthetic Dimension*, London: Macmillan.

Marcuse, Herbert (1989) 'Liberation from the Affluent Society', in S. Bronner, D. Kellner (eds) *Critical Theory and Society: A Reader*, London: Routledge.

Marcuse, Herbert (1998 [1941]) 'Some Social Implications of Modern Technology', in H. Marcuse, *Technology, War and Fascism: Collected Papers Volume 1*, ed. D. Kellner, London: Routledge.

Marcuse, H. (2001 [1965]) 'The Containment of Social Change in Industrial Society', in H. Marcuse, *Towards a Critical Theory of Society: Collected Papers Volume 2*, ed. D. Kellner, London: Routledge.

Marx, Karl (1973 [1939]) *Grundrisse*, Harmondsworth: Penguin.

Marx, Karl (1975 [1843–4]) *Early Writings*, London: Penguin.

Marx, Karl (1976 [1867]) *Capital, Volume 1*, London: Penguin.

Marx, Karl (1992 [1867]) *Capital, Volume 1*, London: Penguin.

Moriarty, Michael (1992) *Roland Barthes (Key Contemporary Thinkers)*, Stanford, CA: Stanford University Press.

O'Neill, Maggie (ed.) (1999) *Adorno, Culture and Feminism*, London: Sage.

Pippin, Robert, Feenberg, Andrew and Webel, Charles P. (1988) *Marcuse: Critical Theory and the Promise of Utopia*, Houndmills: Macmillan.

Plant, Sadie (1993) 'Baudrillard's Woman: The Eve of Seduction', in C. Rojek and B.S. Turner (eds) *Forget Baudrillard*, London: Routledge.

Propp, Vladimir (1984) *Theory and History of Folklore*, Manchester: Manchester University Press.

Ray, Larry (1993) *Rethinking Critical Theory: Emancipation in the Age of Global Social Movements*, London: Sage.

Riesman, David (with Glazer, Nathan and Denny, Reuel) (1950) *The Lonely Crowd: A Study of the Changing American Character*, New Haven, CT: Yale University Press.

Roche, D. (2000) *A History of Everyday Things*, Cambridge: Cambridge University Press.

Sahlins, Marshall (1976) *Culture and Practical Reason*, Chicago: University of Chicago Press.

Salaman, Graeme (1986) *Working*, Chichester: Ellis Horwood.

Seidman, Steven (1998) *Contested Knowledge: Social Theory in the Postmodern Era*, Malden, MA and Oxford: Blackwell.

Smith, Dorothy (1988) *The Everyday World as Problematic*, Milton Keynes: Open University Press.

Smith, Mark J. (2000) *Culture: Reinventing the Social Sciences*, Buckingham: Open University Press.

Strinati, Dominic (1995) *An Introduction to Theories of Popular Culture*, London: Routledge.

Swingewood, Alan (1998) *Cultural Theory and the Problem of Modernity*, Houndmills, Basingstoke: Macmillan.

Touraine, Alain (1974 [1969]) *The Post-industrial Society: Tomorrow's Social History: Classes, Conflicts and Culture in the Programmed Society*, London: Wildwood House.

Touraine, Alain (1988 [1984]) *Return of the Actor: Social Theory in Postindustrial Society*, Minneapolis: University of Minnesota Press.

Touraine, Alain (1995 [1992]) *Critique of Modernity*, Oxford: Blackwell.

Trotsky, Leon (1973) *Problems of Everyday Life, And Other Writings on Culture and Science*, New York: Monad Press.

Truzzi, M. (1968) *Sociology and Everyday Life*, Englewood Cliffs, NJ: Prentice-Hall Inc.

Watson, Tony (1995) *Sociology, Work and Industry*, London: Routledge.

Weber, Max (1930 [1915]) *The Protestant Ethic and the Spirit of Capitalism*, London: Allen and Unwin.

Weber, Max (1978 [1956]) *Economy and Society (2 Vols)*, Berkeley: University of California Press.

Weeks, Jeffrey (1985) *Sexuality and its Discontents*, London: Routledge.

Weigert, Andrew J. (1981) *Sociology of Everyday Life*, New York: Longman.

Wiggershaus, Rolf (1994 [1986]) *The Frankfurt School: Its History, Theories and Political Significance*, Cambridge: Polity.

Wilkinson, Sue and Kitzinger, Celia (eds) (1993) *Heterosexuality*, London: Sage.

Williams, Raymond (1976) *Keywords*, Glasgow: Fontana.

Wittgenstein, Ludwig (1978 [1958]) *Philosophical Investigations* (2nd edn), Oxford: Blackwell.

Index